ALSO BY TERRY MORT

The Reasonable Art of Fly Fishing

Zane Grey on Fishing

Jack London on Adventure

Mark Twain on Travel

Showdown at Verity

The Lawless Breed

Shipment to Mexico

The
HEMINGWAY
PATROLS

*Ernest Hemingway
and His Hunt for U-boats*

TERRY MORT

SCRIBNER

New York London Toronto Sydney

SCRIBNER
A Division of Simon & Schuster, Inc.
1230 Avenue of the Americas
New York, NY 10020

First Scribner hardcover edition August 2009

SCRIBNER and design are registered trademarks of
The Gale Group, Inc., used under license by Simon & Schuster, Inc.,
the publisher of this work.

For information about special discounts for bulk purchases,
please contact Simon & Schuster Special Sales at 1-800-456-6798
or business@simonandschuster.com.

The Simon & Schuster Speakers Bureau can bring authors to your live
event. For more information or to book an event contact the Simon &
Schuster Speakers Bureau at 1-866-248-3049 or visit our website at
www.simonspeakers.com.

Maps copyright © 2009 by Jeffrey L. Ward

Manufactured in the United States of America

1   3   5   7   9   10   8   6   4   2

Library of Congress Control Number: 2009000884

ISBN 978-1-4165-9786-5
ISBN 978-1-4165-9790-2 (ebook)

Permissions and photograph credits appear on page 243.

In memory of Sergeant E. V. Mort,
who spent countless hours flying in a PBY over
the Caribbean and South Atlantic,
looking for U-boats

Contents

~~~

	Introduction	1
Chapter One	A Serious Man	13
Chapter Two	Martha and Spain: Love and War	19
Chapter Three	Two Kinds of Hunters	50
Chapter Four	The Enemy in the Machine	72
Chapter Five	Amateur Hour	109
Chapter Six	The Wandering Angler	123
Chapter Seven	Fathers and Sons	145
Chapter Eight	"And Faded through the Brightening Air"	164
Chapter Nine	In Another Country	193
Epilogue	The Meaning of Nothing	226
	Notes	231
	Bibliography	239
	Acknowledgments	242
	Permissions and Photograph Credits	243
	Index	245

The Hemingway Patrols

Introduction

~~~

E<small>RNEST</small> H<small>EMINGWAY</small> died by his own hand on July 2, 1961. He was sixty-one. If you have ever been to Ketchum, Idaho, which is where he killed himself, and especially if it was July when you were there, you understand that he must have been very ill, both physically and emotionally, to do such a thing at such a time, in so beautiful a part of the world. And so he was.

He was born on July 21, 1899, in Oak Park, Illinois, a middle-class suburb of Chicago. He was the second of six children— four sisters and a brother. His father was a physician, whose primary legacy seems to have been a love of the outdoors, not just hunting and fishing, but simply being in the open air. His other legacy, apparently, was a tendency toward deep, crippling depression. Hemingway's mother was strong-willed with a strict set of conventional moral standards combined with artistic and musical ambitions, but no significant achievement. Hemingway's father committed suicide in 1928. To suggest that the relationship between his parents was the cause of his father's suicide is per-haps facile; but it is certainly fair, if we can believe Hemingway himself, to suggest that their relationship and his mother's impe-rious personality were contributing factors. Unlike many writers, Hemingway never revisited his childhood and adolescence in Oak Park in his fiction. It is as though he preferred to forget it all—all except his boyhood summers at Walloon Lake near Petoskey in northern Michigan, where the family kept a summerhouse. Those were mostly good times, hunting and fishing, swimming and boating, with close friends. All his life he would try to re-create or recapture this kind of high-spirited camaraderie; all his life he would return to the sometimes exhilarating, sometimes calming environment of the woods and water to restore his physical and emotional health.

After graduating from high school (which would be the end of his formal education) Hemingway moved to Kansas City to work as a reporter on the *Kansas City Star.* Then in 1918 he volunteered for the Red Cross, which allowed him to wear a military-style uniform and assume the rank of lieutenant. He was sent to Italy's northern front in the mountains where the Italian army was facing the Austrians and conducting a series of disastrous attacks. Initially he was an ambulance driver, but later he volunteered to supervise a Red Cross canteen located just to the rear of the Italian lines. While delivering chocolates and cigarettes to men in the front line, Hemingway was wounded by an Austrian mortar shell. Shrapnel and debris nearly destroyed his right knee, and he was sent to a military hospital in Milan to undergo surgery and rehabilitation. He was just a few days short of his nineteenth birthday. In the hospital he fell in love with his nurse, Agnes von Kurowsky, one of the most beautiful of all the women in his life—and his first muse. She was eight years older and may not have shared his great passion, but she would become a model for Catherine Barkley in *A Farewell to Arms,* Hemingway's 1929 novel of war and romance in the northern-Italian theater. After a while Agnes was transferred to another hospital, and Ernest returned to his home for further rehabilitation, where Agnes sent him a letter breaking off whatever remained—or ever was—of their relationship.

Hemingway spent that summer and fall in northern Michigan, allowing his knee and his emotions to heal, and in 1920 he moved to Toronto to take a temporary job as companion to the disabled son of the editor of the *Toronto Daily Star.* The connection would prove useful.

His next job took him to Chicago, where he wrote for the *Co-operative Commonwealth,* an agricultural journal. In Chicago he met Hadley Richardson, whom he would marry the following year. Ironically, perhaps, Hadley, like Agnes von Kurowsky, was also eight years older than Hemingway.

In December of 1921, he and Hadley sailed for Europe, where he would cover European political affairs for the *Toronto Daily Star.* The couple settled in Paris, which would become not only their base of operations for travel into Switzerland and Austria, Italy and Spain, but also the vital starting point for Hemingway's literary career.

In Paris he met a variety of artists, some mere bohemian poseurs, others genuine giants of the period—Joyce and Pound and Picasso and, later, Fitzgerald. He made liberal use of Sylvia Beach's lending library called Shakespeare and Company. Beach also ran a kind of starving authors' protective society, making loans of money as well as books. (It was Beach who first published *Ulysses,* when no other publisher wanted anything to do with it.) Hemingway also met and became friendly with Gertrude Stein, who had strong opinions on all things literary and wrote prose that was mostly impenetrable. But she was influential, knew everyone worth knowing in the arts, had a fine eye for modern painting, and ran a kind of literary salon to which she welcomed the eager Hemingway with genuine cordiality. He was an ambitious and alert student; she was well satisfied to give instruction. She and her partner, Alice B. Toklas, would later be godmothers to Hemingway and Hadley's first son, John, aka Bumby. The godfather was Eric Edward "Chink" Dorman-Smith (who later changed his name to Dorman-O'Gowan), a British professional soldier Hemingway had met during the war. The odd trio of godparents reflects some of Hemingway's own interests as well as his complexity, personally and artistically. And one of the baby's middle names was Nicanor, after a matador Hemingway had seen and admired the year before in Spain.

After a brief interlude during which the couple returned to Toronto, where Hemingway continued working for the *Daily Star,* he quit the job and they returned to Paris, where Hemingway felt they could live cheaply enough to allow him to write fiction full-time.

Years later Hemingway would return to these Paris days in his memoir, *A Moveable Feast,* back to the "early days when we were very poor and very happy." It is quite a fine book, made all the more poignant because it was posthumously published.

They were poor in those Paris years, but not desperately so, for Hadley had a modest trust fund that covered their basic expenses. Hemingway was not producing much in the way of income. He was experiencing the usual struggles to get his stories and poetry published. He sold a few stories to German periodicals, but American magazines and publishers were not terribly interested. Fortunately, money went a long way in Paris in those days. They had enough to be happy and enough for him to go now and then to a café where he could write and the waiters were friendly and would not care that he was only nursing a café crème or a cognac. And there was enough money for a little travel. He and Hadley spent winters in Switzerland and Austria learning to ski at a time when there were no lifts and if you wanted to ski down the mountain, you first had to hike to the top. He would revisit those winter days in *A Farewell to Arms,* after Frederic Henry and Catherine Barkley declare their separate peace and flee by rowboat across Lago Maggiore to Switzerland.

Whatever success he had was due in part to his ability to make friends with other writers who had influence, especially Ezra Pound. Pound took him under his wing and helped him find a small publisher for Hemingway's first book, called *Three Stories and Ten Poems,* in August of 1923. Pound also got him some editing work with a new magazine in Paris called the *Transatlantic Review,* which also published some of his stories in 1924.

During that same period his second book, *in our time,* was published in Paris, then with some revisions republished in London by Boni & Liveright, in 1925.

In April of 1925 Hemingway met F. Scott Fitzgerald in Paris. Hemingway's reputation, if not his bank account, had grown because of his modest publishing success and because he seemed to have been adopted by the artistic community in Paris, especially Stein and Pound, and touted as a coming man. Fitzgerald was already well established. He and his wife, Zelda, were international figures based in part on their mutual glamour and in part on the success of Fitzgerald's first novel—*This Side of Paradise*—and his subsequent short stories, which brought him significant income. Though he was not quite three years older than Hemingway, Fitzgerald was already a bestselling author and lived like one. He would reverse the usual progression of a successful writer's life—failure, financial distress, and obscurity would come at the end of his career.

Fitzgerald had mentioned to his editor, the justly famous Maxwell Perkins of Charles Scribner's Sons, that Hemingway was worth considering as a potential author—this on the strength of Fitzgerald's reading of *In Our Time* even before Fitzgerald and Hemingway had met in Paris. Fitzgerald did not have Hemingway's intense and sometimes unappealing competitive instincts, so when he met Hemingway later that same year, he was prepared to be helpful to the younger man. Of course, Fitzgerald was already well established—*The Great Gatsby* would be published that same month—but that only emphasizes his generosity and perspicacity in recognizing and nourishing a major new talent. Many others in his position would not have bothered.

That summer Ernest and Hadley returned to Pamplona for the bullfights. A crowd of friends joined them there, and Hemingway's novel, *The Sun Also Rises,* would come from that experience. The following winter Pauline Pfeiffer, a friend of Hadley's, arrived at Schruns, the Hemingways' favorite winter getaway in Austria.

Pauline was an editor for *Vogue;* she was small and slim and rather different from Hadley, who was literally and figuratively matronly. As Hemingway wrote in *A Moveable Feast,* "The husband has two attractive girls around when he has finished work. One is new and strange and if he has bad luck he gets to love them both."[1]

The next year Hemingway's affair with Pauline led to divorce from Hadley, a sad event for both: "When I saw my wife again standing by the tracks as the train came in by the piled logs at the station, I wished I had died before I ever loved anyone but her."[2]

But he had. And although Pauline's family wealth had little if anything to do with her attractiveness, it nonetheless brought a welcome change to Hemingway's situation. Her uncle Gus, a bachelor who doted on Pauline, was a cosmetics magnate who would provide useful financial support to the Hemingways throughout their married life. Pauline was also a Catholic, and this no doubt raised some memories for Hemingway of being wounded and receiving absolution from a priest in Italy—a priest who routinely assumed that wounded men must be Catholics. From about this time forward Hemingway thought of himself as a Catholic, although he admitted he was not a particularly good one.

The Sun Also Rises was published at the end of 1926 to generally favorable reviews and surprisingly good sales, for a first novel. The hero is Jake Barnes, whose war wounds left him unable to perform sexually, although his desire is unabated and especially aroused by seeing his great love, Lady Brett Ashley, at Pamplona amid the drunken riot of the fiesta there. Jake endures, but only just, and the title is hardly optimistic, nor is the epigraph by Gertrude Stein: "You are all a lost generation." The book would be published by Scribner's, and so began the lifelong business association between Scribner's and Hemingway. Scribner's also bought *The Torrents of Spring,* a minor work parodying the style and content of Sherwood Anderson's stories.

Hemingway and Pauline were married in 1927. They lived in Paris and traveled extensively—he was not yet willing to abandon his old routines or haunts. Meanwhile, the success of his first novel meant his short stories now were being sought by the magazines, and his literary career was well and truly under way. His second collection of short stories—*Men without Women*—was published by Scribner's that same year.

Ernest and Pauline moved back to the United States in 1928. They rented an apartment in Key West, which at the time was a run-down backwater and home to Cuban cigar makers and American bootleggers. But the fishing was good and the living inexpensive. They continued to travel extensively—back to Europe and out West to a ranch near Cooke City, Montana, for hunting and through Piggott, Arkansas, to visit Pauline's family. Their son Patrick was born that year. Hemingway's next novel, *A Farewell to Arms,* was published the following year. Reviews were excellent, as were the sales. In the novel Frederic Henry is a young American soldier in the Italian army who, while on leave, meets Catherine Barkley, a beautiful English nurse; they begin an affair, but Henry must return to the front, where he is wounded by a mortar shell, then hospitalized to recuperate. When he is sent back to the front, he participates in the disastrous battle and retreat from Caporetto, recognizes the futility of it all, makes a "separate peace," and escapes to Switzerland with Catherine, where they spend an idyllic winter in a mountain chalet. It cannot last, though, and in the end Catherine dies delivering a stillborn child, and Henry is left alone. He is another version of Jake Barnes, wounded both physically and emotionally, and left to endure as best he can.

The next few years the Hemingways traveled between Key West and Europe and Montana. In 1931 with financial help from Uncle Gus they bought a house in Key West while Ernest was writing *Death in the Afternoon,* his nonfiction book about bullfighting. That same year their second son, Gregory, was born.

After the publication of his short story collection *Winner Take Nothing,* Hemingway took his first safari to Africa at the end of 1933, courtesy once again of Uncle Gus's largesse. The experience led to *Green Hills of Africa,* in 1935, an experimental nonfiction book that was not particularly well received, certainly not in comparison to his novels. That same year Hemingway bought *Pilar,* his thirty-eight-foot fishing boat and probably his best-loved possession.

In December of 1936 he met Martha Gellhorn—a young and attractive writer of both fiction and journalism. They began an affair shortly thereafter, and when the civil war in Spain broke out, they went there to cover the story. Hemingway's fifth and perhaps greatest novel, *For Whom the Bell Tolls,* came from his experiences in Spain. The hero, Robert Jordan, is a partisan sent to destroy a bridge behind enemy lines. He works with a group of Spanish guerrillas, meets and falls in love with one of them, a girl named Maria, blows up the bridge successfully, but is wounded and forced to stay behind during the retreat. At the end he is lining up an enemy cavalry soldier in the sights of his machine gun.

Pauline turned a blind eye to the affair with Martha for a while, but ultimately started divorce proceedings. Pauline would stay in the house in Key West; Martha and Ernest rented a farmhouse called Finca Vigia near Havana—a house they would buy toward the end of 1940, the year they were married.

Shortly after the wedding the couple took off to cover the war in China. They would spend the first half of the year in the Far East reporting on the various theaters of war. They returned to Cuba in June but then left for Sun Valley, Idaho, for several months.

In the early months of World War II, Hemingway initiated a voluntary counterintelligence operation in Cuba, involving his cronies and associates; this operation soon expanded to include patrols in *Pilar* looking for U-boats and for enemy agents operating from obscure islands off the coast of Cuba. It was a serious business, for Cuba then was a hotbed of fascist sympathizers as well as a strategically important location lying at the center of U-boat routes into the Gulf of Mexico.

The patrols of *Pilar* lasted until the end of 1943. The next year both Ernest and Martha went to Europe to cover the war there. They went separately because the strains in their relationship—strains that had been there from the beginning—grew intolerable. Almost as soon as Ernest landed in London, he met Mary Welsh, a reporter for *Time*. Their affair culminated in a divorce from Martha and a fourth marriage for Hemingway, a second for Mary.

In Europe, Hemingway flew some missions with the RAF, then transferred to the U.S. Army as a correspondent. He spent some time with the French Resistance and the American OSS (forerunner of the CIA), during which time he had the pleasure of entering Paris well before the city was completely under control and before the main body of Allied troops arrived. Later he joined up with the U.S. Twenty-second Regiment and reported on the horrific fighting at Hürtgen Forest.

After the war he returned to Cuba, this time with Mary, who seemed to adapt well enough to life at Finca Vigia. Mary, like all Hemingway's wives, except Martha, made him her number one priority, so that if he liked living in Cuba, she was content to live there, too.

The next few years were rather fallow, although Hemingway did begin work on the book that would eventually become *Islands in the Stream*—the last section of which describes a hunt for the crew of a U-boat. In 1947 he was awarded a Bronze Star for his service in Europe. Hemingway turned his World War II experience into the novel *Across the River and into the Trees*. By this time he had met Adriana Ivancich, who would become another in his series of romantic images and would serve as a model for the heroine in *Across the River and into the Trees*, the story of a middle-aged American professional soldier who is suffering from heart disease and living out his last days in Venice, duck hunting and reminiscing and having an affair with a young Italian woman. This book was not well received by critics, even though Hemingway thought it among his best work. It was published in 1950.

In 1951 he began work on *The Old Man and the Sea,* which was originally intended to be a part of a larger work encompassing "the air, land and sea." It is the well-known story of an epic battle between Santiago, an aged fisherman, and a giant marlin. The book was published in *Life* magazine and then in hardcover by Scribner's. It immediately restored Hemingway's reputation, which had been damaged by *Across the River and into the Trees* and by the lengthy creative hiatus caused primarily by the war years. In 1953 he won the Pulitzer Prize for *The Old Man and the Sea.*

That same year he and Mary went to Pamplona for the bullfights. It was the first time he had been there since 1931. From there they traveled to Africa for a five-month safari, which ended disastrously when the small plane that was carrying them on a sightseeing trip crashed. Worse, the second plane that had come to evacuate them also crashed on takeoff. The first crash caused some bumps and bruises; the second, burns, damaged kidneys and liver, and two broken vertebrae for Hemingway. Mary had two cracked ribs and numerous bruises.

All his life Hemingway had suffered serious injuries in addition to his World War I wounds—a broken arm in a car crash in Montana, a head wound from a falling Parisian skylight, a self-inflicted wound in his left calf (while fishing aboard *Pilar,* he was trying to shoot and gaff a hooked shark and his .22 pistol accidentally went off), another concussion from a car wreck in London when he first arrived there in 1944, a recurrence of concussion while being shelled in France, and now these plane crashes. There is a grim irony in all this, for the man himself seemed the very model of robust health—someone who would dominate any room he entered from the sheer force of his physical presence and from the strength of his personality. At six foot one, over two hundred pounds with a burly upper body, he seemed indestructible, and perhaps his various accidents proved the point, for he survived them all. But after these plane crashes Hemingway was in pain for the rest of his life, and the pain along with the residual effects of the concussions, which were exacerbated by his habitual heavy drinking, must certainly have contributed to his mental state at the end of his life. What's more, he suffered from high blood pressure most of his life, and the medications he was taking for it were not without serious side effects in those days.

In 1954 Hemingway was awarded the Nobel Prize for Literature. From that point until the end of his life he worked mostly on books that would be published after his death—*The Garden of Eden, The Dangerous Summer, Islands in the Stream, True at First Light*. And, perhaps best of all, *A Moveable Feast*. And despite his many accidents and mishaps, he and Mary continued to travel to Europe and the American West.

The last two years of his life were filled with rapidly accelerating paranoia and depression. As a last resort Mary took him to the Mayo Clinic, where they administered electroshock therapy. Hemingway had brief periods of calm afterward but then relapsed. And after several attempts at suicide, he finally succeeded, using his well-loved English, custom-made shotgun, there in his house in Ketchum.

Chapter One

A SERIOUS MAN

Sometimes you know the story. Sometimes you make it up as you go along and have no idea how it will come out.

Hemingway, the *Paris Review* interview

For a moment of night we have a glimpse of ourselves and our world islanded in its stream of stars.

Henry Beston

S AILORS who have studied celestial navigation remember the first time they worked on a complicated navigational fix and their calculations actually came out correctly. Three lines drawn on a chart and derived from the angles of three stars intersect at the same pinpoint, and the navigator knows his exact position in the universe. The pleasure of the moment comes in part because the process of measuring and plotting is not that easy, at least not when you are new to the business. But there is pleasure also in the poetry of knowing you are precisely in this place because the stars have said so. You are at the juncture of three streams of light that began their travels millions of years ago. It's a moment for humility and, at the same time, for a kind of pride of place and an affirmation of self, which is both satisfying and comic, given that you are miles from land and at the complete mercy of that very universe in which you have so accurately and skillfully placed yourself. In calculating where you are, you are reminded that your ship is very small. And you, star plotter, even smaller. Still, you are at the center of it all, "islanded in its stream of stars," and you know it. It is a wonderful conceit. A fine and complicated moment. Full of irony and whatever the opposite of irony is. These moments are fleeting, of course. After all, even the best star fix is accurate only for a short time, for the ship moves on, as do the stars. And that brief period, when everything comes together, just right, passes quickly.

In 1942 Ernest Hemingway must have experienced a similar moment of recognition—that he was just then at the top of his arc, that vectors from many different directions had come together— his writing, his physical well-being, his professional reputation and success, his three sons, his friendships, his pastimes and pleasures. All these major forces had joined to place him at or near his personal and professional zenith. Of course, from the zenith there is only one future direction, and the emotion of the moment would have been complicated by a rueful reflection or two. Still, Hemingway had every reason to savor his position. He had a talented and attractive wife, international acclaim, a farmhouse outside Havana within easy reach of his well-loved Gulf Stream and near also to the little port town of Cojimar, where he kept his fishing boat, *Pilar*. His most recent novel, *For Whom the Bell Tolls,* had been published two years before and had been a smashing commercial and artistic success. A six-figure offer to do a film script was in the works. Though his country was at war, he was in his early forties, still vigorous, but too old to be expected to fight. As with most people and especially artists, his life was not uniformly serene and satisfying; he still had his dark moods, fits of temper, and worries now and then. And Hemingway and his wife, Martha Gellhorn, had periods of tension. But those times aside, it was all just about as good as it *could* get, just then, in Cuba, and he could hardly be criticized for sitting beside his swimming pool, relishing his achievements and enjoying the view from the heights. Certainly he was justified in saying to himself, "Out of all the things you could not have there were some that you could have and one of those was to know when you were happy and to enjoy it all while it was there and it was good."[1]

But from the summer of 1942 through the whole of 1943, Ernest Hemingway did not spend much time resting on his considerable laurels. Nor did he do any writing of consequence. Instead, he spent a great deal of his time cruising in his thirty-eight-foot fishing boat, *Pilar,* along the north coast of Cuba and out into the Gulf Stream. He was looking for German submarines. U-boats.

That sounds like something he would do. It's certainly in line with the popular image of the man, an image created partly by the author himself and partly by the media, for whom he was good copy, always. But this was no publicity stunt. While Hemingway was ostensibly trolling for large fish, he was actually looking for even larger and infinitely more dangerous quarry during a time in the war when the U-boats were winning and America's resources to fight them were absurdly thin. The patrols were his idea, but they were sanctioned by the local American embassy and done in cooperation with the military, both in Cuba and America. In short, this was a serious business.

It's also important to understand that Hemingway was hunting U-boats at a sacrifice to his work—and his income. He could have ridden the wave of critical acclaim in any number of ways. But he did not. He set aside his work to volunteer. And not writing was more than a simple matter of losing revenue, for as he said later, "The time to work is shorter all the time and if you waste it you feel you have committed a sin for which there is no forgiveness."[2] He was at his best when he was working and he knew it; writing defined him. "Writing is a hard business . . . but nothing makes you feel better."[3] Even so, he gave that up for a time—a long time—and went looking for U-boats.

But Hemingway's quest does raise a number of questions, and the most fundamental is—if he ever actually found a U-boat, what did he expect to do with it? It seems like looking for a wolf to grab by the ears. Had he suspended his imagination to the point of fool-hardiness? (As he said in *Men at War,* "Cowardice, as distinguished from panic, is almost always simply a lack of ability to suspend the functioning of the imagination.") Or was his imagination actually in heroic overdrive, like that of some modern Don Quixote? More likely it was the latter. And certainly the project appealed to Hemingway's artistic sense. U-boats were unpredictable, ruthless, impersonal, and fearsome, and as such they were a particularly appropriate metaphor for Hemingway's view of the universe—a universe that alternated between indifference and sudden violence. To Hemingway, *Pilar* versus the U-boat was an irresistible and compelling representation of man's fate: a small wooden boat confronting an iron-and-steel machine of industrial war, knowing the odds against success or even survival were long, but confronting nonetheless, for dignity lay in making the attempt.

But the U-boats were real. The shells and bullets they would be firing were not metaphorical, and wood versus steel is an interesting literary trope but a decided mismatch in battle. To imagine a story is one thing; to go in search of an immensely more powerful enemy is something else. And so it's fair to ask—was Hemingway really serious? If so, was this just part of an ongoing and well-advertised death wish? Who went with him and how did he convince them to go along? Why did he go looking for U-boats in the first place? Was he gathering material for fiction? Does this period tell us anything about the man as artist? Or the man himself? And how many U-boats were in the area, really? Were the occasional sightings merely random, or was this area of the Gulf of

Mexico an active theater of the war? Did Hemingway think deep down that the odds of encountering a U-boat were infinitesimally small and that he could therefore broadcast his intentions, knowing that he would never be put to the test? Was it all just bravado, a farce, an unintentional opera bouffe, the product of a blustering middle-aged man playing at war while actually just fishing? Some thought so; his wife, Martha Gellhorn, for one—especially when she was angry with him. Those who were not his admirers, and there were many, characterized these patrols as little more than self-aggrandizing stunts. Was there any truth in this?

Some, perhaps. But not much. Instead, it's much fairer, and closer to the truth, to realize that Hemingway, like any sailor at the start of a patrol in wartime, did not know, could not know, what lay ahead. And this not-knowing constituted an act of—if not bravery—at least a kind of mental and physical fortitude that is, in itself, worthy of respect. His experiences during World War I and the Spanish Civil War provided hard lessons in the inherent uncertainty of war. As he wrote in the introduction to *Men at War,* "War is the province of chance." Things rarely go the way you think they will; and a great many things could go wrong during a search for a U-boat. And yet he went to sea, not once, but repeatedly from June of 1942 until the end of 1943, each time putting himself, his boat, and the friends who went with him potentially into harm's way. It's easy to look back on history, knowing the outcomes, and make judgments about the way things happened and the way people acted. It's not so easy to be in the moment, when those outcomes are not guaranteed or even fully imagined.

Undoubtedly, Hemingway was thinking over many of these same questions as he guided *Pilar* out the channel of Havana harbor, past the fortress of El Morro, and out into the open water in search of the enemy. The flying bridge of a fishing boat is a fine place for introspection. And when that boat is also a ship of war, and you are in command, responsible for the vessel and crew, the bridge is where your thoughts become most truly serious. It is not a place for illusions. Or self-delusions.

And perhaps in the waters north of Havana, the captain of a U-boat was standing on his own bridge, similarly thoughtful.

Chapter Two

~∾~

MARTHA AND SPAIN:
LOVE AND WAR

*I hear you are marrying one of the most beautiful people I have ever seen.
Give her my best remembrance.*

F. Scott Fitzgerald letter to Hemingway, November 8, 1940

*Granted she's lazy and spoiled, and rather stupid, and enor-
mously on the make. Still she's very beautiful, very friendly,
and very charming and rather innocent—and quite brave.*

The Fifth Column

T HE story of Hemingway's hunt for U-boats has its origins
a few years before the outbreak of World War II. For it was
in Spain, during the 1936–39 civil war, that a number of
themes and events—internecine warfare, espionage, complicated
blood-feud politics, cynical international maneuvering—came
together to solidify Hemingway's understanding of the mortal
dangers of political fanaticism in general and of fascism in particular. The Spanish Civil War was also the source of arguably his greatest literary achievement, as well as the scene of his most complex
love affair. Moreover, his activities in Spain laid the foundation for
political difficulties that complicated his U-boat hunting in Cuba

a few years later. Aside from his service in World War I, the Spanish Civil War was the most formative and important period of his life, personally, artistically, and politically.

Hemingway had loved Spain from his first trip there with his wife Hadley in 1923, so it's not surprising that, when the disastrous civil war broke out, he wanted to go back to witness and share in its agonies. It was a nervous time in 1936. People could not be confident that the timorous or isolated democracies could summon up the will to confront what seemed to be the wave of history, when it seemed possible that the world would soon be divided between the jackbooted totalitarians and everyone else who would either be their vassals or the victims of their charnel houses. Many viewed Spain as the first battle on the first line of defense against fascist dictatorships; to lose there would be to unleash the dogs of war throughout the world. And so it proved.

During the civil war Hemingway went to Spain three times for extended visits lasting several months, both to observe and report, often from the front lines and under fire. And during those times he developed and refined his hatred for the Spanish fascists, who—in league with their Italian and German allies—were despoiling the country. And a few short years later, when the U-boats appeared in the waters around Cuba in 1942, Hemingway knew well that the Nazis who were sinking unarmed merchant ships in the Gulf of Mexico were the same people who helped supply the artillery shells that rained down on Madrid while he was there and whose pilots bombed helpless Spanish civilians in Guernica. These Germans were well-remembered enemies whose ruthlessness and military professionalism had been on display in Spain.

*   *   *

Toward the end of 1936 Hemingway was already thinking about going to Spain. Just then, another writer entered the picture, a woman who also wanted to cover the civil war there: Martha Gell-horn.

The story goes that she came into his life in Sloppy Joe's in Key West. It was December in 1936. The civil war in Spain had been under way since July, but although he was following the news there with intense interest, Hemingway's plans to go there were not firm yet. What's more, he was still working on his novel *To Have and Have Not.* But not on that day. Instead, he was in his accustomed place at the bar when Martha walked in with her mother and her brother. Martha's black dress set off her long blond hair nicely. Some say she was there hunting for him. If she was, she never admitted it and in fact went out of her way to deny it. Whatever the truth—and neither Hemingway nor Martha was completely reliable when it came to truth telling—the result would be the same. She was twenty-eight. Hemingway, thirty-seven. He was famous. She was a published author who had been featured on the cover of the prestigious *Saturday Review*. Her book of short stories, *The Trouble I've Seen,* had been published in England and America to favorable reviews. There had been an earlier novel, too, as well as some freelance journalism. At her age she had every right to think well of herself as a writer not only of promise but of some solid achievement.

At the time Hemingway was married to his second wife, Pauline, and living in Key West. That meeting in Sloppy Joe's was the start of a love affair that lasted more than three years and culminated in Martha's becoming wife number three—much to her, and his, eventual chagrin.

People said Martha was beautiful. Hemingway thought so. And Scott Fitzgerald, who could fairly be regarded as having a good eye for that sort of thing, certainly said so. Anyone who has written about her, or quoted people who knew her, has said the same.

Her photographs, though, suggest something different.

Attractive, yes. But hardly beautiful. Not even conventionally pretty, really. She must, therefore, have had something else, a physical allure that communicated itself instantly, especially to the men she encountered, something that a camera could not capture. Martha must have radiated a rare combination of intelligence, energy, sexual appeal—and good humor. A long line of lovers, both before and after Hemingway, could attest to that. Many people observed that she had glamour—an attribute the other Hemingway wives manifestly did not. Even Pauline, who had worked in Paris for *Vogue* and who knew something about fashion, could hardly be called glamorous.

And there was something else about Martha—a kind of sexual ambivalence . . . an attitude that must have suggested availability mixed with a paradoxical lack of real interest. Her response to attempts at seduction seemed to be "Well, all right, if it means that much to you, but don't expect me to get all that involved." Many men would consider this a challenge; that suggestion of indifference would only enhance her allure.

By nature and by profession Martha wanted to be where the action was. She liked to be around men who were part of what was going on. Sex was one means to make those connections; she understood perfectly the effect she had on men. It would have been easy to fall in love with Martha Gellhorn; lots of men did. It would not have been so easy to *be* in love with her; lots of men found that out. She didn't really care for the physical part of the arrangement; sex was not a necessary evil so much as a necessary bother.

As she wrote in one of her many self-exploratory letters:

Now back to love and sex; what a fascinating topic. I don't know whether I'm prim; I sure haven't lived it. I started living outside the sexual conventions long before anyone did such dangerous stuff and I may say all hell broke loose and everyone thought unbridled sexual passion was the excuse. Whereas I didn't like the sex at all; I only believed in honesty and besides the man wanted it and what I wanted was to live at top speed. . . . I never ever thought you got something for nothing in this life, and fair's fair, and besides all my life idiotically, I thought sex seemed to matter so desperately to the man who wanted it that to withhold was like withholding bread, an act of self-ishness. But myself, I was not 'awakened' if that's the word; often attracted, often horribly in love, but the bed part didn't come off—I think due to the clumsiness of the men and partly (largely?) due to a Victorian upbringing; sex and love were different. . . .

I accompanied men and was accompanied in action, in the extrovert part of life; I plunged into that; that was something altogether to be shared. But not sex; that seemed to be their delight and all I got was a pleasure of being wanted, I suppose, and the sort of tenderness (not nearly enough) that a man gives when he is satisfied. I dare say I was the worst bed partner in five continents.[1]

It would seem that the earth did not often move for Martha, if at all.

Living at "top speed" did not mean living a life of pleasure, not in the usual sense. As a journalist and an author of fiction—and the two would overlap from time to time—she was in many ways a pioneer. Throughout her long life, work, that is, writing, was her main concern—and her primary source of strength. As she said, only work gives one "a real sense of life, of the wonder and surprise and joy of being alive."[2] Early on she adopted a motto from André Malraux—*Travail—opium unique*.[3] Or, "Work, the only drug." And while her relationship with Hemingway certainly opened many opportunities for her professionally, she had already achieved a measure of professional success before she ever met him. She would go on to future successes while they were together, and to other successes after they had parted.

Like her adored mother before her, Martha went to Bryn Mawr, a prestigious women's college in suburban Philadelphia with a reputation for turning out independent women. She quit after her junior year, having become bored with academics. After a few years of traveling in Europe, living with Bertrand de Jouvenel, the married son of a French politician—an affair that resulted in two abortions and a difficult breakup—she returned to America, where she got a job working for Harry Hopkins, veteran New Dealer and future head of the WPA. Hopkins had an idea that the only way to find out what was going on in America was to send writers out there to see for themselves and report back. His first hire was Lorena Hickok, a bulky, pipe-smoking, hard-drinking close friend of Eleanor Roosevelt's—their relationship sparked a number of rumors of the predictable kind. Hickok spent a year driving around the country and sending back reports of widespread misery—creating a kind of anecdotal *Grapes of Wrath*.

The obvious objective was to gather evidence to justify the New Deal programs. Hopkins was apparently satisfied with Hickok's roving reports, thinking that they conveyed nuances of misery that mere statistics could not. So he decided to expand the staff. Martha, having been introduced to Hopkins by a reporter friend, got the job of covering the textile mills of North and South Carolina as well as New England.

It was just the thing for her. Though she found the experience thoroughly depressing, it gave her the opportunity to work and to exercise her considerable talent for indignation. The misery she saw was profound, the attempts to relieve it through government programs, inept to the point of criminality. The bosses who kept the pathetic workers in thrall through credit schemes at the company stores were hopelessly venal. She wrote, "It is probable—and to be hoped that one day the owners of this place will get shot and lynched."[4] As for the workers themselves, they were fast becoming "useless human material," beset by venereal diseases and ignorant hopelessness. No one involved in this triangle of misery—the bosses, the workers, the government agencies—seemed to be able to break free from ignorance, incompetence, or venality. To Martha everyone was contemptible; only the victimized workers deserved any sympathy, perhaps because she did not believe they had either the means or the imagination to change their lot. Still, the phrase "useless human material" suggests her complicated response toward them—a mixture of empathy with revulsion at the victims themselves, much the way a fastidious person might regard a ragged, reeking street person: pity and loathing mixed together. Her emotional connection to society's casualties, while real, remained abstract. Her first lover, de Jouvenel, said she "combined 'an ever-flowing deep rage against injustice, imbecility and weakness,' with an odd lack of real compassion."[5] De Jouvenel found this combination interesting and attractive; others would find it frustrating and inconsistent.

Her work led her to an introduction to the White House—an introduction facilitated by her mother's friendship with Eleanor Roosevelt (they had attended Bryn Mawr together). The friendship with Mrs. Roosevelt became a constant in Martha's life, for she admired the older woman's passionate devotion to the causes that touched her, mostly involving the suffering of the forgotten and helpless. Eleanor became something of a role model for Martha—"She gave off light. I cannot explain it better."[6] Martha, though, understood that she lacked something that Eleanor had—an ability to concentrate and stay focused for the long term. All her life Martha alternated between bouts of furious energy and work, including travel to far-off and difficult and dangerous places, with a sudden need to escape from it all, to stay put and be alone. This would last until boredom sent her back into action, so that she came to live her life as a series of exciting episodes strung together by periods of solitude, refreshing at first and then gradually becoming intolerable. She did not have the kind of constancy that she admired in Mrs. Roosevelt. She was like the submarines her husband would later be searching for—always in need of time to recharge batteries. This is not an unusual human trait, but in Martha's case it was more pronounced than in most.

From that first meeting at the White House she corresponded with Eleanor Roosevelt as long as the latter lived, sometimes asking for advice, sometimes telling her about the latest love affair and signing "love, Marty."

Though she was politically liberal all her life, Martha's experience in the Depression made it hard for her ever to accept the idea that any government or institution was an effective solution. This stance is contradictory, of course, since dedicated liberals generally place great faith in the efficiency of government, but it stemmed from her belief that market economies or private action were even less efficient. In fact, she came to doubt the effectiveness of any system—not as a result of careful analysis, really, but more because of her eyewitness observations of the people in charge and her streak of haughty contempt for almost anyone she met in a position of power, with the possible exception of the Roosevelts. She dwelled on the left side of the political spectrum because, in her view, people there at least seemed to care about injustice and poverty and all the other social ills, whereas the right didn't give a toss for any of it and cared only about accumulating wealth.

Her political ideas also shared a distinct snobbery common among intellectuals of the thirties, and beyond. Like many of her contemporaries in the arts and journalism, Martha came from a comfortable background. She grew up in St. Louis, a thoroughly Middle American city. Her father was a physician, her mother well educated and cultured. That Martha was half-Jewish never seemed to matter to her in a religious way, but it might have given her a sense of being somewhat apart from the Babbitts[*] of her world—that and the fact that her extended family, parents, and brothers had distinguished careers and solid achievements in their lives. Martha's mother was an early feminist and activist in a variety of social causes. So Martha undoubtedly grew up thinking she was somehow different from Main Street America, the people Richard Nixon would later call the Silent Majority. She maintained this prejudice her entire life. Speaking of Alger Hiss, she once said, "He doesn't understand why Whittaker Chambers and Richard Nixon were out to kill him, I do; he was the very embodiment of everything they were not and could not be, an educated upper class American, an American gentleman; they hated him."[7] Hiss was also a Communist spy, but Martha and the people who believed as she did would not accept this; to them, the charge was all part of a middle-class conspiracy against the well educated and well tailored—the revenge of the envious "booboisie," to borrow H. L. Mencken's priceless term. Still, reading Martha's comments, it's hard not to think that style—or the lack of it—was part of the intelligentsia's indictment of Middle America; and style in this case meant something much more important than fashion; it meant the way ideas are expressed, including the behavior of the people who expressed them.[†]

It's hard to determine which aspect Martha detested more—American mainstream values or the way they were presented and

---

[*] George Babbitt, a character in Sinclair Lewis's 1922 novel, *Babbitt*—real estate agent, enthusiastic civic booster, somewhat harried family man, thoroughly conventional middle-class archetype. His name became a shorthand for Main Street America.

[†] Martha lived much of her later life in England, where, not surprisingly, she had nothing good to say about Margaret Thatcher—"I really am a snob," wrote Martha, "I cannot bear that counter jumper woman."[8] The British term *counter jumper* drips condescension, as Martha understood perfectly: it suggests that Mrs. Thatcher would have been better off staying behind the counter of some small shop, dispensing ribbons or notions, instead of bothering the best and the brightest with her theories and shrill hectoring.

represented. Perhaps she never bothered to separate the two. All those eager men in rumpled suits endlessly scurrying after the next dollar, the hardware clerks and insurance agents, Rotarians and Elks, all the potluck suppers and church bazaars, all the unimaginative wives who stayed contentedly at home and thought Modernism meant better refrigeration and gave little if any thought to the plight of society's victims—none of it was for her. Even worse were the ostentatious nouveaux riches or the country-club people who spent their weekends playing golf. She disliked most of what Middle America stood for and never changed her mind about that. She sympathized only with the intellectual elites and the underclasses, albeit in an abstract way, whereas she regarded the vast majority with profound suspicion: "I never for a moment feared Communism in the US but have always feared Fascism. Fascism, it's a real American trait."[9]

Occasionally her contempt for politicians and political theory drifted into cynicism: "It does not matter in the least that Communism does not work, nor bring 'economic justice and happiness'; hope in the unknown is always powerful if the known is dreadful."[10] This assertion is stunning and could be used as a text for any would-be tyrant: "Let them eat hope." Either that or it is entirely nihilistic: "Nothing works anyway, so what does it matter?"

The comment is also indicative of her tendency not to care all that much about the means employed as long as the ends were, in her view, noble, and this relates to her attitude toward truth in journalism, something that challenged her throughout her career. Perhaps she believed in a higher truth, one in which the facts were simply one component—which means simply that she believed a little poetic license was justified if the resulting story more effectively dramatized the plight of the victims she was interested in portraying and thereby assisting. She had no patience for what she called "all that objectivity shit."[11]

Martha's tendency surfaced first in a story she did in 1936 about the lynching and burning of a black man in Mississippi. She wrote the piece as if she had actually witnessed the event, but she had only heard about it secondhand when she met a drunken redneck who told her the story, which may not have been true. She sent the story to her agent in London, who sold it to the *Spectator,* and from there it found its way to *Reader's Digest.* Somewhat embarrassed, Martha confessed the deception to Mrs. Roosevelt: "The point is, that article was a story. I am getting a little mixed up around now and apparently I am a very realistic writer (or liar), because everyone assumed I'd been an eye-witness to a lynching whereas I just made it up."[12] Mrs. Roosevelt advised her to keep quiet about the whole thing—this from a woman Martha described as "a moral true north."[13]

Well, that could be excused as a youthful journalistic misjudgment. But interestingly Martha had the story reprinted in her 1988 collection called *The View from the Ground.* Apparently she was no longer troubled by the deception. Or, more likely, she could not bring herself to omit what she considered a good story from the collection. For it was a good story. But to call her a journalist is inaccurate—she was a writer who went into the world to experience it and write down her impressions. Her first object was simply to be where history was happening, and her second object was to effect change where she thought change was needed, although she did not much believe in the possibilities: "And of course I do not believe in journalism; I think it changes nothing."[14]

Ironically, Martha expressed a lifelong distaste for what she called *apocryphiars,* a word she made up to describe people "who rewrote history, particularly to their own advantage."[15] She apparently saw no inconsistency between the concepts of "apocryphiars" and "objectivity shit." And when she met Hemingway, she was willing, at least temporarily, to overlook his outsize apochryphying tendencies.

But Martha was far from being the only young activist who

was willing to bend the truth and the facts to fit a particular set of ideals or objectives. Nor was she the most radical. The 1930s were a breeding ground of leftist ideas and programs, and many of the most active, unsurprisingly, were the young intellectuals and artists—few of whom seemed to have risen from the ranks of the proletariat. For example, consider the manifesto created in 1932 by Edmund Wilson (son of a lawyer, graduate of the exclusive Hill School and Princeton University, friend of Fitzgerald's, critic and novelist):

a. The ruling castes, hopelessly corrupted by the very conditions of their emergence, must be expelled from their present position.

b. A temporary dictatorship of the class conscious workers must be set up as a necessary instrument for abolishing all classes based on material wealth.

c. A new order must be established, as swiftly as can be, in which economic rivalry and private profit are barred; and in which competition will be lifted from the animal plane of acquisition to the human plane of cultural creation.[16]

In those times being on the left was expected of an artist or intellectual; it was the norm. (Even Norman Rockwell endorsed the WPA in some of his *Saturday Evening Post* covers.)[17] Individuals might, and did, squabble violently over various doctrines within the faith, but disagreed little about the essential idea that something was fundamentally wrong about Main Street America and capitalism. The Depression was proof of that. And so were the Babbitts.

Martha pretty much agreed. But although she was probably unconscious of the irony, she shared with the Babbitts of the world a fundamental belief in individualism. She only differed from them in her vision of how to spend her freedom. While she was perfectly willing to have government organize other people's lives for their own good, she would draw the line at having anyone organize hers: "I want to be myself and alone and free to breathe, live, look upon the world and find it however it is."[18] Or, again: "I have lived my life exactly as I thought best and it is a perfectly good life and I don't give a goddam what anyone . . . thinks about it."[19]

This, then, was the person who walked into Sloppy Joe's and who would become Hemingway's third wife—an attractive, sexually experienced woman at the peak of her physical perfection, aggressive and ambitious, impressed with Hemingway's work and reputation and willing to tell him so—to his great satisfaction; a woman with numerous talents, especially for writing and for indignation and disapproval; a woman who was available physically, but strangely unreachable and disengaged and therefore all the more maddeningly desirable; an independent operator with an ingrained suspicion of authority and a thorough contempt for bourgeois ideas and ideals; an outspoken advocate who believed that if she could only expose the truth of an evil in her writing, people might (but probably would not) respond, and if she had to adjust the facts a little, well, so be it; an adventuresome traveler who quickly grew bored if tethered to any one spot, or activity, too long; an athlete who all her life sought out lonely beaches where she could swim naked and then soak up the sun in solitude; a woman who loved being around men and loved the action of politics and war but would not submit to being ordered around or to playing second fiddle to anyone, either as a writer or a reporter . . . in short, a woman who was exactly the wrong sort for Hemingway to marry. He wanted his wife to be a junior partner in the Hemingway firm, someone who would look after things and leave him alone while he traveled and wrote and relaxed; someone who might also be taught to enjoy his great passions for fishing and shooting and the good things of life and be available when wanted—but never to be demanding. Martha didn't exactly meet these criteria. They would both learn those hard lessons later, though they should have known better from the start.

But that afternoon in Sloppy Joe's, as he got to know her over drinks, basking in her obvious admiration, Hemingway wasn't thinking about any of that. After all, he already had a wife who fit that bill. No, just then he was undoubtedly thinking that this woman might be just the right sort to have an affair with . . . and to share the excitement of the immediate future with. And if he detected an indefinable trace of coolness about her, he probably dismissed it, thinking she just needed the right sort of man.

As for the immediate future—it certainly *would be* exciting. For there was a war in Spain, and suddenly the idea of going there became even more compelling to Hemingway, for now a new element was added to an already powerful brew. Spain offered the excitement of war, the opportunity to participate in important events and write about them, passionate devotion to a cause and a people, association with like-minded comrades—and at night, a young and desirable woman to take to bed. The temptations were overwhelming. Hemingway did not resist.

* * *

But the best writing is certainly when you are in love. If it is all the same to you, I would rather not expound on that.

Paris Review interview

It's not clear when their affair began. Martha says she was not really interested at first and in fact had a dalliance with an anonymous Swedish sailor while still in Key West and before heading home to St. Louis. On the way home she stopped in Miami; Hemingway happened to arrive there, too. He was on his way to New York to make arrangements for Spain. They had dinner, then traveled together as far as Jacksonville. After that they corresponded by mail and phone, and when Hemingway came to New York again in February, this time on his way to Spain, his letters and phone calls to her carried a sense of urgency, and that was as close as anything to an aphrodisiac to Martha. She arrived in New York at the end of February, and most likely the affair began there, following dinners at the Stork Club and parties with Hemingway's friends.

Hemingway was going to Spain as a correspondent for the North American News Alliance (NANA). Martha meanwhile made a handshake agreement with *Collier's* magazine to do free-lance articles on the war. It wasn't what she wanted, exactly, as an assignment, but it was enough to get her there. Hemingway reached Madrid on March 17; Martha toward the end of March. Though they didn't travel together, they would end up in adjoining rooms in the Hotel Florida on the Plaza de Callao, a mere seventeen blocks from University City, where the Loyalists and the Nationalists were exchanging machine-gun fire. At various times during the war the Florida was the temporary home of most of the journalists and writers who were there to cover the fighting—John Dos Passos, André Malraux, Lillian Hellman, Antoine de Saint-Exupéry, among others. The hotel was also the target of Nationalist shells now and then, so that the assembled writers and journalists occasionally experienced a nervous moment or two.

By this time the war had been raging for nine months. Madrid was partially surrounded. Nationalist troops under Francisco Franco were shelling the city, but they did not seem to be in any hurry to take it. The roads east to Valencia and north to Barcelona were still open, so it was possible to get in and out of Madrid, though it involved some hardship and risk. Martha joined Sidney Franklin, an American bullfighter and Hemingway's unofficial factotum, in Valencia, and Franklin drove her to Madrid.

The day she arrived, Martha met Hemingway in the Gran

Via restaurant, gathering place of journalists, army officers, spies, hangers-on, and prostitutes. On seeing her, Hemingway said, "I knew you'd get here, daughter, because I fixed it so you could." This probably kindled a slow burn in Martha, who had a right to think that she had managed the trip on her own. As for Hemingway's habit of calling his younger female inamoratas "daughter," it seems a strange affectation, to say the least. It wasn't as though he was trying to hide their relationship; indeed, he would be proud of her, for Martha was the kind of woman who turned heads.

This time of great intensity was ideal for writing and for being in love. Hemingway was lucky in that way, for he had been in Paris in the twenties when it was equally as vibrant and welcoming to writers and lovers, and he had been both things there. And now there was Madrid, ravaged by war, true, but also alive with the kind of stories that draw writers like sirens *and* alive with the kind of commitment to a cause, to an idea, that intoxicates intellectuals and artists, perhaps because it gives them a means to escape self-absorption and become a part of something that seems to have meaning beyond anything the individual self can create. And when the enemies are the despised bourgeoisie and reactionary militarists, so much the better. As reporter Herbert Matthews said, "I know as surely as I know anything in this world that nothing so wonderful will ever happen to me again as those two and a half years I spent in Spain. . . . It gave meaning to life."[20] "Meaning" lay in the commitment to the cause, and the cause was antifascism. That was the glue that bound the otherwise incompatible elements, the incompatible doctrines, the incompatible people from around the world who came to Spain for that war. Some came to fight, some came to write about the fighting, some to make films, some just to look, so that they could say they had been there, and perhaps to catch an exciting whiff of cordite. But all had the same sense of what this war was about, for it seemed a clear case of black and white, right and left—the Nationalists, i.e., the fascists, versus the Republic. As Martha said, looking back on her experiences there:

"I think we . . . cannot help but be deformed because of Spain. Spain was where our adult hope was (the sum total of the remaining hope of youth, with a reasoning and logical hope of adults) . . . Spain was a place where you could hope, and Spain was also like a vaccination which could save the rest of mankind from the same fearful suffering. But no one important cared."[21]

In the thirties, many of the same Marxist political theories that were bandied about among American intellectuals had taken root in Spain and grafted with some indigenous movements of revolt, such as anticlericalism, land reform, and the desire for independence in Catalonia and the Basque country.[*] These "movements" united more or less with the republicans, socialists, communists, and anarchists to form a motley coalition of reformers that somehow swept into office in 1931, at which point the king abdicated and a new order seemed about to be born. The new government began instituting a number of reforms that attacked the prerogatives of the Church, tried to redistribute land to the peasants, and tried to provide some autonomy to Catalonia (the district in which Barcelona is the major city).

All of this outraged the main conservative elements and institutions—the army, the Catholic Church, and the owners of capital—albeit in different ways. The army viewed itself as a protector of the nation and therefore detested the idea of Catalan autonomy. What's more, they found the messy corollaries of reform—strikes and civil disturbances—distasteful in the extreme. The Republican government had apparently initiated disorder, which to the army seemed a derogation of any government's first obligation. The Catholic Church detested not only the assault on its preroga-

---

[*] Catalans and Basques each have a language of their own, although Catalan is similar to Spanish, while Basque is sui generis. These independence movements are another obvious indication of the link between language and national identity.

tives (such as requiring civil marriages) but also the fundamental atheism of the left. Republican politicians were denounced as Jews and Freemasons as well as Marxist atheists. Additionally, a deep strain of anticlericalism existed in some quarters because the Spanish Church was perceived, with good reason, as a defender of the old order. Numerous attacks on the property and persons of the Church occurred—attacks that were properly described as atrocities. (One Barcelona demagogue, Alejandro Lerroux, "enjoined his followers, the 'young barbarians,' to murder priests, sack and burn churches and 'liberate' nuns.")[22] The large landowners and businessmen saw socialism and communism for what they were—an attack on the concept of private property; moreover, they wanted nothing to do with the idea of unionized peasant workers whom they preferred to pay subsistence wages.

On the other side, the frustrated Republicans in the coalition could do little to stop the leftward progress of their government, while the "workers," through a number of large unions, generally supported the radical reforms, even though each large union had its own agenda and political philosophy. Civil violence, much of it fomented by Falangists, the Spanish fascist party members acting as *agents provocateurs,* plagued the country for the next several years. The political turmoil dragged on until 1936, when the army, finally having enough of both civil disturbances and economic and social reforms, revolted, and Francisco Franco eventually emerged as the leader, though at the beginning he was just one of several generals leading the rebellion. Thus, in an ironic turn of events, the rebels were the political conservatives, and the actual government—the Republic—were the "liberals." And the Republic was a squabbling collection of socialists, anarchists, separatists, Stalinists, and Trotskyists, along with a few frustrated true Republicans, who were not radical enough to suit their coalition partners and too radical to suit the rebels. To say that the coalition contained both anarchists and communists, and that the communists contained

Stalinists and Trotskyists, says all that is needed to be said about its possibility for cohesion or survival. It is a wonder that it lasted as long as it did.

Part of the reason the coalition did manage to hold out for three years of bitter fighting was the passion of its various components. True, each was passionate to its own particular creed—the Stalinists were loyal to Stalin, the trade unionists to their unions, the loyal army officers and troops (who did not join the rebellion) to the legitimate government, the agricultural workers to the idea of land reform, the separatists to their region—but despite their differences they were clear about who the enemy was. And so when the revolt broke out the government issued arms to the "workers" and later introduced conscription to fill out the ranks. This ragtag conglomeration was reinforced almost immediately by foreign volunteers—the famous International Brigades. All told, somewhere between forty thousand and sixty thousand volunteers from some fifty countries came to Spain to fight. Some were embittered refugees from fascism in Germany and Italy, others were idealistic Englishmen, such as George Orwell, still others were American leftists and idealists who formed the celebrated Abraham Lincoln Brigade. And in the three years of fighting, 20 percent of these volunteers would be killed, and a great many of the rest wounded.[23]

These were the people Martha wrote about for *Collier's* magazine, "men who came all this distance, neither for glory, nor money and perhaps to die," and they "knew why they came, and what they thought about living and dying, both. But it is nothing you can ask about or talk about. It belongs to them."[24]

There are echoes of Herbert Matthews's sentiments here, of course, but even stronger stylistic echoes of the man Martha was there with: "And each man retained now, better than any citation or decoration, the knowledge of just how he would act when everything looked lost."[25]

* * *

When war broke out, Franco's troops were based in Spanish Morocco, where they had earlier been fighting against local rebels, so it was logical for him to take command of the rebellion in the south of Spain, while his brother generals dealt with the north. His army of about forty-seven thousand men had a large contingent of Moors, so in another irony, the Moors would be returning to Spain in the name of Spanish nationalism and the Catholic Church—after having forcibly been expelled centuries before by their Catholic majesties, Ferdinand and Isabella. But first Franco would have to find a way to transport his army from Africa to Spain.

The rebel generals also faced the problem of financing and equipping their rebellion, so they turned to the governments that would naturally be sympathetic to their ideals and attitudes—Germany and Italy, both of which eagerly jumped in with offers of money, equipment, and men to help in the fight. Both countries wanted to try out new weapons systems and to train their troops, airmen, and sailors in actual combat conditions. (By the war's end Italy had sent over one hundred thousand troops to fight in Spain.) What's more, in political considerations, a Spain that was friendly to Germany and Italy would add to France's uneasiness and perhaps render her a little more pliable during the future expansions that Hitler in particular had in mind. France did sit on the sidelines during the war, even closing its borders periodically so that arms and ammunition for the Republic could not get through. This was simply French nervousness about offending the fascist states, despite France's socialist government, which had theoretical sympathy for the Spanish Republic. Meanwhile, the British, who had some economic ties with Spain that made them lean toward the Nationalists, i.e., the rebels, made it clear to the French that they would prefer a position of noninterference. As for faraway America, the mood was largely isolationist; if the

Spanish people wanted to kill each other, that was their business. Also, the large Catholic lobby supported the Spanish Church and thereby effectively blocked any action to aid the Republic that FDR might have considered, though he did not appear to be particularly interested in the conflict, having numbers of other New Deal irons in the fire. America remained officially on the sidelines throughout the war, though of course opinions about Spain were divided and much debated—as they were in Britain and France. But officially, all three stayed out of the war. Meanwhile, Stalin initially regarded the whole thing with indecision. His main worry was Germany, and to counterbalance that threat he needed the support of the British and the French. Nor did he want to antagonize Hitler. It was a difficult problem because his country's interests seemed to conflict directly with what one would assume would be its natural solidarity with the Spanish leftists, and especially, of course, the Spanish Communist Party. Ultimately, though, Stalin decided to send arms and ammunition, and the aid along with some Russian advisers arrived in time to prevent the collapse of the Republican defenses around Madrid and elsewhere, thereby prolonging the war for another two years.[26] His action was not altogether a matter of geopolitics, though—or international communist solidarity—for he sold the arms for substantial amounts of Spanish gold in a transaction that looked suspiciously like making a profit, although communist commentators would have called it something else.

As the major powers in the world considered their own interests, Franco solved his African transport problem by calling on Spain's new allies. His troops were moved into Spain in German planes and ships. The German navy, including some of the same officers who would eventually wind up commanding U-boats in the waters off Hemingway's Cuba, shielded the operation from the ill-equipped and ill-prepared Republican navy, while German and Italian fighter planes provided air cover.

When Franco's African army landed, Spain's most intense suffering began.

Military historians do not regard Franco as a particular genius. He was slow-moving and cautious, but steady. And he had a clear view of the political nature of the war, which explains why he would depart from a logical line of advance and detour to a city or town that had no strategic value except that it contained some Loyalist soldiers to be eradicated. For Franco viewed this as a war of political extermination—it was not enough to conquer territory: the scourge of the left must be erased, and that meant, simply, killing unionists, workers, Republicans, socialists, communists, anarchists, and anyone else marginally sympathetic to the Republican government. As he said, "We must carry out the necessarily slow task of redemption and pacification, without which the military occupation will be largely useless. The moral redemption of the occupied zones will be long and difficult because in Spain the roots of anarchism [i.e., leftists] are old and deep."[27]

This was not a matter of winning hearts and minds. To cleanse the "occupied zones" the enemy within must be annihilated. Franco turned that task over to his Moors and Spanish Legionnaires, who raped and looted their way north toward Madrid, killing the opposition they encountered and leaving a trail of terror and desolation in their wake. No one deemed to be an opponent was spared—captured soldiers, local politicians of the wrong stripe, wounded men in hospitals, women—even, in at least one case, pregnant women in a maternity ward in Toledo, who were taken out and shot.

This was not a case of troops running wild; it was policy. Traveling with the army were the Falangist special squads—fascist party hit men who routed out anyone who might have escaped the army. In one captured town a reporter for the *Chicago Tribune* "saw Falangist patrols stop workmen in the streets and check if they had fought to defend the city by ripping open their shirts to see if their shoulders bore the telltale bruises of recoiling rifles."[28] Those who did were taken to the bullring and machine-gunned. When it was over, there were eighteen hundred corpses.

Nor were the terror tactics unique to Franco's operation. In the north, Franco's colleague General Mola said, "It is necessary to spread terror. We have to create the impression of mastery, eliminating without scruples or hesitation all those who do not think as we do. There can be no cowardice. If we vacillate one moment and fail to proceed with the greatest determination, we will not win. Anyone who helps or hides a Communist or a supporter of the Popular Front [the leftist coalition] will be shot."[29]

This was no posturing. During the war and its aftermath Nationalist troops and political assistants killed approximately two hundred thousand people.[30] Even today researchers are trying to determine the precise numbers, for Franco's long reign after the war retarded the effort for many years.

As historian Antony Beevor noted, "Not surprisingly, people wondered if Franco wanted to repeat the deathbed answer of the nineteenth century General Navarez when asked if he forgave his enemies: 'I have none. I have had them all shot.'"[31]

In the Republican zone, which comprised mostly the districts of the eastern half of Spain, the violence was equally as loathsome although the numbers of dead were smaller. Some thirty-eight thousand conservatives and fascist sympathizers were killed, many by impromptu *checas*—leftist gangs of self-appointed secret police. Hemingway in *For Whom the Bell Tolls* tells the story of Pablo's capture of his village and the subsequent murder of the police and rightist-leaning villagers, including the priest who so disappointed Pablo because "he died very badly." This was fiction, but only technically and stylistically. Such things happened in many places.

The feeling is, though, that some slight shade of difference existed between the atrocities both sides committed. The Nationalists did so as a result of stated policy; the leftist killings were more

the result of gang violence, in many cases local score-settling—
something that is common in civil war. The victims in either case
were nonetheless dead, but the Republic's hands seem somewhat cleaner than the Nationalists'—in terms of policy. Once
the Communists gained power, however, certain political killings
accelerated, and the targets were their rivals *within* the Republic's
patchwork coalition. (In Barcelona in May of '37 a civil war within
the Civil War broke out between the Communists/Stalinists and
the POUM, which was the party of Trotskyists who had allied
themselves with the anarchists; the Stalinists won and promptly
arrested hundreds of POUM supporters.)[*]

Not all civilian deaths came from the barrel of a gun. The
most infamous military atrocity of the war was the bombing of the
Basque city Guernica. This was carried out by German aviators of
their volunteer Condor Legion. The city was destroyed, although
its military significance was negligible, if that. Picasso famously
recorded the event, which has the distinction of being the first
time defenseless civilians were targeted for aerial bombardment.

Those who said this altogether terrible war was merely the beginning of something worse were quite right. It was a war against
civilians, a war fought by guerrillas and by massed armies as well
(the pivotal battle for Teruel alone cost the Loyalists sixty thousand casualties and the Nationalists fifty thousand), a war of spies
and counterspies, of firing squads and sabotage, atrocities and mass
graves, refugees, siege and starvation, cynicism and devotion, a war
in which competing faiths intensified and justified existing ha-
treds—Catholic nationalism versus communism and anarchism,

---

[*] To oversimplify an impossibly confusing political situation—the Trotskyists were
communists who wanted not only to defeat the Nationalists but also to institute
revolution within Spain, and elsewhere; the Stalinists were primarily interested in
defeating the Nationalists without alienating the "bourgeois democracies"—Britain
and France—who were vital to Stalin because of his fear of Germany. George Orwell, who was a low-level POUM militiaman, describes these events in *Homage to
Catalonia*.

the landowners versus the land hungry, industrialists versus the workers. In the war the fascist states tested their weapons systems, while the Loyalists squabbled among themselves, and the cynical policies of faraway governments determined who would live and who would disappear, sometimes mysteriously; and the Communists gradually filled the power vacuum created when the Loyalist government fled from Madrid to Valencia as Franco's legions approached the capital. This consolidation of power along with the aid from Stalin meant that those of the other Loyalist faiths, especially the Trotskyists and the anarchists, were just as doomed as if they had been surrounded by Franco's Moors. In this perplexing war, only the insightful were able to sort through the confusion. All the rest were willing to see it in simple partisan terms, right and wrong, good and evil, whereas in fact the countless bodies in mass graves attested to evil being everywhere and good being "something rare."

In his short story "Night Before Battle," Hemingway needed only fourteen words to express a central truth of the war in Spain: "I guess he's nuts all right. Or has he got politics?" "He's got politics."

A person "had" politics. Like a disease. Right or left. Both equally fatal. To someone else and perhaps to yourself. Fascism and communism were the twin malignancies of the twentieth century. And both metastasized in Spain.

* * *

The war lasted three years. Hemingway and Martha went to Spain three different times in 1937 and 1938. The first visit resulted in a film called *The Spanish Earth,* made by Joris Ivens, a communist propagandist, with the text by Hemingway. The film was financed through an American collection of writers, called Contemporary Historians, in which John Dos Passos played a significant role.

Originally the voice-over narration was done by Orson Welles, but his basso profundo delivery was judged too melodramatic, so Hemingway capably rerecorded his own script. His baritone and his clipped and restrained delivery seemed to fit the tone of the film.

Back in New York, Martha helped Ivens with the editing of the film, inserting music as well as sound effects to suggest explosions and machine-gun fire. These postproduction inserts were necessary because of the difficulty and danger of handling bulky sound-recording equipment on the battlefield, but the obvious absence of ambient sound makes the film seem slightly unreal. For its time, though, *The Spanish Earth* was an interesting documentary, despite its overt and entirely intentional political motives.

The film was shown in the United States to raise money for the Loyalists, and through Martha's contacts it was shown at the White House, where Hemingway was unimpressed with the quality of the food and the presence of FDR—"Very Harvard charming and sexless and womanly, seems like a great Woman Secretary of Labor."[32] The film was then shown in Hollywood to a group of show business people at actor Fredric March's home, where Ivens made a speech, saying in part, "This is a war in which there are no rewards or medals. Wounds are the only decorations and the only reward is that of a good conscience."[33] It is a good line, though not quite true, for as John Dos Passos said,

> Behind the lines a struggle almost as violent as the war had been going on between the Marxist concept of the totalitarian state and the anarchist concept of individual liberty. More and more as the day-to-day needs of the army become paramount . . . the Communist Party forges ahead as the organizer of victory. The anarchists and socialists with their ideas of individual and local freedom and self-government have given way step by

step before this tremendously efficient and ruthless machine for power.[34]

Dos Passos was one of the founders of Contemporary Historians, but he gradually became disenchanted with the way the Loyalist government was co-opted by the Communist elements for whom Ivens was a spokesman and propagandist—clear conscience or otherwise.

Given Hemingway's involvement with the film, it's hard to make the case that he was apolitical. But as Robert Jordan says, he was not a communist, he was an antifascist. Also, it would be hard for a man like Hemingway to separate the comradeship of war from the comradeship of politics. A good deal of "my enemy's enemy is my friend" was in this war, so the politics of it all could be confusing, especially to someone like Hemingway who was not politically minded in the first place. ("All you can be sure about in a political-minded writer is that if his work should last you will have to skip the politics when you read it.")[35] Yet in June 1937 when Hemingway and Martha showed excerpts of *The Spanish Earth* and gave speeches before the second American Writers' Congress in New York—Hemingway nervously, Martha adeptly—some would interpret his comments as a leftist or even communist position. This went down well with the audience, who were mostly true believers. But it would not later be forgotten when some in the government and the FBI in particular would wonder about Hemingway's loyalties. To some in the FBI, mere participation on the Republican side in Spain was evidence of communist sympathies. Many artists and writers were tarred with that brush, and Hemingway was no exception, despite his oft-stated belief in a minimum of government, "an opium of the people, along with a belief in any new form of government. What you wanted was the minimum of government, always less government."[36] The great irony of the Spanish Civil War is that, regardless of their politics, almost all—journalists, artists, zealots of every stripe, and even the FBI—saw it in binary terms, when in fact it was a complicated, multifaceted tragedy.

Between the first and the second trip to Spain, Hemingway returned to Pauline, who had a wife's unerring nose for romantic wandering and recognized in his moodiness the same sort of dilemma that he had suffered through twelve years earlier, when he was trying to balance his marriage to Hadley with his love affair with Pauline. If she saw the irony of that, it did not give her any grim pleasure. Nor did she fall for her husband's predictable ploy of using his erratic and abusive behavior as an opening for her to throw him out and thereby solve his problem for him. In fairness, he was still ambivalent about the marriage. He wanted it both ways but was not insouciant enough to carry it off. His irritability showed that his rather conventional conscience was troubling him: "I know only that what is moral is what you feel good after and what is immoral is what you feel bad after."[37] His predicament was not letting him feel good, no matter which woman he was with.

*   *   *

If the republic lost it would be impossible for those who believed in it to live in Spain. But would it? Yes, he knew that it would be, from the things that had happened in the parts the fascists had already taken.

For Whom the Bell Tolls[38]

In the end the Republic did lose. In October of 1938 Hemingway and Martha were in Barcelona to see the last of the International Brigades march out to the harangue of La Pasionaria, the doughty Communist orator. As Martha and Hemingway watched the sad parade, Hemingway broke down and wept, and at that moment, Martha later wrote, she truly loved him. They had been together more than a year, but this show of vulnerability touched her in ways their previous relationship had not. Indeed, she had characteristically been ambivalent about it from the start, going to bed with him "as little as she could manage"[39] and describing the experience as "an invention of excuses and, failing that, the hope that it would soon be over," but attaching herself to him publicly, so that journalists and war tourists in Spain had no doubt about what was going on. Her reservations about him must have been strengthened if and when she read his play *The Fifth Column,* an obvious "drama à clef," in which the portrait of the female lead is hardly flattering and her identity unmistakable:

"She has the same background all American girls have that come to Europe with a certain amount of money. They're all the same. Camps, college, money in the family, now more or less than it was, usually less now, men, affairs, abortions, ambitions. . . . This one writes. Quite well, too, when she's not too lazy. Ask her about it if you like. It's very dull, though, I tell you."[40]

How Martha could read this without telling its author to go and "obscenity thyself" is difficult to imagine. Maybe she did. But most likely it was also just one more low spot in a relationship that had moments of great excitement and even passion, of a kind, punctuated by arguments and doubts and recriminations, then by separations that made the doubts disappear for a while. And all of it taking place in the midst of one of history's great maelstroms, so that everything seemed important and worthwhile, and if a little passion spilled over the bounds of good taste and manners now and then, well, how could it be otherwise? Hemingway, after all, she regarded as a genius, which bought him a good deal of latitude with her and with most everyone else, while he regarded her as beautiful and desirable—as well as quite brave—so that the asset side of their balance sheet looked stronger than the liabilities. There was enough net worth to keep them both going.

Aside from its scathing picture of Martha—and their relationship—*The Fifth Column* reveals Hemingway's intensified interest in spies and counterspies, an interest that would stay with him in Cuba and be a partial motivation for his U-boat-hunting adventures. In the poisonous, sinister atmosphere of Madrid everyone was always looking over his shoulder; a friend today might denounce you tomorrow. With his acute sensitivity to atmosphere, Hemingway would have been well aware of the lethal machinations going on below the surface of the war. The very term *fifth column* can be traced to General Mola, who said four columns were converging on Madrid but the city would be taken by a fifth column, that is, people in Madrid who sympathized with the rebellion and would rise up and take over the city when the time was right. This statement dramatically increased the fear and panic among the Loyalists and led to further atrocities aimed at suspected Franco sympathizers in the city. (In one incident alone twelve hundred rightists who had been jailed for political reasons were taken out and shot.) It seems fair to say that Hemingway's experience in Madrid, in which the atmosphere was murky with political and military intrigue, either created or sharpened his awareness of operations behind the scenes, of clandestine action and treachery, of menace lurking in the shadows. "'There's always more to it than we know about,' Nick said."[41]

Ultimately, the Nationalists drove the remnants of the Loyalist army out of their last stronghold in Catalonia, out of Barcelona, and over the border into unwelcoming France, where they were herded into wretched refugee camps while the Nationalists consolidated their power and began the postwar phase of political cleansing via the firing squad. Franco declared final victory on April 1, 1939. Meanwhile, Hitler and Mussolini prepared for the next war. When the Germans overran France, they scooped up the refugees who'd fled Spain after the civil war. Some fifteen thousand were sent to concentration camps in Germany and Austria, where at least half of them died, while another fifteen thousand were sent to forced-labor camps to build the Atlantic wall on the French coast, which would not be breached until D-day in 1944. Franco made no objections to any of this; it saved him trouble.[42]

Martha, ever energetic and indignant, made a lecture tour through the United States talking about the war in Spain as it slowly ground to its tragic end, then later went to Prague to cover the growing crisis with Hitler. She wrote her articles for *Collier's* and wondered about the future with Hemingway—"I believe he loves me, and he believes he loves me, but I do not believe much in the way one's personal destiny works out."[43]

Hemingway returned to New York in November of 1938 to join Pauline and to have some awkward conversations, for she was aware of what was going on—the signs and the reports were too obvious to ignore. From there he and Pauline went to Key West for Christmas. After a short stay he boarded *Pilar* and went to Havana, alone; his second marriage was essentially over. He booked a room at the Ambos Mundos Hotel, where he would begin to write his novel of the Spanish Civil War.

Meanwhile, refreshed and renewed by separation, Martha would arrive in Havana a couple of months later. She decided to look for a more permanent place to live than a disorderly hotel room and discovered Finca Vigia—Lookout Farm.

Perhaps she detected a trace of irony in that name.

Chapter Three

~~~

TWO KINDS OF HUNTERS

Certainly there is no hunting like the hunting of man. And those who have hunted armed men long enough and liked it never really care for anything else thereafter.

Hemingway, "On the Blue Water"

Be harsh.

Admiral Karl Dönitz, general orders to all U-boat commanders, 1942

HEMINGWAY called it the Great Blue River. The Gulf Stream starts in the Gulf of Mexico and runs along the north shore of Cuba, outside Havana harbor, and just beyond the hill where Hemingway's house, Finca Vigía, looked to the north. From there the current travels east and north through the Straits of Florida between the mainland and the Bahamas, then along the Atlantic coast to Cape Hatteras, where it veers off toward the North Atlantic and ultimately warms a section of Scotland enough to grow tropical plants there, a bizarre anomaly in the otherwise chilly Highlands.

When World War II came, Hemingway had been fishing the Gulf Stream for years, first from his base in Key West aboard *Anita,* a charter boat owned by Joe Russell, proprietor of Sloppy Joe's bar in Key West and model for Harry Morgan in *To Have and Have Not.* Later Hemingway fished from his own boat, *Pilar.* People familiar with his writing but less so with his biography may assume that the boat was named after the character in *For Whom the Bell Tolls,* but it was the other way around. The boat came first, in 1934, well before the Spanish Civil War and the novel he would make of it. Pilar was his pet name for his second wife, Pauline, a code name they used when they were having their affair while he was still married to his first wife, Hadley. So when he accumulated enough money to buy his own boat, he named her *Pilar.** No doubt he felt the irony of this a few years later, as he continued to fish from *Pilar* even as his marriage to Pauline dissolved and was replaced by his relationship with Martha Gellhorn. But a man given to romantic adventures must learn to live with these kinds of ironies. Besides, it's bad luck to change the name of a boat, and Hemingway was always careful about preserving what luck he had:

> "My," she said. "We're lucky that you found this place."
> "We're always lucky," I said and like a fool I did not knock on wood. There was wood everywhere in that apartment to knock on too.[1]

Pilar was a wooden boat. Undoubtedly many days and not a few nights passed when Hemingway was alone on the flying bridge, remembering those early days in Paris with Hadley, the one he had been lucky with in Paris and, later, careless with, and when nightmarish thoughts or worries about what might happen came to him, he knocked gently on his boat, just in case.

Pilar was thirty-eight feet long and cost $7,500, which was fairly

---

*He also said that it was named after a shrine in Zaragoza, a town where he had gone to bullfights. Perhaps he told Pauline one thing and others something else. It would not have been the first time.

expensive in 1934. America was still suffering through the Depression, and $7,500 could sustain a family with modest needs for a few years. (A public-school teacher averaged $1,227 a year; a physician, $3,382.) Hemingway borrowed some money from his publisher, Scribner's, and made a deal with *Esquire* for a series of articles that would cover the balance. Arnold Gingrich, the founder and editor of the magazine, was also an ardent angler who later produced some good writing of his own on the subject. Gingrich was attracted to Hemingway because the cachet of his name would help the fledgling *Esquire* grow. He was willing to pay Hemingway to write whatever he wanted, and the result was a series of "letters" about fishing in the Gulf, among other things. In this way, *Pilar* helped pay for herself—a nice arrangement. As Hemingway wrote to Gingrich, "The boat is marvelous. Wheeler 38 footer, cut down to my design. 75 horse Chrysler and 40 h. Lycoming. Low stern for fishing. Fish well, 300 gal gas tanks. 100 gal water. Sleeps six in cabin, two in cockpit. Can turn on its own tail burns less than three gals an hour trolling and four at cruising speed with the big engine. Will do sixteen with the two motors. The little one will do five hooked up."[2]

Pilar's hull was black and her superstructure dark green. The two engines provided some security in case one broke down and also allowed Hemingway to economize on fuel by using the smaller engine while trolling. That *Pilar* could "turn on its own tail" was useful in fighting fish, for a hooked marlin was apt to go in any direction, and the person at the controls needed to be nimble in adjusting course and speed. Perhaps that nimbleness gave Hemingway some (misplaced) confidence in his plan to search for U-boats. The engines were not big, though, and conditions had to be right—calm seas and a following wind—for *Pilar* to get up to sixteen knots. But she probably didn't like running at maximum speed for long. No boat does.

Hemingway said the boat could accommodate eight people,

and once wartime patrols were under way he would sometimes have that many in his crew. But it was an uncomfortable arrangement in a thirty-eight-foot boat. There was a fighting chair, and the specially lowered stern had a roller across the top, the better to haul large fish aboard. The controls on the flying bridge were added later and consisted of a car steering wheel attached to the lower steering mechanism. Hemingway was therefore literally standing on the overhead of his main cabin when he was at these upper controls. But a flying bridge provides the best visibility in all directions, visibility that is useful regardless of the kinds of fish you are looking for. It's also the best place for a skipper to be alone. Or to shout orders from.

As a blue-water fishing boat, *Pilar* was on the small side. True, some local fishermen went to sea in skiffs; the Old Man, Santiago, for one. But Santiago and others like him had no choice. They were of the have-nots, at least economically. But for sportfishing, *Pilar* was little more than adequate, especially for long voyages lasting several days and nights. Thirty-eight feet may look reasonably impressive when tied to the dock, but once out of sight of land, reality sets in quickly, and Hemingway was a realistic and careful sailor, always: "There's no danger from the fish, but anyone who goes on the sea the year around in a small power boat does not seek danger. You may be absolutely sure that in a year you will have it without seeking, so you try to avoid it all you can."[3]

When he made the crossing from Havana to Key West during a storm in 1936, he learned the truth of his own statement. *Pilar* barely managed to handle fourteen hours of huge waves, and the experience "scared you somewhere between your ankles and your balls. My balls felt very small."[4]

But *Pilar* survived that scare and a few others while serving her skipper well, and then some. Hemingway would probably have agreed with Kenneth Grahame's Mr. Water Rat when he said, "Believe me, my young friend, there is nothing—absolutely noth-

ing—half so much worth doing as simply messing about in boats."
Hemingway plainly loved *Pilar,* and his affair with her lasted longer
than any of his other affairs, or marriages.

* * *

What was it about big-game fishing that attracted Hemingway?
What does it say about him?

It is, first and foremost, the hunt. There is no use trying to
explain the appeal of the hunt. There are people who like it and
know about it and others who do not and who do not approve of it.
These two groups will never convert one another, although people
who like the hunt are more sympathetic to their quarry than the
others would imagine, and because of this sympathy they are more
able to understand the feelings of those who disapprove. Hunting
for a large fish, trolling through salt water in some of its more ami-
able moods, is part of the appeal, even when nothing happens—
for there is always the chance that a fish will rise, that the surface
of the water, so apparently empty, will suddenly come alive. The
hunter is looking for more than just his quarry; he is looking for
a moment that will register in his imagination and memory. Such
moments are the sporting equivalent of an epiphany and are rich
in both adrenaline and metaphor. What's more, the hunter wants
to accumulate as many of those moments as he can, and so he goes
out as often as possible. The writer Zane Grey, another passionate
angler, once went eighty-two days fishing for marlin off Tahiti and
never sighted a fish. Only on the eighty-third day did he hook a
huge marlin, which he fought for hours, until the sharks came and
he and his crew fought them off with gaffs and oars and cleavers
while they tore off chunks of meat, so that when the marlin was
finally brought in, it was nothing like what it had been before.
Hemingway was a fan of Zane Grey's angling books and even gave
some to his friends as presents. He kept a copy of one of them on

board *Pilar,* so it's fair to wonder whether the idea for *The Old Man and the Sea* originated with Grey rather than with a story Hemingway heard about an old Cuban fisherman who had suffered a similar experience.

So the hunt drew Hemingway to big-game fishing, but there was also the lure of the sea. More specifically the Gulf Stream: "You tell them that the biggest reason you live in Cuba is the great, deep blue river, three quarters of a mile to a mile deep and sixty to eighty miles across that you can reach in thirty minutes from the door of your farmhouse, riding through beautiful country to get to it, that has, when the river is right, the finest fishing I have ever known."[5]

Pilar would be rigged and ready to go almost immediately after leaving Havana harbor, for the Gulf Stream lies just outside the harbor entrance. Hemingway would have his two outriggers streaming baited lines as well as two rods trolling baits from the cockpit. He'd also trail a white wooden teaser that danced directly astern to attract the attention of a cruising marlin.

He was after marlin most of all. They were the biggest and the toughest and the most beautiful, as well as the most interesting, creatures that roamed the Gulf Stream. Finding them was a matter of understanding the Gulf Stream and knowing how these fish behaved. ("Marlin travel from east to west against the current of the gulf stream. No one has ever seen them working in the other direction.")[6] Hooking them and fighting them was a matter of willpower and physical strength. The sport challenged your intellect and experience, took place in a fascinating environment that could at any moment turn hazardous or worse, and presented you with an adversary that was many times stronger than you and could only be vanquished through determination and an unwillingness to quit. The sport had all the important elements. Luck was involved, too, for a leader might break or the fish might sound beyond your ability to raise it from the depths, or a hook might pull out, or the fish might throw it during one of the jumps you hoped for and came there to see. Any number of things might happen, but the key was to apply your understanding and your willpower and your physical strength so that you minimized your chances of failure, so that when failure came, you could at least tell yourself that you had done all you could. It was just you and a great fish. Fighting a fish was something you must do alone, like writing, and therein lay much of its appeal. "All art is only done by the individual."[7]

The death of the fish was not the object, not really, but the final act in a well-constructed drama—necessary, as any final act must be, but not the whole point.

On the other hand, maybe not: "One of its greatest pleasures, aside from the purely aesthetic ones . . . is the feeling of rebellion against death which comes from its administering. Once you accept the rule of death 'thou shalt not kill' is an easily and naturally obeyed commandment. But when a man is still in rebellion against death he has pleasure in taking to himself one of the God-like attributes: that of giving it."[8] Hemingway was talking about bullfighting here, but it doesn't take much imagination to believe the same sentiments applied to marlin fishing. Or to any of the other things he liked to hunt.

To Hemingway, killing the fish was not in any way inconsistent with catching it in an ethical manner, which included fighting the fish yourself and not using the boat as a sea anchor that would ultimately exhaust the fish while you sat there with the drag screwed down. That sort of thing was all right for a single man fishing from a skiff to feed his family, but not all right for a sportfisherman. There were ways things should be done and ways they shouldn't.

When we read Hemingway's writing on marlin fishing, we come away with the impression that he was indeed an ethical sportsman who followed a well-thought-out code of conduct.

There were, however, dissenting voices:

Ernest was a meat fisherman. He cared more about the quantity than the quality, and was more concerned about the capture of the quarry than the means employed to do it. He was also—and this is what no true angler is—intensely competitive about his fishing, and a very poor sport. If the luck was out, then nobody around him could do any right, and he was ready to blame everybody in sight, ahead of himself. When things were going right, he was quick to promote everybody in his company to high rank as good fellows, and was jovially boastful about their every least accomplishment, as well as his own. But let a hook pull out and his attitude was never to praise the fish that managed to bend it, but only to blame the hookmaker.[9]

Arnold Gingrich wrote this in 1965, a few years after Hemingway had killed himself and after the inevitable and predictable revisionism had begun. But the words have the ring of truth. Many anglers, especially fly fishermen such as Gingrich, regard competitive fishing—and fishermen—with disgust and disdain. Worrying about poundage instead of simply relishing the experience and the art of the sport is considered bad form. Also, trolling from a boat in which the principal actor in the hunt is the skipper, not the angler, had little appeal for Gingrich. And once a fish was hooked, landing it seemed a matter of brute strength and doggedness rather than anything like skill. A victory of willpower and stamina, not art. But this very aspect appealed to Hemingway's competitive nature—the contest with an opponent and the chance to prove that he was stronger, if not physically, then mentally and emotionally.

There was something unpleasant about Hemingway's competitiveness that was inconsistent with his ideas about the way a man should behave, at odds with his admiration for "grace under pressure." Someone with that sort of code might be expected to take the loss of a fish a little more philosophically. This competitiveness shows in too much of what he did—such as in his sophomoric comparisons between himself and other writers ("I can beat [Tolstoy]")[10]—and, most egregiously, his unconscionable trashing of Scott Fitzgerald, his friend and, in many ways, benefactor. It's impossible to read about this sort of thing without wondering how he could have allowed himself to lose control that way. It was gracelessness under no pressure at all. The amateur psychologist might well wonder just how strong his outsize ego really was. As Toni Morrison once said, "A large ego can be generous and enabling, because of its lack of envy."[11] Hemingway could be "generous and enabling" when things were going well, but less so when facing frustration and failure.

So Gingrich's recollections are consistent with how Hemingway behaved much more often than his admirers would wish. Whether Gingrich was being objective is another question. Few completely objective opinions about Hemingway, either the man or the writer, exist. He was much better at creating partisans, for or against. During his professional life he converted many friends into enemies—through just the sort of competitive blustering and mean-spiritedness that showed up now and then aboard *Pilar.*

But Hemingway's marlin fishing had an aesthetic element that critics such as Gingrich seemed to overlook. Despite the premium on strength and persistence that seemed to be the essence of big-game fishing, being attached to a creature that is utterly wild and of another world is somehow magical. When a marlin comes flying suddenly out of the water, shaking itself, then falling back with the kind of splash, as Hemingway said, "a horse dropped off a cliff might make," then you are seeing something that rewards your efforts and stays with you. Gingrich fished with Hemingway a number of times over three seasons but never hooked a marlin. Had he done so, he might have looked at things a little differently.

What's more, Gingrich portrays Hemingway as a poor sport, but that is offset in part by Hemingway's thoughtful observations about the ethics of the business—as illustrated by his concern for the proper balancing of tackle and quarry. Too light a rod left too many fish hooked and then lost or, worse, hooked for too long and therefore exposed to shark attack. On the other hand, heavy tackle that let the angler winch in a fish without giving it a fair chance to escape through sheer power and willingness to outsuffer the angler was equally wrong, and he said so. A pure "meat fisherman" does not worry over such things. "Our ideal is to catch the fish with tackle that you can really pull on and which still permits the fish to jump and run as freely as possible."[12] The art and the ethics lay in finding this proper balance. Apparently Gingrich did not see this side of Hemingway; it's hard to say whose fault that was.

In this as in most things about Hemingway, the truth is a mixture, with plenty of nuances, rather than a simple "this or that." One suspects that Hemingway as sportsman was at his best when he was fishing without an audience, when only his Cuban mate, Carlos Guttierez, was along to manage the boat, leaving Hemingway alone with his fish. Or maybe when he was out with just his three sons, for he genuinely loved the boys and cared for them and took pains to show them how things were done, fishing being only one of the important arts that a man should master. But hangers-on and sycophants rarely brought out the best in him—despite his love of having them around. After all, the best of him was in his writing, which was something he could only do when he was alone. When he was with a gang of cronies or admirers, he tended to drink too much and talk too much and tell stories about himself that were not always strictly true, which is ironic given his constant emphasis on making his written stories as true as possible. "The most essential gift for a good writer is a built-in, shockproof, shit detector. This is the writer's radar and all great writers have had it."[13] But with a crowd of friends and well-wishers around him, he didn't always have his radar turned on, it seems. Maybe his writing was the only thing that really mattered—that and his sons—so that the rest of it, his pals and his recreation, were mere sideshows that did not require either self-discipline or truth telling. Or maybe they were an escape from the hard work of truth telling and from the self-discipline it requires.

Fighting a great fish and conquering it was appealing not only for its own sake but also as a metaphor, like boxing, bullfighting, and hunting for big game. All are elemental contests involving danger and requiring strength and dedication, willpower and perseverance. But big-game fishing was not just a metaphor and a way of testing yourself against nature's best adversaries. It was also an inexhaustible field of study, an opportunity to learn things that were by themselves interesting, a chance to acquire knowledge that was an end in itself as well as a means to catching more and bigger fish. Hemingway had a scientific bent and kept careful journal notes about the fish he caught, the weather conditions, when and how they were caught, and he invited a number of scientists aboard *Pilar* to fish with him, as he developed and tried to verify his theories on marlin (he believed that all marlin were essentially the same fish at different stages of their development).*

This careful attention to the details was consistent with the way he approached any subject that interested him. As his friend John Dos Passos said of him, "For Hem it was different. He had an extraordinary dedication to whatever his interest was for the moment. Whether it was six-day bicycle racing or the bullring or skiing or fishing a trout stream, he stuck to it until the last dog was hung.

"He stuck like a leech till he had every phase of the business in his blood. He worked himself into the confidence of local professionals and saturated himself to the bursting point. Outside of an occasional scientist I have known struggling with a tough line of experiments I've never known anyone with that sort of

---

*Most scientists disagree and divide the marlin into four species: blue, black, white, and striped.

stickatitiveness. Some of Hemingway's best writing stems from this quality."[14]

This "stickatitiveness" was more than just the zeal of an interested amateur. The more Hemingway knew about a subject, the better he could write about it. And, ironically, the more he knew, the more he could leave out of his stories: "If a writer of prose knows enough about what he is writing about he may omit things that he knows and the reader, if the writer is writing truly enough, will have a feeling of those things as strongly as though the writer had stated them. The dignity of movement of an iceberg is due to only one-eighth of it being above water."[15] Properly crafted, the writing was not only lean and efficient but also evocative and suggestive.

In fishing, as in all his education, Hemingway was essentially an autodidact. (He read voraciously and eclectically, routinely running through hundreds of books a year.) He wanted to master any activity that interested him, and marlin fishing interested him more than just about anything else he encountered, other than writing: he was "completely satisfied on [*sic*] this as sport, living, spectacle and exercise."[16]

Something else about the Gulf Stream, though, attracted him as much as the chance to attach himself to a great fish: "In the first place the Gulf Stream and the other great ocean currents are the last wild country there is left. Once you are out of sight of land and of the other boats you are more alone than you can ever be hunting and the sea is the same as it has been since before men ever went on it in boats."[17]

Yes, perhaps that's how it was before the war. But when war came, the captains of merchant ships heading east from Gulf ports and then turning north through the Straits of Florida were only too keenly aware that they were not alone, regardless of how empty the surface of the sea seemed to be. The Gulf Stream was a highway of predators who, like the marlin, swam into the current. These were the U-boats coming from their bases in France across to the killing grounds off Cape Hatteras, then traveling down the Atlantic coast, their noses into the Gulf Stream.

* * *

A great killer must love to kill.

Death in the Afternoon[18]

The U-boat captains who came to the Gulf and the Caribbean in the spring of 1942 thought of their mission as killing ships, and they did indeed love doing it. Many of them had a sort of jaunty swagger, much like the aviators of World War I; they were interested in sinking as many ships as possible during a patrol; killing men was not the primary object, for most of them. In fact, many would fire their first torpedo, then wait as the merchant crew scrambled into the lifeboats before firing the coup de grâce. The commander of *U103,* Werner Winter, rescued some floating crewmen of one of his victims and after personally treating one of them for a wound said, "Sorry we had to do this, but this is war."[19] Others would surface and give the men in lifeboats some provisions and a course toward a safe landfall. Some captains were kinder, better sportsmen than others; and as the war went on and the bombing over Germany intensified, the humanitarian urges diminished and shipwrecked crews were left to their own devices. What's more, U-boat captains grew more and more wary of counterattack from the air or from escort vessels and therefore could not stay surfaced long enough to conduct rescue operations without endangering themselves. Further, many of the merchant ships had been equipped with naval guns, serviced by U.S. Navy personnel, and the Germans therefore considered these as no longer helpless merchantmen, but enemy warships. Finally, they had orders from Admiral Dönitz: "Be harsh. Bear in mind that the enemy takes no regard of women and children in his bombing attacks on German cities." Dönitz's irrefutable position was that a merchant crewman who was killed when his ship was sunk would never sail on another. What's more, stories of crew losses would make recruiting new merchant sailors that much more difficult.

Regardless of how the U-boat captains felt, the very nature of submarine warfare against merchant shipping meant that hideous casualties were unavoidable, most of the time. For the prime target was oil. And gasoline. The tankers carrying this cargo originated in the Gulf ports of Texas and Louisiana, and in the early days of the war they crossed the Gulf alone, passing by the north shore of Cuba and through the Straits of Florida and up the Atlantic coast to the Northeastern ports, where they either joined a convoy headed for England or unloaded their fuel and started the equally hazardous voyage home. Traveling alone, they were easy targets, and once struck by torpedoes the more flammable cargos would ignite, incinerating ship and crew alike, while the less volatile crude oil might spill into the sea, covering struggling crewmen and suffocating them or weighing them down so that they sank helplessly. Many a U-boat captain and his sailors watched as merchant sailors, some of them on fire themselves, jumped from their burning ships into the burning water and perished.

The tankers were not the only targets—any merchantman traveling in the war zone was fair game, for all cargoes were in some way or other a part of the Allied war effort. If the ship was too small to justify using an expensive torpedo, the U-boat would surface and blast the merchantman with an 88 mm or 105 mm deck gun. A few well-placed shells would suffice. Banana boats coming north from the tropics were sunk, leaving bodies and bananas alike floating on the surface in an absurdist tableau of war. Bauxite carriers from Trinidad went down, too, as well as sugar carriers, ships crammed with war material of all kinds, ore carriers—in fact, anything that steamed through this gauntlet was a potential target, whether the ship was from a neutral country or not. Some neutral ships painted large flags on their superstructures in an attempt to elicit mercy from the U-boats, but to no avail. The German policy was that any ships coming into war zones were legitimate targets. Their registry—with only a few exceptions—did not matter.

When the U-boats first arrived in the Gulf and the Caribbean, there was little if any defense against them. Surfacing to use a deck gun and save a torpedo carried with it almost no risk of counterattack. Merchant ships traveling alone chose their own courses, for the masters of merchant ships were notably independent-minded and would do as they thought best even as their colleagues were being sunk in increasing and alarming numbers.

This early period of the war—the whole of 1942—was a time of great success for the U-boat captains, and many went home with torpedoes expended to a hero's welcome and generous shore leave while their boats were being refitted and rearmed for another trip to the hunting grounds. Some called this period the Happy Time, though it's fair to wonder whether the officers and crews of the cramped and uncomfortable submarines were really all that happy—except when they returned safely to their home port after a successful patrol.

Happy or not, it was a period of repeated victories. During his testimony at the Nuremberg war-crimes trials Admiral Dönitz was asked how many merchant ships had been sunk by German U-boats during the war. He replied, "Two thousand four hundred and seventy-two, according to Allied statistics." In the first six and a half months of 1942 his U-boats sank over 360 ships in the waters off the U.S. east coast and in the Gulf of Mexico and the Caribbean. That's nearly 15 percent of their total for the entire war. They did this at a cost of seven U-boats sunk in combat. In the cost-benefit ratio of war, that is very successful indeed.

By many accounts, the Germans were as surprised by the Japanese attack on Pearl Harbor as the United States was. But they lost no time in declaring war on America and sending U-boats to attack American and Allied shipping near the source. They were perhaps relieved to have the political fig leaves of the previous months removed, for the U.S. Navy had been in the war long before the public knew much about it. The United States had been cooperating with the Canadian and British Royal Navies to provide escorts for the North Atlantic convoys that carried supplies to Britain provided in part under the Lend-Lease Act and protected in part by World War I–vintage destroyers ("four pipers") that America had transferred to the British in exchange for some naval bases. U.S. Marines had occupied Iceland (ostensibly at the request of the Icelandic government, but with pressure brought by the British, who were keenly aware of Iceland's strategic location and importance to the survival of the convoy system). America had established important weather stations in Greenland. One American destroyer (USS *Kearny*) had already been attacked and damaged by a U-boat, and another, the USS *Reuben James,* torpedoed and sunk with the loss of 115 out of a crew of 160 men. And this was all before war had been declared.

But once the war came, the U-boats flocked to American waters with a vengeance. They came from their bases in France. (It's interesting to speculate how the precipitate collapse of the French affected the battle against U-boats. By using French bases far in advance of their natural home bases in the constricted Baltic or North Atlantic—bases that the British Royal Navy could have bottled up with relative ease—the U-boats got to their hunting grounds faster and stayed there longer. Whether patrolling the Atlantic coast or the Atlantic convoy routes, the typical U-boat of the period had a range of forty-two days, without refueling. Many a merchant ship went down because the French surrendered so quickly. These losses at the margins may be impossible to calculate, but common sense suggests they were significant.) The U-boats came first to America's east coast, where they happily targeted merchant ships silhouetted against the night sky by the lights of the cities along the eastern seaboard. Desperate measures were called for. As historian Samuel Eliot Morison noted, "The submarine situation was so serious in early 1942 as to tempt the Navy to try anything; the fact that President Roosevelt proposed and Admiral King, not addicted to romantic methods, authorized mystery ships, proves how serious the situation was."[20]

At the urging of FDR the Navy authorized civilian yachtsmen up and down the Atlantic coast to cruise and look for U-boats. The Navy also converted several civilian ships into "Q-ships"— the "mystery ships" that appeared to be merchantmen but were actually armed and commissioned naval vessels. Their armament was concealed, and their mission was to cruise shipping lanes in an attempt to lure U-boat captains into thinking the Q-ships were easy game, so that they would surface for an economical kill. At that point the Q-ships would open fire with deck guns, then follow up with depth charges as the surprised and frantic U-boat captain ordered an emergency dive. That was the plan.

But the Germans weren't fooled. They had experience with similar ruses during World War I, and when the newly converted Q-ship USS *Atik* went on active patrol for the first time in March of 1942, she was promptly sunk with the loss of all hands by *U123* after a running gunnery battle on the surface.[*]

Another experiment involved the USS *Irene Forsyte,* which was a converted schooner. Whoever believed that such a vessel could be a match for a U-boat was seriously misguided, but fortunately for the crew they did not have to test their mettle in combat, for the *Irene Forsyte* nearly foundered on her first cruise and had to be removed from service.

---

* *U123* lost one man during this action and was one of the most successful boats in the war. She sank forty-two merchant ships totaling 219,924 tons. She survived the war and was turned over to the French navy, which commissioned her into their fleet.

Gradually U.S. coastal defenses along the Atlantic seaboard were tightened, so in the spring and summer of 1942 the U-boats shifted southward, into the Gulf of Mexico and the Caribbean in search of easier pickings. In either case they would use the Straits of Florida, which would lead them along the north shore of Cuba and westward into the Gulf, or eastward along the north shore and then south through the Windward Passage between Cuba and Haiti and thence into the Caribbean. Either way the north shore of Cuba lay squarely in their path as they headed for their hunting grounds. And the north coast of Cuba was Hemingway's territory; it was also the main highway for most of the shipping going either to or from the Gulf ports. He was directly astride the combat zone.

*   *   *

Normally the Gulf Stream current runs at about four knots—nothing too difficult for a giant marlin to manage but something else again for a U-boat whose top speed while submerged was about seven knots. Running into a four-knot current consumed time and energy. And while a U-boat could run on the surface and preferred to because she could make a top speed approaching eighteen knots, the surface was where danger lay. But those were the choices—struggle into the stiff current while submerged and waste time getting through the Florida Straits and into the Gulf, or travel on the surface and risk being sighted and attacked. The obvious tactic would be to travel on the surface at night, and in the early days of the war this was not very dangerous because the U.S. patrols were few and far between, and the aircraft that flew over these areas were not yet equipped with radar. What's more, it was absolutely necessary for a U-boat of that time to run on the surface for long periods because it had two distinct methods of propulsion—diesel engines for surface running and battery-powered electric motors for submerged running. The diesels charged the batteries, in concept much like a car's engine charges its battery. But the diesels operated only when the boat was on the surface,* and the U-boat's batteries ran down after six hours of submerged running. Therefore the U-boat had to operate on the surface a good deal of the time to keep its batteries charged.

Despite the adverse current and the proximity to the Florida coast, the Straits of Florida were the shortest way into the Gulf and therefore a preferred course of the U-boats. Commanders were always mindful of fuel consumption, since in the early days of the war the Germans had not yet deployed tanker submarines (called milch cows) that could refuel U-boats at sea. (These came on line quickly, though, in the spring of 1942, though they tended to operate in the mid-Atlantic.) The first U-boat captains therefore had to rely on what fuel they could carry from their home port. Throughout the war, secret refueling dumps were rumored to be on Cuba and other islands—dumps established and maintained by fifth-column units. Little if any hard evidence existed of these facilities, but people believed in them at the time, and they were a secondary target of Hemingway's surveillance missions. Finding a supply dump would in some ways be more valuable than spotting a cruising submarine, which could easily escape before help arrived. Also, this kind of mission was well suited to a small boat such as *Pilar*, which could poke her nose into the shallows around the mangrove islands along Cuba's north shore. And it suited a crew of men armed only with Thompson submachine guns, handguns, and grenades, since presumably any fuel dump hidden in the mangroves would not be heavily garrisoned.

A glance at the map will show that U-boats—always concerned to maximize their fuel supplies—had few alternatives to the

---

*Later in the war U-boats were equipped with *Schnorchel*—ventilation devices that let them run submerged on diesel engines.

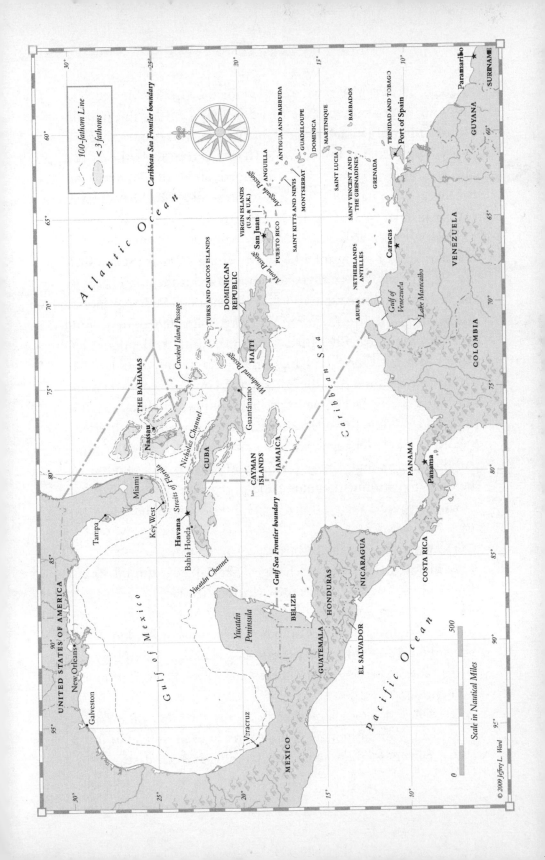

Straits of Florida if they were headed for the Gulf of Mexico. The only other choice involved a fuel-devouring detour through the Crooked Island Passage in the Bahamas—a riskier course because to get to the Gulf the U-boat would have to creep along the narrow channel of deep water close to the north shore of Cuba to avoid the Great Bahama Bank, which was too shallow for U-boat comfort. A U-boat needed depth, both for protection and as a means of stealthy attack and escape. Merely being able to submerge was no guarantee of safety, for a U-boat running submerged at a shallow depth could be spotted and attacked from the air. Therefore the U-boats preferred to travel through the deep Straits of Florida against the Gulf Stream current. If danger threatened, they could dive into the Great Blue River—disappear into its depths in less than a minute. Once the danger had passed, they could rise to periscope depth and scan the horizon for a merchant ship traveling north at a stately pace. One torpedo to stop her, perhaps a second to sink her. A few minutes to watch the target go down, perhaps a word or two exchanged with the survivors to verify the ship's name, tonnage, and cargo. Then a southerly course, bound for the Gulf, to continue the hunt—and perhaps through the Yucatán Channel to the Panama Canal area, the obviously vital link between the two oceans.

How deadly were the U-boats?

A memo from General George Marshall to Admiral Ernest King on June 19, 1942, states the situation clearly:

> The losses by submarines off our Atlantic seaboard and in the Caribbean now threaten our entire war effort. The following statistics bearing on the subject have been brought to my attention:
>
> Of the 74 ships allocated to the Army for July by the War Shipping Administration, 17 have already been sunk. Twenty two percent of the bauxite fleet has already been destroyed.

Twenty percent of the Puerto Rican fleet has been lost. Tanker sinkings have been 3.5 percent per month of tonnage in use.

We are all aware of the limited number of escort craft available, but has every conceivable improvised means been brought to bear on this situation? I am fearful that another month or two of this will so cripple our means of transport that we will be unable to bring sufficient men and planes to bear against the enemy in critical theaters to exercise a determining influence on the war.[21]

The significant words as far as Hemingway was concerned were "every conceivable improvised means."

Chapter Four

≈≈≈

THE ENEMY IN THE MACHINE

He who sees first, wins.

From the U-boat commander's handbook

ANDLING *Pilar,* or merely being aboard her, was a pleasure for Hemingway, as it would be for any blue-water sailor, except when the weather was foul or threatening. *Pilar* had a wooden hull, decks, and bulkheads—forgiving material that accommodated itself to the motions of the sea, smooth to the touch and comforting physically and aesthetically. And she had an open-air conning station on the flying bridge, a place to savor the sights and smells of the sea, a place where, barefoot, Hemingway could synchronize his body with the movement of the boat and let his imagination run loose for a while as he simultaneously kept his eye out for seabirds diving on frantic baitfish that could perhaps be fleeing from a marlin. *Pilar*'s outriggers were like antennae on some delicate aquatic insect, her wake foamy white against the blues and greens of the Gulf. Seen from afar or up close, she was a pretty thing. Small wonder that Hemingway named her after a lover.

By contrast, U-boats did not have names, only numbers.*

---

* World War II U.S. submarines were all named after fish: *Dace, Gudgeon,* etc.

(Some individualized themselves with designs painted on the conning tower, much like the devices on a knight's shield.) Nor did they have much in the way of creature or aesthetic comforts. A warship of any kind, surface ship or submarine, is first and foremost a machine. Seen from a distance, it is easy to romanticize the beauty of a Navy ship or submarine cutting a creamy bow wave, an elegant haze-gray silhouette—and no sailor would disagree with that image. But any sailor would also know that on board the ship, within the ship, the human element largely gives way to the requirements of the ship itself, the machine—the endless miles of cables overhead, and vents and steel bulkheads and steel decks, heavy watertight doors and hatches that seal off men working in a magazine or gun turret or engine room, where the smell of fuel oil and the myriad valves and gauges, the oppressive heat and the deafening sound of the power plant, make life uncomfortable on the best of days. Just about the only soft thing on a warship is the sailor's bunk, and he will tell you he doesn't get to spend nearly enough time there. At least on a surface ship a sailor can enjoy the sea breezes on weather decks. Not so in a submarine, for the main decks, narrow and slippery, are dangerous places to work, while the confined area of the conning tower leaves little room for anyone other than the men standing watch.

Inside a World War II submarine the sense of living in the workings of a machine was doubled and redoubled, intensified and inescapable. Crewmen had to cooperate with each other merely to move from one part of the boat to another. There was little color to soothe tired eyes; clothing, which inevitably got soaked, had little chance of drying; the bulkheads were damp and moldy, as was some of the food, notably the bread; and little if anything reminded the sailor of home except the picture in his pocket or the one pasted to the steel bulkhead by his bunk, the bunk that must be shared with another—one man sleeping while the other was on watch. The stench of oil in the engines and the traces of diesel exhaust mixed with the smell of the food being cooked or simply in storage, and that mingled with the smell of mildew and mold and the odors of the men who served for weeks without the chance of bathing—taken all together, it was a hard and uncongenial environment to live and work in, much less to fight in. Only when the U-boat surfaced did the men on watch have a chance to breathe the sea air for a time while they searched the surface of the ocean for targets and the air for potential threats and tried to stay dry against the inevitable spray.

When a threat appeared, the alarm was sounded and the U-boat began to dive. The bridge was cleared of lookouts and the watch officer was the last down the hatch into the control room as the boat was already beginning to submerge. A World War II submarine submerged by changing the angle on the hydroplanes in the bow of the boat, slanting them downward to drive the bow down (the faster the boat was going on the surface, the faster the dive) while simultaneously blowing air from the buoyancy tanks along the sides of the boat and letting the seawater rush in to fill the tanks. Unlike most ships, the U-boat was not naturally buoyant, and without the air in these tanks it would simply sink. When the boat wanted to surface, air had to be pumped into these tanks from compressors and the water driven out. While the boat was running submerged, air had to be pumped into or bled out of trim tanks to keep the boat on an even keel. This tricky operation required constant vigilance, primarily from the chief engineer.

The workhorse of the German submarine fleet was the Type VII. During the war 568 of this type of boat* were commissioned. While boats in this class varied slightly, their general characteris-

---

*Traditionally submarines are referred to as *boats,* even though their size might qualify them as *ships.* As a rule of thumb, a *boat* is anything that can be lifted out of the water and placed aboard another vessel. A *ship* is too large for that. Thus people sailing for Europe on a liner who refer to catching the boat are incorrect. But it is a common mistake.

tics were basically the same. Each boat carried fourteen torpedoes and could fire them from five tubes—four in the bow, one in the stern. On deck was an 88 mm gun, for which the boat carried 220 rounds of ammunition in a waterproof magazine near the bow. Some were also equipped with antiaircraft machine guns later in the war, when it became clear to everyone that the airplane was the chief menace to the U-boat.

The Type VII boat's top speed was almost eighteen knots on the surface and something less than eight knots submerged, and it had a range of eighty-five hundred miles at ten knots on the surface but only eighty miles at four knots underwater, after which point the batteries had to be recharged, which meant the U-boat would have to surface. This was a critical factor in antisubmarine warfare— the job started with and depended upon vigilant surveillance. No one knew when or where U-boats would surface, but all knew that they would have to surface sometime, and so the more eyes that were watching, the better the chances of engaging and destroying the U-boats. Surface ships and boats, volunteers and military personnel, civilian and military aircraft, fixed-winged aircraft and blimps—anything that could float or fly was pressed into service to be on the lookout. The mission of these surveillance crews, Hemingway's included, was not simply to wander around the Gulf hopelessly looking for periscopes. The mission was to patrol a sector and to be on hand if and when a U-boat came to the surface. Sighting was the opening act of battle, followed by communication to headquarters, dispatch of ships and planes, and finally, attack.

The Type VII was 67 meters (about 218 feet) long overall but only about 50 meters long within the pressure hull—the actual interior living and operating space. The width or beam of this space was 4.7 meters. That's roughly 15 plus feet—narrow enough to be sure, but the crew of fifty men or so did not have the luxury of even that much elbow room, for the interiors of the boats were lined with lockers for storage, bunks, compartments, so that the actual passageway down the center of the boat was a mere few feet. The aft third of the boat housed enormous diesel engines that allowed only a couple of feet passage between them. Those given to claustrophobia were not suited for the submarine service. Comfort was something you left in home port.

The maximum diving depth of the Type VII was 722 feet—according to its design specifications. At that point the seams in the pressure hull—the inch-thick cylindrical steel skin that is the true hull of the sub—would begin to weaken and, at some undetermined lower depth, collapse, crushing machines and men alike.

The Type VII submarines were the key to Admiral Dönitz's wolf-pack strategy in the Atlantic. There were two elements to the strategy. First, the targets were convoys, dozens of merchant ships sailing in formation. Therefore the more U-boats that could be gathered, the greater the havoc they could wreak on the convoy. But the other rationale for the wolf pack stemmed from the difficulty of finding convoys. The ocean is large, and the electronics and satellite surveillance that are taken for granted today were nonexistent. Dönitz therefore deployed his U-boats in an extended line covering the usual convoy routes, and when one boat spotted a convoy, it would radio to headquarters, which would in turn signal all the U-boats in the area to gather at the target. In other words, wolf-pack tactics were developed in part because of the difficulty of locating targets. Vigilance was therefore critical to submarine and antisubmarine warfare, alike. As the U-boat commander's handbook said, "He who sees first, wins."

In the Gulf of Mexico and the Caribbean, though, it was different—at least early in the war. Convoys were not the norm, and many independent-minded merchant ship captains steadfastly stuck to their preference for sailing alone. What's more, in the comparatively constricted waters of the Gulf, where extensive shoals restrict the navigable waters, it would not be hard for U-boats to find shipping targets. So the U-boats did not come in packs, but rather singly, and started to arrive at the end of April 1942. The first was *U507*.

U507, under the command of Harro Schacht, left Lorient[*] on April 4, 1942. On April 30 she was patrolling off the northeastern coast of Cuba when she spotted a small tanker, a molasses carrier named *Federal*, heading west along the Cuban coast to pick up cargo. Not wanting to waste a torpedo, *U507* surfaced and at 450 yards opened fire with her 105 mm deck gun. After absorbing dozens of rounds, the tanker rolled over and sank as the crewmen abandoned ship, having left five dead behind. This encounter took place five miles off the Cuban coast near the port city of Gibara. An hour after the one-sided battle, a single U.S. Navy aircraft arrived on the scene, no doubt dispatched in response to *Federal*'s calls for help. By that time *U507* was long gone.

Patrolling the Gulf until May 16, *U507* sank seven merchant ships. Flushed with success and emboldened by the meager defensive response, *U507* sighted her ninth and last victim, the Honduran freighter *Amapala*. *U507* surfaced and fired her last torpedo, which malfunctioned. The Germans then fired some machine-gun bursts across the merchant's bow. Recognizing the inevitable, the *Amapala*'s crew abandoned ship. Two German sailors then volunteered to swim to the target ship and open her sea valves. The *Amapala* partially sank but was later salvaged. During the operation a single U.S. bomber arrived in response to *Amapala*'s calls for help. *U507* crash-dived and endured a few bomb blasts without damage, and when the bomber departed, the U-boat surfaced and recovered the boarding party and headed for home, arriving after a patrol of sixty-two days on June 4, all torpedoes expended, and a score of some forty-five thousand tons of shipping.

---

[*] One of the five U-boat ports in France, where bombproof concrete pens protected the boats from air attacks; the others were Brest, Saint-Nazaire, La Pallice, and Bordeaux.

Her sister boat *U506* arrived on May 10 and spent the next ten days nearly matching *U507*'s score, sinking seven ships and damaging an eighth.

Both of these U-boats were a Type IXC—a long-range submarine that was larger than the Type VIIC. The new *U166* carried twenty-two torpedoes, a 105 mm and a 37 mm deck gun along with a 20 mm antiaircraft gun. It had a crew of up to 56 men, a range of 13,450 miles, a surface top speed of 18.3 knots, and a submerged speed of 7.3. The boat was 251 feet overall. All told, the German navy commissioned fifty-four of these boats—one-tenth of the number of Type VIIs. These boats were not as nimble as the smaller Type VIIs and so were judged to be less appropriate for the wolf-pack tactics used against the Atlantic convoys, during which the increasingly dangerous cat-and-mouse game played with escort vessels demanded maneuverability and fast-diving capability. But the greater range and hitting power of the Type IXs made them ideal as lone-wolf operators—ideal, in fact, for the Gulf of Mexico and the Caribbean, where unsuspecting or stubbornly independent merchant ships still steamed alone.

In the summer of 1942 twenty different U-boats cruised into the Gulf of Mexico. When their patrols were finished, seventy-eight merchant ships were on the bottom of the Gulf. (The Caribbean toll was even worse—from May through September 153 ships were sunk by U-boats.)[1]

* * *

These, then, were the enemies that Hemingway went to sea to find—the Germans were in the Gulf in force, and they were supremely dangerous and ambitious. And successful.

Hemingway's mission was more complicated than merely cruising around and scanning the horizon for enemy submarines, for much of the time the U-boats traveled beneath the surface, and *Pilar* had no underwater detection equipment. Hemingway might sail *Pilar* through an apparently empty sea and never know that a submerged U-boat was lurking nearby, perhaps watching him through the periscope and trying to decide whether *Pilar* was worth destroying. Aside from spotting a periscope, the only way to detect a submerged U-boat was to entice it to the surface.

The experience of some local fishermen suggested a way to do that.

U-boats, which had traveled far from their bases in France and had been on patrol for weeks, had long since run out of fresh food and were often attracted by the sight of a fishing boat. Having spotted a potential target, the U-boat would suddenly surface in a massive display of foam and streaming water, no doubt astonishing the fishermen. The Germans would then send over a boarding party to relieve the locals of their catch, as well as any fruits or other fresh foods they might have on board. This happened to commercial fishing boats more than a few times during the war. If the fishermen were lucky, the Germans would go on their way with no further harm done, beyond the loss of the catch. If they were not lucky, they would be set adrift in life rafts and their boat sunk with gunfire, for a U-boat would not waste a torpedo on a fishing boat. And if they were very unlucky, they would be machine-gunned along with their boat (though most, if not all, U-boat commanders drew the line at this sort of thing, despite orders from the commander of the U-boat fleet, Admiral Dönitz).[2]

Hemingway reasoned that a fishing boat such as *Pilar* would offer a tempting opportunity to U-boat captains on the lookout for fresh food. He would have to hope, though, that the U-boat he attracted was not having a run of bad luck. No U-boat skipper wanted to go home with little or nothing to show for the patrol. Even sinking a fishing boat such as *Pilar* would be something positive to report.

As he considered this plan, Hemingway must have smiled

ruefully at the irony of the situation, for the hunter would now become the hunted, and *Pilar* would be the bait.

But his plan had a potentially fatal flaw—once the U-boat surfaced and once Hemingway had reported the contact, help would be delayed. (The hour that it took for aircraft to respond to the *U507*'s surface attack on the *Federal* proves the seriousness of this problem; this was not the result of inefficiency so much as the lack of available ships and planes.) Hemingway would have to find a way to prolong the enemy's stay on the surface, since U-boat captains did not linger there longer than necessary. But then, when either aircraft or surface ships arrived, he would need some way to escape the coming attack and avoid becoming the victim of friendly fire. Besides, for all the Navy knew, *Pilar* might be an enemy craft based clandestinely in Cuba and used for resupply. Numerous German agents were rumored to be on the island cooperating with U-boats; Hemingway's secondary mission was to be on the lookout for just these kinds of rendezvous.

The only solution he could devise was perhaps characteristic— he would attack the U-boat and try to damage it sufficiently to cause casualties, confusion, and mechanical malfunctions that would prevent the U-boat from submerging and escaping.

How did he intend to do it? *Pilar* had no armament aside from some Thompson submachine guns—handheld weapons that were useful at close range. These were antipersonnel weapons that could do little if any serious damage to the U-boat itself. Hemingway had originally considered mounting twin fifty-caliber machine guns on *Pilar*, but that plan was impractical—the wooden vessel could not support such heavy equipment nor withstand the recoil. What's more, the U.S. government agencies in Cuba were reluctant to provide the guns. And finally, it would be difficult, if not impossible, to disguise the gun mounts on the relatively small *Pilar*, which would mean that, as an armed vessel, *Pilar* would be a legitimate target of war to any U-boat commander. Having heavy machine guns installed would actually make Hemingway's mission more dangerous, for they would give a U-boat captain more than enough justification to sink *Pilar* and so add "an armed patrol boat" to his score.

Without installed armament of any kind, Hemingway reasoned that his only option, once he had reeled a U-boat to the surface, was to get alongside close enough to throw hand grenades up and into the U-boat's conning tower—as well as an explosive charge packed in a fire extinguisher—a device Hemingway designed. Ideally, these would tumble down the open hatch and explode in the control area of the sub, possibly killing the captain and various officers along the way. Perhaps the explosions would not only ruin some of the controls but also damage the hatch between the exterior bridge of the conning tower and the control room below and thereby prevent it from closing and sealing the interior, so that the boat would not be able to submerge until after it had made some time-consuming repairs. Meanwhile, Hemingway and his crew would use their Thompson submachine guns to discourage the Germans from using their own deck guns against *Pilar* as she fled the scene.

Could this work? In theory, maybe. Certainly grenades exploding in the confined spaces of the control room would do fearsome damage to men and equipment as well.

But Hemingway's plan of attack assumed that the German captain would allow *Pilar* to come alongside, whereas a naturally wary U-boat commander would in all probability heave to maybe fifty yards away, man his deck guns, then send an armed boarding party in an inflatable boat to relieve the "fishing boat" of its catch. After all, U-boat commanders were in the business of stealthy attacks; they were especially cautious when surfaced in enemy waters during daylight, and they would have enough imagination to consider any vessel a potential threat. Hemingway would not be allowed to get close enough to throw grenades,[*] let alone a fire extinguisher; nor would the Thompson submachine guns be a match for the German deck guns.

Further, Hemingway must have known that no matter how many officers he killed in his initial attack, someone would still be left in the chain of command, and once *Pilar* turned to flee the area, the German sailors would use their deck guns and destroy her with ease. Their heavy-caliber machine guns would turn the boat into splinters, to say nothing of what a four-inch-caliber gun with an explosive shell would do. In an instant *Pilar* would simply cease to be. And *Pilar* was nothing like a PT boat, which could scurry away at forty knots, zigzagging to avoid the fall of shot. At best *Pilar* would do maybe sixteen knots, with both engines straining. Running away at top speed, *Pilar* would still be in range for a good half an hour. German gunners could take their time before opening fire and still reduce *Pilar* to so much flotsam with a single shot. Not that they would bother to wait.

Perhaps Hemingway intended to heave to while the Germans were preparing to send over their boarding party, at which point he would suddenly push *Pilar*'s throttle to full speed ahead so that he could rush alongside the U-boat, throw his grenades, then escape while the Germans tried to recover from the shock of sudden attack. But this could hardly succeed, for the Germans were old hands at this business. They would see *Pilar* suddenly getting under way; they would have her covered with deck guns, and when she made her turn to attack the U-boat, they would open fire on her, and that would be the end of *Pilar* and her crew. Nor did it make sense to try to use the boarding party as hostages in some way, for

---

[*] Hemingway discussed his plans with a friend, Marine Colonel John Thomason, Chief of Naval Intelligence for Central America, who told him that no U-boat commander would be foolish enough to let him "throw beanbags down his hatch," at which point Hemingway dubbed him "Doubting Thomason."[3]

they would be well armed and well trained to deal with any such foolhardiness.

So, looking at the plan objectively, Hemingway must have known that it was a forlorn hope. He might be able to do some damage to the U-boat and thereby delay its escape, but with little chance that he and his crew would survive the encounter. But given the difficulties inherent in *Pilar*'s pose as a fishing boat, there seemed to be few alternatives available to him.

* * *

If Hemingway contemplated his plan with a degree of rueful fatalism, nothing about it seemed to worry his wife, Martha. She was not convinced that there was any danger at all. She did not know about the carnage in the Gulf that summer, but she did know Hemingway and suspected his plan, indeed his whole self-designed mission, was little more than a grown-up boy playing at war while the real war was raging in Europe and the Pacific. She had lived with him now for five years, married for two of those years. Much of the glow had faded.

Perhaps at one time Hemingway's audacious plan would either have impressed or horrified Martha. Perhaps when they were first together in those exhilarating days in Spain, a plan so bold and apparently dangerous would have stimulated a trace of awe or respect. Or after the Spanish Civil War at the end of 1939 when she was on another assignment in Finland. Then it was possible for her to write to him, "As I love you I love your work and as you are me your work is mine."[4] The work she was referring to was the novel he was writing just then in Cuba—*For Whom the Bell Tolls*.

The language is uncharacteristic of Martha, the last woman in the world to surrender her individuality or let it be invaded by another, although she probably thought she meant what she said at the time, since her work as a journalist had sent her away from him, and separation always cast their relationship in rosier colors than constant togetherness ever could. Ironically, she later said in her book *Travels with Myself and Another,* "Loving is a habit like another and requires something nearby for daily practice."[5] That may be true for many people, but in Martha's case she needed just the opposite—periodic distance and time apart to allow the irritations and disappointments of regular contact to recede and to let the better memories come forward. (Also, she needed time by herself, for its own sake, and would probably have escaped even from a comfortable relationship, now and then.)

When she wrote this letter, she was in Helsinki covering the Finnish-Russian war for *Collier's* and suffering in the December weather and thinking of the warmth of Cuba and Finca Vigia. The "you are me" line foreshadows the ending of *For Whom the Bell Tolls:* "'You are me now,' he said. 'Surely you must feel it.'" But although Martha used the line in her letter, it's hard to imagine that the thought originated with her. It sounds more like something Hemingway might have said to her in the evening after a few glasses of Tavel, the wine that he said goes best with love. (He used similar lines in his 1929 novel, *A Farewell to Arms:* "There isn't any me. I'm you. Don't make a separate me."[6]) This may have been one of his standard ideas that Martha picked up, and it became a kind of shorthand between them, although in the back of her mind Martha must have cringed a little when she said those words. The sentiment was so unlike her. As literary dialogue, the line lacks credibility. We accept it at the end of *For Whom the Bell Tolls* because Robert Jordan and Maria are in extremis at that moment and should be allowed some latitude. But even so, reading that scene requires a little suspension of disbelief and raises memories of other works in which Hemingway's romantic dialogue falls short of the rest of his writing. Hemingway might legitimately counter that the line seemed to work pretty well in real life, but there is a difference between the foolish, albeit seductive, things lovers say to each other on the one hand, and literary merit, on the other.

In the early days of their relationship, as the first year of the war in Europe came to a close, Martha was happy to think of her coming role as Hemingway's wife. The divorce from Pauline was being finalized, and by January of 1940 Martha was back in Cuba, writing to her editor at *Collier's*, "It is perhaps wrong to be so happy in this present world, but My God how I love this place and how happy I am."[7] The weather was certainly better than in Finland.

But being together again, so far from the war in Europe where history was being played out at enormous costs, soon lost much of its appeal for Martha. Not only did she become bored with being the lady of the finca, she also began to chafe under Hemingway's often overbearing and controlling attitudes toward their relationship.

Hemingway had a way of indoctrinating and dominating, if not psychologically inhabiting, his wives and anyone else who associated with him (which gives a slightly different shading to "you are me"). Martha herself says that she had to fight against the inroads of Hemingway's infectious writing style, and she did not always win the fight. Then there was the Hemingway style of living—a combination of vast enthusiasm, real expertise in any subject that interested him, and an energy level that simply overwhelmed everyone, so that, Tom Sawyer–like, he converted all and sundry to his passion of the moment. This power of personality was useful in selling the idea of the patrols to the U.S. embassy and the Navy and also in recruiting his friends for the crew. But it was less attractively displayed in his relationships with his wives. It's hard to imagine that his second wife, Pauline, really wanted to go off on safari to shoot a lion, but she did, only to be characterized for her troubles as "Poor Old Mama" in *Green Hills of Africa*. Pictures in Martha's biography show her in the hunting field, shotgun under her arm, with Hemingway—probably in Sun Valley,* probably shooting pheasants or ducks. She later refers to live-pigeon shooting in Cuba—something she had never done and would not do again, so far as can be determined, yet something that was a passion with Hemingway in the Havana days. In fact, once she broke with Hemingway, she apparently never picked up a shotgun again. In short, Hemingway as a force of nature tried with no little success to convert his various friends and wives into people with whom he could feel compatible and to whom he could act as mentor and expert leader. And even Martha succumbed to some extent. He was an artist, after all, always working not only on his writing but also on his latest Galatea. But as Scott Fitzgerald (no stranger to relationships with complicated women) remarked when he heard Hemingway was marrying Martha, "I think the pattern will be somewhat different than with his Pygmalion-like creations."[8] Fitzgerald knew Martha and recognized that she would only go so far before rebelling against being molded into a shape that didn't suit her—which was any shape other than the one she chose to adopt at the moment.

* * *

About the time that Martha was returning to the warmth and rich colors of Cuba, where the ceiba tree in the finca's front yard had sprouted eight new orchids, Hans-Gunther Kuhlmann, twenty-six years old and an officer in the German navy, reported to *U37*, where he would serve for the next thirteen months, eventually rising to first watch officer (second-in-command). While Kuhlmann was aboard, *U37* would torpedo forty-six ships during her eight war patrols, and her three different captains would all win

---

*About Sun Valley, Martha said, "I hate it like holy hell. It is the west in an ornamental sanitary package. But . . . anyhow, I'm going, because that is my job."[9] This was in September of '41—after they had been married awhile.

the Knight's Cross of the Iron Cross—symbol of particular success in the *Kriegsmarine*. Successful U-boat commanders were the naval equivalent of the ace pilots, the Red Barons of the ocean war, and they were feted and petted by Admiral Dönitz, commander of the U-boat fleet, who ran his operation as a virtually independent fiefdom under Hitler. Dönitz had great latitude because he was successful. (By contrast, the surface navy, insecure and cautious to the point of being useless, was essentially sitting it out in various ports and fjords. The pocket battleship *Graf Spee* had been trapped and scuttled in Montevideo early in the war; the German battleship *Bismarck,* true, had sunk the redoubtable battle cruiser HMS *Hood,* pride of the Royal Navy, but it, too, would be sunk by the British in May 1941. From that point on the German surface navy—which had not been prepared for war and which had been promised by Hitler that it would not have to be ready until 1944—ceased to be much of a factor. Not so the submarines. The German navy looked to the U-boats for success.)

The youthful Kuhlmann would have been less than human—or, perhaps, less than a professional naval officer—had he not wanted a share of the U-boat glory. An ambitious young officer longs for two things: command of his own ship and the opportunity to distinguish himself and his crew in action. Kuhlmann was no less ambitious than his brother officers.

When Kuhlmann was aboard *U37,* in the early days of the war, the U-boats were winning the Battle of the Atlantic, roaming the seas without much opposition and devastating the convoys that ran between the United States, Canada, and Great Britain, laden with war material, food supplies, and in some cases Canadian troops. The great prizes were the eastbound convoys, with the double benefit from sinking them—loss of both ships and cargoes. But any U-boat skipper was almost as pleased to sink a returning, westbound merchantman, empty of cargo and sailing "in ballast," for that ship and most, if not all, of its crew would sail no more.

The United States was still formally neutral, and the British were struggling to organize and protect their convoys from the depredations of the German submarine campaign. Ideally, convoys were escorted by warships that were armed with asdic (underwater sound-detection devices) and depth charges and that could and eventually would traverse the Atlantic shipping lanes and fight off, and sink, the U-boats along the way. But that strategy required large numbers of escort ships, especially destroyers and corvettes, and at that moment the British did not have nearly enough. The Royal Navy was large and superbly professional, but it was stretched very thin; even the fifty "four-piper" U.S. destroyers, outmoded as they were, would be welcome additions to the fleet. But these would not begin to arrive until September 1940.

Thus Kuhlmann and his colleagues enjoyed great success. True, the submarine service was inherently dangerous. Simply operating such a complicated piece of machinery involved risk. But going to sea at any time involves the possibility of danger, and at this time the risk of death from enemy action was slight and easily offset by the rewards for success. (This would drastically change as the war went on, however—of the forty thousand men who went to sea in U-boats, thirty thousand were lost by war's end.)

In March 1941, Kuhlmann was transferred from *U37* and given his first command—the *U7*, a small "coastal" submarine carrying only five torpedoes and no deck guns. Boats of this type were mostly used for training.* No doubt when Kuhlmann first took command of *U7* he felt proud, but he was hoping that something more impressive would soon come his way. And so it did. Four months later he was given command of *U580*.

U580 was a new boat; Kuhlmann would be its first skipper. As with all newly commissioned naval vessels, there was a period of

---

*As an example of the inherent risk of the service, *U7* sank with all hands in February 1944 as a result of a diving accident.

shakedown and training—shakedown for the boat, to make sure its systems operated properly, and training for the crew. When the Germans acquired their U-boat bases in France they moved their combat operations there, but training of new crews and boats was mostly conducted in the Baltic Sea.

Operating out of Kiel on the Baltic Sea, *U580* went through the standard training routine until November 1941 when, during an exercise, she collided with a target ship, the *Angelburg,* and promptly sank, losing twelve men out of the crew of forty-four. So Kuhlmann's second command ended almost as quickly as his first.

Normally a collision at sea is the death knell for a commanding officer's career, especially if his vessel sinks, and so it's reasonable to assume that Kuhlmann was not at fault in this incident, for the following March he was given command of *U166*—another newly commissioned boat. Moreover, most of the crew who survived the *U580* accident came aboard his new command with him. Both his crew and his senior officers must therefore have had faith in him—no small matter in the submarine service, in which the decisions of the skipper can literally mean life and death to the entire crew. This is true of course in any branch of the navy, but especially so in the intense, psychologically fragile environment of a submarine, where the close quarters and dismal living conditions and the routine of endless days on patrol are punctuated by a few minutes of action followed by perhaps the most difficult of all combat situations to endure—the depth-charge attack of your enemy.

As U-boat ace Wolfgang Luth observed, "'It is common knowledge that when the depth charges start to explode, everyone looks to the officers.' . . . A captain had to be especially careful, for his attitude was all too quickly transferred to his men. If he looked worried, they would panic. If he looked confident, they would at least be quiet. And if he smiled through the worst of it, they would look at each other and smile, too. Appearances in such a case were everything."[10]

Though Hans-Gunther Kuhlmann apparently had the respect of his crew, despite the loss of *U580*, one wonders what he thought about himself. He was, after all, a very young man still. In this he was no different from the rest of the U-boat service, in which a thirty-year-old captain was unusual. (Of the 203 new submarine captains in 1941, only fifteen were older than thirty-two; most were in their twenties, like Kuhlmann.)[11] But the collision must have given Kuhlmann some doubts, if only now and then, that his luck was not what it should be. Or had been. Sailors are, as a breed, superstitious, and a U-boat had little wood to knock on when doubts appeared.

There must have been something else, too, perhaps the opposite side of doubt; he had been captain of two U-boats and was now taking over his third, but he had not yet been on a war patrol, much less fired torpedoes at an enemy—not as a commanding officer. He must have been especially eager to prove himself. He may have been exonerated over the collision, but senior officers have long unofficial as well as official memories. Kuhlmann could easily imagine some of his seniors sitting around the officers' club in the evening and, when Kuhlmann's name came up, hearing one of them say, "Oh, yes, Kuhlmann. The one who had that collision. Lost his boat. Not his fault, apparently. But still . . ."

Yes, Kuhlmann must have said to himself in his private moments, he had only one way to erase that mark against his name. What's more, a Knight's Cross medal was virtually guaranteed to a skipper who sank two hundred thousand tons of enemy shipping. The likelihood of such exploits in the Atlantic was diminishing, somewhat, as the Americans and the British were cooperating to provide better, though still far from perfect, protection for the Atlantic convoy runs. But in the summer of 1942 new fields of opportunity were opening up—the U.S. coastline and, farther south, down through the Gulf Stream and into the Gulf of Mexico.

Kuhlmann's new boat was ideally suited for that sort of mission, for it was a Type IXC—a long-range submarine that was larger than his previous Type VIIC.

U166's home port was in Lorient, France. "Lorient was not a pretty place, but it had that French 'flair.' The people all were nice, we drank a lot of wine and champagne, and it all was free."[12] Apparently, being occupied was not that oppressive a situation for some of the locals, although the town suffered from errant British bombs intended for the U-boat pens and the dockyard facilities. Still, when the U-boat was not on patrol, the crew had ample opportunity to relax:

"One third of the crew lodged ashore, where hotels, brothels and a country rest house were provided, while one third went on leave to Germany by special train, and one third worked at repairs and upkeep. Thus each member of the crew had nine days work, nine days rest, and nine days leave between cruises."[13]

No doubt at some point before *U166* was scheduled to leave on her first patrol, Kuhlmann went back to Germany for a quick reunion with his new bride, Gertrude. Looking at pictures of them as they were then, smiling, obviously happy with each other, painfully young, Gertrude truly beautiful and Kuhlmann handsome and apparently carefree—it all seems inconceivable that in the next few weeks that same young man would be at sea, prowling the shipping lanes looking for unarmed merchants to torpedo, while always on alert for enemy planes and ships, piloted by other pleasant young men with pretty young wives at home, men who would cheerfully send Kuhlmann, his boat, and all his men to the bottom. How and why such things can happen is one of the many mysteries of war, one that looks out at us from old photos. These people don't seem so very different, after all, and of course they aren't.

We don't know what Kuhlmann and Gertrude thought about Hitler. But a professional naval officer such as Kuhlmann, who had gone through the naval academy and trained on surface ships before transferring to U-boats, would probably have appreciated the buildup of Germany's military forces and the professional opportunities that provided, while most likely grumbling that the navy seemed to get the short end of the funding and development stick when compared to the army and the *Luftwaffe*. He would, at this time, have had great faith in the leadership of Admiral Dönitz and would probably therefore have leaned toward Dönitz's Nazi sympathies, simply out of loyalty to his commander, if nothing else. But no political commissars were aboard the German U-boats. Sailors were allowed to think whatever they liked, as long as they did their jobs and more or less kept their political opinions to themselves. In this as in all matters pertaining to the running of the boat, the skipper set the tone and the boundaries. But of all branches of the service the navy seemed to be the least politically indoctrinated, perhaps because of its traditions, perhaps because Hitler knew next to nothing about naval issues and didn't meddle or interfere as much as he did with the army and the air force, or perhaps because the crew of a ship or a U-boat is a self-contained entity under the command of one man—the skipper. Loyalties and allegiances get pared down to their essences—to your mates, to your skipper, and to your vessel. When land sinks below the horizon, you are, after all, very much alone.

On June 17, 1942, *U166* left Lorient for the Gulf of Mexico. Just before they left Kuhlmann wrote to Gertrude:

"In three days it will be two years that we have been married. . . . Have these two years not been beautiful and we, completely lucky? How I am to be envied, my all dearest. It hurts that I cannot be with you on that day, but 'c'est la guerre.'"

Then, on the morning of departure: "Keep me dear. I always think of you."[14]

* * *

The first leg of the voyage was perhaps the most dangerous, for Lorient was on the southern end of the Brittany peninsula, within easy reach of Britain's Royal Air Force. Kuhlmann reported on June 20 that he had been caught on the surface at night by an aircraft using searchlights. The plane had dropped bombs, but *U166* suffered no damage after, presumably, making an emergency dive.

In this era of GPS and satellite surveillance and navigation, it's difficult to imagine how important the human eye was to the combatants in World War II, especially in the early years of the war. A ship that was out of sight of land was dependent on celestial navigation—locating its position by measuring the angles of various stars. Days and weeks of stormy weather when clouds obscured the stars meant that the ship could be miles and miles off course, blown by winds and currents in directions and speeds that were undetectable until the clouds cleared away and the navigator could again use his sextant. True, the navigator could set a compass course and a speed and assume that the ship was following that line drawn so hopefully on the chart (called dead reckoning), but the sea and the winds are rarely calm enough to allow that luxury, and the currents are not generally as obvious as the majestic Gulf Stream and can send a ship unknowingly off its course, pushing it sideways, even though the helmsman is steering the compass course perfectly and the ship's bow seems to be pointing where the navigator wants it to go.

The human eye was key to combat, too, both to initiating it and avoiding it. The conning tower of a U-boat was relatively low in the water, and because of the curvature of the earth, a lookout perched at the highest point on the U-boat could only see at most around a half dozen miles, and this on a perfectly clear day.* What's

---

*A rough formula for the distance to the horizon is 1.32 miles times the square root of the distance in height, in feet. If a lookout was sixteen feet above sea level, the horizon would be 5.28 miles away, but of course if a target ship's mast was a hundred feet high, that would add another 13.2 miles, i.e., the tip of the target's masthead

more, if the lookout was scanning the sea for merchant ships at that distance, all he might see was just the top of a mast and perhaps a smudge of smoke—contacts that might easily be missed by a tired or inefficient lookout; four hours of staring at an empty sea through binoculars will test the alertness of the best of sailors, and lookouts on U-boats were enlisted men, boys, really, of eighteen or twenty, easy victims of boredom or daydreams—young men who were perhaps not quite as eager as their officers to find a contact, not because they feared combat, so much, as because little glory would be in it for them, aside from the glory of being associated with a successful U-boat. Then, too, the movement of the U-boat plowing through the water made it hard to hold binoculars steady, and that alone might cause a lookout to miss a tiny masthead far off in the distance. Add in the possibility of bad weather, and it's not surprising that simply finding a target was a major problem.

The lookouts also scanned the sky for planes. Aircraft were the great enemy of the U-boat because of their speed and ability to appear out of nowhere and attack with bombs or depth charges while the startled U-boat was still frantically diving. In the early days of the war, planes used visual sighting in the same way U-boats looked for their targets. But by the spring of 1943 planes equipped with undetectable microwave radar were able to locate surfaced U-boats from well beyond visual range, and then swoop down. In his war crimes testimony Admiral Dönitz said:

"The airplane, the surprise by airplane, and the equipment of the planes with radar—which in my opinion is, next to the atomic bomb, the decisive war-winning invention of the Anglo-Americans—brought about the collapse of U-boat warfare."

---

would just be visible to the U-boat lookout, theoretically. Smoke, however, might be visible up to thirty miles.[15] The Germans even experimented with towing a primitive helicopter at an altitude of up to four hundred feet. A man was perched up there with binoculars and a telephone. Allied airpower made these contraptions impractical.

But Kuhlmann's boat in the summer of '42 did not have these worries, and the danger from air attack, while still real, could in some ways be mitigated by sharp-eyed lookouts who could spot a cruising aircraft before the aircraft spotted the cruising submarine.

As mentioned, Admiral Dönitz's wolf-pack strategy was designed to deal with the inherent problems of finding the enemy convoys. He would send his U-boats to various sectors, and when one spotted a convoy that boat would report back to Dönitz's U-boat command (BdU), which would then radio other U-boats in the area, ordering them to gather at a particular point to intercept the convoy. When all were in place, the attack would commence. Interestingly, this centralization of control would lead in part to increased combat casualties for the U-boats because the Allies began using HFDF ("huff duff"), which stands for "high frequency direction finders"—an electronic device that could pick up the radio signals from one U-boat to another or from a U-boat to headquarters. HFDF did not capture the *content* of the message, just the fact of its *transmission*. But the transmission itself located the U-boat and allowed merchant convoys to change course to avoid it, while at the same time vectoring surface ships and aircraft, where available, to attack it.[*]

But *U166* was not part of a wolf pack, so it's unlikely that Kuhlmann communicated much, if at all, with other U-boats; his exposure to detection would therefore be minimized. (Dönitz did require regular reports, though, and so unwittingly exposed all his U-boats to HFDF.) Kuhlmann was on his own and on his way to the Gulf of Mexico, where he had every right to believe the danger from the air as well as the danger from surface ships would be

---

[*] The actual messages were transmitted in code by the German Enigma machines; the code was cracked by the famous Bletchley Park cryptographers initially in December 1942. Breaking the code was facilitated when the British captured *U110* and recovered an Enigma machine in May 1941.

far less than in the Atlantic. The defenses there, including HFDF installations, were still being developed, and air surveillance was largely visual. Long-range PBYs—flying boats—patrolled the immense spans of water looking for U-boats on the surface, and even stately blimps flew along the coastlines as far down as Trinidad. Their slow speed and long range made them useful platforms for visual surveillance, but even though they were armed with bombs and machine guns, they did not see much combat (one blimp was shot down during the war by a U-boat's antiaircraft machine guns; no blimps recorded any U-boat sinking). Their value was more psychological than anything, for as they hovered above a convoy, the merchant sailors could feel that they were not so completely alone. However, a blimp escorting a convoy greatly simplified the U-boat's problem of spotting targets, for the blimp was obviously visible at a much greater distance than the surface ships it was escorting, which might well be below the horizon and therefore invisible to the U-boat.

Running submerged, U-boats had ears as well as eyes—hydrophones that could pick up the noise from other ships' propellers:

"Our listening devices were very effective. . . . Under good conditions we could detect a ship thirty miles away, because we heard the propeller noise. Not only that, we could identify the type of ship and whether it had diesel engines, steam turbines, or steam pistons, and we could count the propeller revolutions and know whether it was a warship or a merchant ship."[16]

The key phrase here is "under good conditions." Proximity to land, the salt content of the water, water temperature, the different temperature gradients affected by season and weather conditions—all affected the hydrophones. Often conditions were so poor that the hydrophone operator could pick up little or nothing until it was too late, at which point all he could hear was the sound of a target disappearing, or, worse, a destroyer beginning a depth-charge run.

* * *

On July 11, 1942, the crewmen of the Dominican schooner *Carmen* were no doubt horrified when a few hundred yards away a U-boat surfaced.

Carmen, only eighty-four tons, was certainly nothing worth wasting a torpedo on. Still, Kuhlmann had come a long way. They were off the north shore of the Dominican Republic. It had been a long time since Kuhlmann's last combat action—not since he'd been a junior officer aboard *U37.* The *Carmen* was better than nothing. And so he ordered his gun crew to man the 105 mm deck gun, no doubt reminding them to remove the tompions (barrel inserts that sealed the gun against seawater), for he knew that more than one boat had lost men who forgot to remove these before they fired the gun, thereby blowing up the gun barrel and the gun crew alike.

Seeing this distressing apparition, the Dominican crew immediately took to their boats. Whether they understood Kuhlmann's order to abandon their schooner or not, they understood what it meant to look into the barrel of a 105. Kuhlmann then opened fire and sank the *Carmen.* It was not much, but it was a start. A victory, if only a small one.

Two days later, Kuhlmann was cruising off the eastern tip of Cuba when his lookouts sighted a more likely target—it was the U.S. steam freighter *Oneida,* of 2,309 tons.

The preferred method of torpedo attack was from the surface. It was easier to aim torpedoes from the bridge, using the instruments there, than to squint through a periscope when submerged. The optimal range for a torpedo was between five hundred and a thousand yards, so assuming Kuhlmann followed standard procedures, he would have stood off for a while as he scanned the target for potential armament (e.g., Naval Armed Guard gun crews), then, seeing none, he would have approached to within a thousand yards or so. While he was approaching and evaluating, he would have loaded two of his bow torpedo tubes. When he was satisfied with his position, he would have sighted the target using his targeting optics to communicate aiming instructions to the torpedoes. (World War II torpedoes were, in concept, cruise missiles with their own electric propulsion and guidance systems that received their instructions from the aiming devices operated by the skipper. Later in the war they detonated magnetically, when they encountered the magnetic field of the target; but at this stage Kuhlmann's torpedoes were most likely the type that detonated on contact with the target.)

By mid-1942 German torpedoes had a range of seventy-five hundred yards and a speed of thirty knots, so there was no reason to get much closer than a thousand yards before firing. At sea a thousand yards (half a nautical mile) does not seem so far away, especially if the target vessel is carrying flammable or explosive cargoes. And so while the crew of the *Oneida* were frantically lowering their lifeboats or throwing rafts overboard, Kuhlmann sighted through his aiming binoculars and, when satisfied, fired one torpedo. The *Oneida,* a smallish vessel, probably required only one shot to send her to the bottom. Probably, too, Kuhlmann motored slowly over to the surviving merchant sailors, asking them the name of their ship and verifying its tonnage and cargo and then, if necessary, giving them directions to the nearest land. Then he turned his boat away and headed west along the north shore of Cuba, at some point during the day reporting the sinking of the *Oneida* to Dönitz at BdU.

Two days later Kuhlmann was just off Havana. At night he would have seen the glow of the city. Kuhlmann must have begun to question his luck, for he had only two kills to his score, neither a particularly impressive vessel. On the evening of the sixteenth this busy sea-lane seemed to be empty of contacts; the only target in sight was a smallish trawler, most likely a tramp of some sort traveling from Cuba to Key West and back again. If the *Carmen* was not worth a torpedo, this wretched thing was hardly worth an artillery shell. But nothing else was on the horizon, so Kuhlmann ordered his engines "ahead standard" to overtake the vessel that had turned away and seemed to be trying to escape. It took hardly any time to close the range, and as Kuhlmann pulled within hailing distance, he warned three crewmen to abandon ship. They complied with alacrity, piling into their only lifeboat and pulling away from their vessel as fast as possible. Kuhlmann then ordered the gun crews into action, and a few shots later the target was smashed and sinking, her cargo of onions littering the surface of the sea and mingling with the splintered wreckage. As was his habit, Kuhlmann edged his U-boat close to the lifeboat of the ragged crew. He didn't have to ask about the cargo—that was obvious; onions were everywhere. Twenty tons of them. Probably the men on deck grappled a few crates that were not damaged—it was fresh food after all, albeit only onions. Perhaps the cook could make soup. And onions contain vitamin C, which would come in handy, since *U166* was by this time running low on lemons, their usual source of antiscorbutic.

It only remained to identify the vessel for the war diary and for the report to Dönitz.

"Are you men all right?" Kuhlmann asked first. They nodded glumly; they were in no position to register complaints.

Then Kuhlmann shouted, "What was the name of your vessel?"

The answer was no doubt unnerving.

"Gertrude!"

* * *

The fate of the *Gertrude*—the destruction of a small, militarily insignificant vessel just off Havana in July 1942, just as Hemingway was organizing his patrols—meant that Hemingway was truly engaged in a dangerous business. The Germans would attack anything, it seemed. A July 28, 1942, article in the *New York Times* describes the attack:

"Axis submarines, ranging from the Straits of Florida to the coast of Canada, have taken to preying on 'small fry' and have sunk two fishing boats, costing the United Nations the loss of 40,000 pounds of onions and nineteen swordfish."

Although the writer implied that the attack resulted from a starving U-boat crew's desperate need for food (only to their exasperation when they discovered a cargo of onions), the truth was plain to anyone who thought about it. The only thing the Germans were desperate for was tonnage sunk—and a Knight's Cross. While German raiders did now and then strip a target of her cargo before sinking her, their main object was destruction, not spoils.* Hemingway was an inveterate reader of the newspapers, and although this report was not a wire-service story and therefore might not have been picked up in the local papers, it seems incredible that Hemingway would not have learned about something that happened in the middle of his usual fishing grounds. After all, the attack took place within the range of Havana's lights.

The destruction of the *Gertrude* should have proved to Hemingway that his planned tactics were hopeless—something that reason should have told him in the first place. And probably did. No U-boat commander would allow any target vessel, regardless of how harmless it seemed, to come alongside close enough to toss grenades onto the submarine's bridge. The standard doctrine was

---

* Raiders were more likely to take their time and strip a target early in the war when the threat of swift enemy reaction was minimal. The German surface raider *Atlantis,* a ship fitted out to look like a harmless merchant, generally removed cargo and crew before sinking the target. Captured film shows footage of them even removing a piano from a target before sending her to the bottom. But the *Atlantis* was sunk by the Royal Navy in November 1941, and by that time German raiders were becoming more wary.

to stand off and sink the enemy—whether a man-of-war, merchant ship, or wretched onion boat. Early in the war the targeted
crews were allowed to abandon ship as long as there was no potential danger to the U-boat. But that was pretty much the limit of
sportsmanship among the German commanders. (Some U-boat
commanders, though, followed Dönitz's "Be harsh" order to the
letter. Early in 1942 the SS *Cardonia*'s and the *Esso Bolivar*'s crews
were machine-gunned while lowering their lifeboats in the Windward Passage between Cuba and Haiti. The SS *Oregon*'s men were
machine-gunned in the water in the Mona Passage between the
Dominican Republic and Puerto Rico.)[17]

So how should we think about Hemingway's plans for using
his weapons? The least charitable explanation is that they were so
much bravado—grown-up boys playing with dangerous toys. That
is certainly possible, and throughout his lifetime Hemingway provided plenty of justification to those who thought him a blowhard
and a poseur. After his death when biographies, revisionist and
otherwise, had begun, Martha wrote, "Well, what the hell, I am
doomed to go down to posterity as some sort of second rate witch
in the Master's life, and the Master himself is probably getting what
he deserved, for he did fake things—events, people, emotions—
himself."[18] Were the patrols another of these "fake things"? Martha
seemed to think so. This comment of hers would no doubt have
infuriated Hemingway, for whom the word *true* become almost a
cliché from overuse and emphasis. To be called a fake would have
been intolerable. But by the time she said it he was past caring.* It's
interesting to contrast Martha's view with George Plimpton's in
his introduction to the Hemingway interview in the *Paris Review*:
"The fact is that Hemingway, while obviously enjoying life, brings
an equivalent dedication to everything he does—an outlook that is

---

* It's not clear whether Martha was using *fake* as a verb or adjective. Possibly both,
simultaneously.

essentially serious, with a horror of the inaccurate, the fraudulent, the deceptive, the half-baked." Of course, Martha knew Hemingway rather better than Plimpton did.

Looking at Hemingway's plans objectively, and remembering General Marshall's memo to Admiral King ("has every conceivable improvised means been brought to bear . . . ?") and remembering how vital the visual aspect of naval warfare was at this time ("He who sees first, wins") and remembering that hundreds of other civilian volunteers, both airmen and mariners, were doing much the same sort of thing all along the Gulf and Atlantic coasts in support of the Navy and Army Air Corps that were stretched so thin, we have to conclude that Hemingway's self-designed and entirely voluntary mission was potentially useful and welcome. As for the grenades and the Thompsons, given the very real danger involved (witness the *Gertrude*), what would we have him do—go to sea unarmed? It would be against all his natural instincts, and against the instincts of any mariner going into harm's way. As mentioned earlier, *Pilar* was not sturdy enough to mount heavy machine guns, and besides, that sort of visual evidence of hostility would make her more vulnerable, not less. But hand grenades and submachine guns that could be hidden in the main cabin would at least offer some semblance of defense, if only the cold comfort of knowing you were not unarmed. And if you were going to take these things on board, did it not make sense to have some sort of plan for using them? And who could say? Perhaps Hemingway would encounter a U-boat captain made careless by strain or fatigue or overconfidence. Perhaps he would get lucky.

Curiously, Martha's initial skepticism about the mission and its potential for benefit and danger remained intact. Maybe Hemingway failed to explain it to her. Perhaps Martha merely dismissed his explanations the way she dismissed the few news stories that did get through censorship:

During that terrible year, 1942, I lived in the sun, safe and comfortable and hating it. News reached us at regular hours on the radio and none of it was good. But we didn't understand how bad it was; piecemeal and (now I see) wisely censored, the news gave us no whole view. . . . I think my ignorance was typical. We did not realize that the fatal danger was on the sea. . . . Then American news broadcasts began to tell, with great excitement, of German submarines sinking ships along the eastern seaboard of the U.S., and in the Gulf of Mexico and the Caribbean and as far south as Brazil. I was leery of the tone; it sounded boastful as if suggesting that we too, in our impregnable safety, were endangered. Which we weren't.[19]

The key phrase here was "leery of the tone; it sounded boastful," for that also summed up her attitude toward the patrols of *Pilar*—and now and then toward Hemingway himself. In the summer of '42 Martha regarded Hemingway's proposed patrols as little more than an excuse to go fishing and thereby avoid the hard work of fiction and, worse, avoid covering the real war in Europe. She did not know the extent of the calamity occurring in the Gulf. Nor did she think Hemingway's self-designed mission posed much in the way of danger to him and his boat. After all, why would the Germans be interested in destroying a thirty-eight-foot fishing boat?

* * *

The three men in the *Gertrude*'s lifeboat drifted for three days and finally made landfall in Key West, Florida. They were lucky. But what of Kuhlmann and *U166*? So far the patrol had hardly been a success. Just one decent-size vessel torpedoed, and now he had sunk a boat with his wife's name on the transom. It was hard to convince himself that this was a good omen; quite the contrary, it was unsettling. He probably told himself that when he got back to Germany on leave, the two of them would have a good laugh about it, and she would tease him and tell him it was somehow Freudian. But that day was far away; for now he was in enemy waters.

For two weeks Kuhlmann could not find another target that was practicable. No doubt during that time he saw many potential targets in the crowded sea-lanes of the Gulf, but none offered a realistic chance of success, either because of their distance or speed or, possibly, their convoy protection. But on July 30 his radioman intercepted a message from a U.S. patrol ship (*PC566*) advising the commander of the Gulf Sea Frontier (headquarters for the Gulf Naval Command) that the ship it was escorting, the *Robert E. Lee*, which had been bound for Tampa, was changing course and heading for New Orleans, because no pilot was available to bring the ship into Tampa.*

This was more like it. The *Robert E. Lee* was a passenger liner, 375 feet long and 5,184 tons. She was carrying a crew of 141, en route from Trinidad to the United States. On board also were 270 passengers, many of them American construction workers and their families; others were shipwrecked victims of earlier U-boat attacks in the Caribbean. The ship had come in convoy as far as Key West, but the convoy then dispersed and the *Robert E. Lee* and her escort went on alone.

After intercepting the message, Kuhlmann easily located the *Robert E. Lee*. He made his approach submerged. Through the periscope he could see the elderly ship, painted navy haze-gray in a pitiful effort to camouflage the ship against precisely the danger that it was now unknowingly facing. Kuhlmann could also see *PC566*, a Navy patrol craft 178 feet long with a three-inch gun for-

---

*A pilot is a local contractor who brings ships in and out of a particular port; even Navy ships in foreign ports will use pilots, much to the nervous apprehension of captains and officers of the deck, who reluctantly turn over the handling of their ship to a local civilian mariner.

ward, a 40 mm aft, and two 20 mm mounted near the bridge. She also carried depth charges, which could be rolled off the stern and fired off both sides of the ship. It was not the most formidable of adversaries but still nothing to tangle with unnecessarily, so Kuhlmann decided to stay submerged to attack the *Robert E. Lee*. He probably considered trying for the patrol boat first, which would then allow him to surface and sink the *Robert E. Lee* at his leisure, but he decided against it. Maybe the position of *PC566* made the shot difficult, so that, if Kuhlmann fired and missed, he would give away his position before he had a chance to sink the liner. Better to take the sure thing.

It only took one torpedo. The explosion occurred in the number three hold, then blasted up through two decks, knocked the engines out of commission, and started a fatal list. Water came rushing in through the hole in the hull and open portholes, and passengers and crew alike started jumping overboard, while other crew members lowered six lifeboats and threw life rafts into the sea, which luckily was calm that day. In minutes the sea was covered with swimmers and rafts and lifeboats and debris, while the *Robert E. Lee* began to settle by the stern. Soon her bow was pointed toward the sky as she slipped downward and disappeared into five thousand feet of water.

A lookout on *PC566* spotted Kuhlmann's periscope, and the little ship turned and started a depth-charge run, much to the amazement and distress of the people in the water, for the exploding depth charges were as lethal to them, perhaps more so, than to the enemy U-boat. As the *Lee*'s captain said afterward, "We paddled around looking for anyone alive in the water. Those we reached were dead, either from the concussion of the depth charges or having their necks broken by jumping into the water with a cork life jacket on. Then the sharks came and took over."[20]

Meanwhile, having dived deeper into the Gulf, Kuhlmann and his crew listened as the depth charges exploded around them and held on as the explosions rocked their boat, throwing some of them to the unyielding deck or against the hard corners of the lockers, dimming the lights and perhaps starting leaks at weak points in the pressure hull, and all the while Kuhlmann was remembering that this was the moment when his men would be watching him for signals that would help them manage their fear, even as he struggled to control his own emotions, perhaps silently reciting technical information to keep his mind fixed on something. He knew that water transmitted pressure much more intensely than air, and if an intense pressure wave hit a submerged boat, it would tear it apart at the seams. The depth charges did not have to land on the boat; if they exploded anywhere within 350 feet, the damage would be lethal. Depth charges dropped from a warship weighed about five hundred pounds and came in patterns, so that the U-boat was straddled and could only rely on guile and the steadiness of the crew and the strength of the boat's construction to survive.

As the depth charges kept coming, despite Kuhlmann's maneuvers—changes in the U-boat's depth and course—it became harder and harder not to let the fear and doubt overwhelm him. He and his men were trapped in their machine.

*   *   *

Is it stretching a metaphor too far to suggest that the fight between *PC566* and *U166* was like the fight between the Old Man and his great fish? Perhaps. But Hemingway would probably have thought the metaphor was apt. After all, he called the U-boats "tin fish." In *The Old Man and the Sea* he made at least one direct comparison: "The fish's eye looked as detached as the mirrors in a periscope."[21] Certainly parallels exist between the two fights. In both cases the drama was between the hunters and the hunted, who were tethered together—the one by fishing line, the other by sonar. The nervous, sweating men in the U-boat could hear the electronic signal from the patrol craft pinging off their pressure hull, a sure indication that they were caught, that the depth charges would continue to follow them, that their captain's desperate maneuvers were not working. The hunters in both cases wished the death of their quarry; the frantic quarry wished primarily to escape. It's hard to say whether the sailors aboard the hunter felt the same degree of sympathy for the enemy they were trying to kill—the same degree, that is, that the Old Man felt for his great fish. Most likely some did; others did not. There is generally less hatred among sailors at war since both sides are facing what seems to be a mirror image of themselves—a ship at sea manned by mostly unseen men like themselves and facing the same intrinsic perils of seafaring. Somehow it is different from warfare on land. (When the *Bismarck* sank HMS *Hood,* the initial reaction among the German sailors was shock, not jubilation.)

The transformation from something to nothingness is stunning even to the hunters whose object it was. Of course, that sentiment applies more to the battle between surface ships; the contest between the hunter patrol craft and his unseen U-boat quarry is more clinical—almost abstract. Nor does any potential sympathy for a trapped and doomed enemy lessen the hunters' desire for victory. But perhaps many if not all of the sailors aboard *PC566* would have preferred to capture the U-boat than to sink her. Capture was a more unusual event, and it was difficult in many cases to be sure of a kill, for a stricken U-boat might limp away undetected, leaving behind a trace of fuel oil as a tease, so that a frustrated PC commander could only report a "probable."[*]

---

[*] At least three U-boats were captured during the war, two by the British and one by the U.S. carrier *Guadalcanal* and escorts.

So it was in this case. *PC566* finished her depth-charge patterns, then turned to survey the surface for clues, to listen to the sonar for contact. But nothing was seen or heard. No debris was on the surface of the water, other than the debris, human and otherwise, left behind by the *Robert E. Lee,* and no return ping came to the sonar's searching signal. Kuhlmann and his crew had escaped, it seemed. So *PC566* returned to see what could be done about the survivors of the *Lee.*

But Kuhlmann and *U166* had not escaped. The last pattern of depth charges tore apart the bow of the U-boat, and she sank with all hands into a mile of water and came to rest on the bottom, where she lay undiscovered until 2002, when an oil-exploration device stumbled across her. There she lies still, and video images confirm the manner of her death. We are left to wonder what the last few moments aboard *U166* were like. Did Kuhlmann maintain his façade of sangfroid or ironic humor or whatever pose he had decided on till collapsing bulkheads and the inrushing Niagara of water made further demonstrations impossible? At what point did the hideous realization of imminent death by drowning overtake him and render all human poses irrelevant and absurd? Perhaps only a few seconds passed between self-control and oblivion. Any sailor would wish it so. All true hunters want a clean kill.*

---

* From the start of the war in 1939 till its end, 766 German U-boats were sunk.[22]

Chapter Five

~~~

AMATEUR HOUR

The massacre enjoyed by the U-boats along our Atlantic coast in 1942 was as much a national disaster as if saboteurs had destroyed half a dozen of our biggest war plants. . . . If a submarine sinks two 6,000 ton ships and one 3,000 ton tanker, here is a typical account of what we have totally lost: 42 tanks, 8 six-inch howitzers, 88 twenty five pound guns, 40 two pound guns, 24 armored cars, 50 Bren carriers, 5,210 tons of ammunition, 600 rifles, 428 tons of tank supplies, 2,000 tons of stores, and 1,000 tanks of gasoline. Suppose the three ships had made port and the cargoes were dispersed. In order to knock out the same amount of equipment by air bombing, the enemy would have to make three thousand successful bombing sorties.

Samuel Eliot Morison, *The Battle of the Atlantic*[1]

Loose lips sink ships.

Slogan on the ubiquitous World War II poster

FROM spring through the summer of 1942 Hemingway spent some of his time working on a massive edition called *Men at War,* a selection of articles, histories, and stories about war. Hemingway, with no false modesty, included some of his own work alongside that of Tolstoy, Herodotus, Stendhal, Crane, and others of equal literary and military prominence.

But he did not neglect the war or his planning for his patrols. Authorizations from the Navy and the embassy were delayed, as well as the permission for and access to the small arms he needed to carry out his plans. Whether these delays were the result of bureaucratic inefficiency or official hesitations about the project is hard to say. Hemingway would have gone out on his own—and did in fact undertake a few patrols prior to official authorization—but without radios, small arms, and reporting procedures, these patrols could accomplish little or nothing. Official sanction was also important because any casualties among his crew would be recognized as legitimate wartime injuries, and the men or their families would be eligible for government insurance.

Despite these frustrations, he was not idle, for there was the Fifth Column to worry about—not his play, but the real thing.

*   *   *

In 1942 Cuba issued a series of postage stamps. The first showed a hand ripping an innocent-looking mask away from a sinister character with the face of Bela Lugosi; the inscription read, "Unmask the Fifth Columnists." The second stamp said, "Destroy it. The Fifth Column is like a serpent," and showed a woman struggling with what seemed to be a python. The third stamp said, "Fulfill your patriotic duty by destroying the Fifth Column," and showed some muscular workmen using an I beam to batter down the fifth out of a row of columns. The last one showed a sort of Greek warrior goddess, complete with spear and shield, about to attack an ape-necked villain, with the inscription "Don't be afraid of the Fifth Column. Attack it."

What did all this mean? Several things, at least. First, the Cuban government was worried about foreign agents and, even more, about Falangist sympathizers within Cuba, people who supported Franco's efforts in Spain and would be just as happy to see their

German and Italian friends win this war so that they could then, no doubt, seek their assistance in taking over Cuba. Second, Cuba, at least officially, was in the war on the side of the Allies. In fact, historian Samuel Eliot Morison says that of all our allies in this area, Cuba, with its small fleet of patrol vessels and gunboats, was among the most cooperative in providing whatever it could to the war effort.[2] Third, people in Cuba were nervous, just as their allies to the north were nervous, about the possibility of sabotage and subversion, and meanwhile ships were being torpedoed all along the Atlantic coastline and down into the Gulf of Mexico. The people who were worried had a right to be:

"Early in 1942 Hitler declared the Atlantic coast and the Caribbean to be 'blockaded' in order to justify sinking neutrals, and the vessels of Sweden, the Argentine, and almost every neutral country trading with the United States *except Spain* were among those sunk in the campaign."[3]

Spanish ships came and went, though they, too, were theoretically neutral in a blockaded area and were therefore legally subject to potential sinking. (Hitler's bothering to declare a blockade is a glaring irony; invoking international maritime law seems unusually fastidious, for him.) That Spanish ships were not targeted[*] indicated a not-very-shadowy nexus among Franco's Spain, Hitler, and their fascist sympathizers in Cuba—certainly it would if you were living on the island and shared the general nervousness. Then, too, Spanish Republican refugees in Cuba had clear memories of what Franco's firing squads had done to their comrades, so their attitudes and behavior would have been governed by a volatile mixture of fear and the desire for revenge.

In short, the stamps indicate a climate of intrigue and suspicion on the island, an atmosphere that would have appealed to

---

[*] "Mr. Winfield Scott, U.S. Consul at Tenerife, reported a U-boat refueling at Santa Cruz on 2 Mar 1942, and stated that the Spanish minelayer *Marte* and sailing ship *San Miguel* carried oil and supplies out to meet submarines at sea."[4]

Hemingway, reasonably fresh from the war in Spain, in which the infighting and double-dealing among the competing political parties in the Republic, as well as the dangers, real and imagined, from the fascist fifth columnists, were enough to generate intense, feral wariness, if not paranoia—as well as some pleasurable excitement. At the start of the World War II the atmosphere in Cuba would have aroused Hemingway's appetites for, and sensitivity to, the murky underworld of spies and saboteurs, and he decided to do something about it. He assembled a group of his friends—local fishermen, jai-alai players, Cuban cronies, and assorted shadowy characters—into an unofficial spying ring designed to gather information about Falangist activities on the island, about the very people who would make up the Fifth Column that so worried the governments of both Cuba and the United States. As Martha wrote in July of 1941,

There are 770 Germans here (how many in Mexico) and 30,000 Spaniards who are organized into the Spanish Fascist secret society, the Falange. . . . I tell you that the American Ambassador here is constantly and intensely concerned with the local Nazi activities, and that the English minister is equally so. . . . They feel that while the Nazi activities here are small, they are a perfect sample of how it begins and they think it significant that Cuba, itself useless, should attract Nazis and they are following all their work, and the Falange, very closely*

* Martha wrote this to Charles Colebaugh, her editor at *Collier's,* who had rejected her story on Nazi activities in Cuba. Apparently Colebaugh initially wanted something dismissing the Nazis as "hard working little fellows who were not getting anywhere," then rejected the article as too light. Martha had seen Nazis and fifth columnists at work in other countries and had no illusions about how things worked, so while she was not an alarmist, she was also not dismissive of the threat. That she referred to Cuba as "itself useless," though, is puzzling; surely she had a better strategic sense than that.[5]

It seemed like a worthwhile idea—this amateur counterintelligence business. Hemingway named this operation the Crook Factory. (He was apparently addicted to giving nicknames. Almost everyone he loved or liked was assigned some sort of moniker, often tipping over the line to childish absurdity. Here again he influenced those around him. Martha, for example, signed her letters to him sometimes as "Bongie," "Mook," or "Mrs. Bug," and nothing in her life before or after Hemingway suggested a strain of juvenile playfulness.) Calling his outfit the Crook Factory seems to trivialize the operation, but in the climate of the times the idea was not so trivial after all. Hemingway knew lots of locals who would have known of his sympathy for the Spanish Republican cause and his corresponding antifascism. Further, the many refugees from the Spanish Civil War had keen memories and a strong interest in exacting some sort of revenge against the party that had despoiled Spain. Why not use them, Hemingway reasoned, to look around a little, see what could be learned, and maybe uncover something useful to the Allied cause? Perhaps he was thinking of a scene he wrote not that long before in his play *The Fifth Column*:

> Philip: Twelve bloody months, my boy, in this country. And before that, Cuba. Ever been to Cuba?
>
> Antonio: Yes.
>
> Philip: That's where I got sucked in on all this.
>
> Antonio: How were you sucked in?
>
> Philip: Oh, people started trusting me that should have known better. And I suppose because they should have known better I started getting, you know, sort of trustworthy. You know, not elaborately, just sort of moderately trustworthy. And then they trust you a little more and you do it all right. And then, you know, you get to believing in it. Finally you get to liking it.[6]

The "all this" and the "it" here were counterintelligence work. With the very real climate of intrigue in Cuba, why not let nature imitate art?

Hemingway proposed the idea to the local American embassy officials with whom he was friendly. The proposal received the blessing of the U.S. ambassador to Cuba, Spruille Braden, who shared the general nervousness about infiltration of saboteurs and Fifth Columnists. Looking back on this period, it is constantly important to remember that the people then did not know what was going on or what might happen. Just as a U-boat might surface anywhere at any moment, so, too, might some lurking gang of saboteurs attack important installations. Also, at this period of the war there was precious little good news—not in Europe, the Atlantic, or the Pacific—to counterbalance public anxiety and doubt. Things seemed to be going badly everywhere. Not until June 1942 did the Battle of Midway suddenly and stunningly signal a change of fortunes in the Pacific. But the Battle of the Atlantic against the U-boats was still raging and apparently still being lost (115 ships sunk in June in the Atlantic). Meanwhile, Hitler controlled all of Europe, and his army was besieging Leningrad, where Russian civilians were starving to death by the thousands.

So, in May 1942 when America was well and truly in the war, and things looked pretty bad wherever you looked, the U.S. embassy in Cuba agreed to bankroll Hemingway's gang—the price tag was not excessive: $500 per month.* The local FBI agents seemed to go along with the operation at first, although they resented the embassy's co-opting of a business—intelligence gathering—that, with some justification, they considered their turf. What's more, they had genuine and legitimate doubts about the wisdom of turning an amateur like Hemingway loose with little or no operational control over his activities. They also had their doubts about

---

* Approximately $6,541 in 2009 dollars.

Hemingway personally and politically—to the point that they had begun to maintain a file on him.* Reading it leads to some inescapable conclusions:

First, the FBI felt that Hemingway harbored some unhelpful hostility toward the Bureau—and should therefore be regarded warily. In an October 8, 1942, letter to J. Edgar Hoover, local Havana agent Raymond Leddy raised two red flags: "1) It is recalled that when the Bureau was attacked early in 1940 as a result of arrests in Detroit of certain individuals charged with Neutrality Act violations for fostering enlistments in the Spanish Republican forces, Mr. Hemingway was among the signers of a declaration which severely criticized the Bureau in that case; 2) in attendance at a jai alai match with Hemingway the writer [i.e., Leddy] was introduced by him to a friend as a member of the Gestapo." Obviously the FBI in the person of Leddy seemed to be a little thin-skinned and humorless, and Hemingway later dismissed the Gestapo comment as a joke. In the climate of the times, though, when people were beginning to understand just what the actual Gestapo was really up to, it's easy to understand why the remark might rankle a starchy professional who took pride in his Bureau and the wartime job it was doing and would resent being compared to Nazi thugs. The same would be true for Hemingway's signing a declaration criticizing the FBI, although anyone who thought about it would understand that that's what writers and activists did—and do—especially when one of their chief causes is being obstructed by government actions, in this case the Neutrality Act, which the United States passed to avoid becoming entangled in the Spanish Civil War. That war aroused the interest of the vigorously anticommunist Bureau, which was apparently uninterested in or dismissive of the lunatic complexities and murderous doctrinal disputes

---

*The FBI's dossier on Hemingway runs to 120-plus pages; the first entry is in 1942 and the last is dated 1955.

among the various leftist parties and which viewed the whole affair in simplistic terms—fascist versus communist—ironically in much the same way as did most of the idealistic volunteers and journalists. Nor did the Bureau seem to understand the political naïveté of so many of the artists and idealists who went to Spain and who, in many cases, ultimately outgrew their early orthodoxy. (John Dos Passos, for example, started life on the far left and gradually became an anticommunist as a result of what he witnessed in Spain; this caused him some discomfort with former friends who retained their earlier sympathies, if not their policies.) Thus by definition—that is, the Bureau's definition—Hemingway and many of the other American volunteers, journalists, and war tourists were legitimate subjects of official scrutiny. Hemingway, being probably the most famous, was naturally of particular interest, even though he was never really politically minded—his individualism would never let him submit to any party line, especially the Communist's: "I cannot be a communist now because I believe in only one thing: liberty. First I would look after myself and do my work. Then I would care for my family. Then I would help my neighbor. But the state I care nothing for. All the state has ever meant to me is unjust taxation. . . . I believe in the absolute minimum of government."[7] Or: "I can't be a communist because I hate tyranny and, I suppose, government."[8] Like Martha, he had seen people in power, politicians and generals, and was correspondingly skeptical.

But other incidents along the way had also aroused the notice of the highly sensitive FBI—the speech before the Writers' Congress, for example, a group well-known to have leftist sympathies, to say the least.

Moreover, the FBI and the State Department were at odds, at least in regard to the way the ambassador in Cuba, Spruille Braden, handled his business. Braden is described as "hotheaded" and similar unflattering adjectives. It should surprise no one that different agencies and departments competed—to the detriment of the gov-

116

ernment's efficiency and budgets, to say nothing of the public's best interests. Ambassador Braden was friendly with Hemingway and, in the FBI's view, endorsed Hemingway's various intelligence-gathering schemes without much scrutiny or careful thought—not one of Braden's strengths to begin with, in the Bureau's view. The local FBI agents, such as Leddy, who were called legal attachés, sent memos back to the Bureau that criticized Hemingway's schemes initially because they, the FBI, had no say in managing them—the embassy was handling that—and later because Hemingway seemed to be out of control entirely and, worse, was dipping into allegations of corruption involving the Cuban chief of national police and other possibilities of official malfeasance that could embarrass both governments and damage the war effort. In 1942 Cuba's president was Fulgencio Batista, the same Batista who had led the earlier coup, called the Revolt of the Sergeants, in 1933 and who had been running things from behind the scenes since that time. In 1940 he stepped forward to run officially for president.[*] This is the same Batista who was friendly with mobster Meyer Lansky and who later made Havana an agreeable haven for a variety of mafiosi, and it is the same Batista who decamped unceremoniously in 1959 when Castro's revolution reached Havana. So, if Hemingway did start to tug on a string of corruption in government circles, it would not be surprising if he unraveled some schemes that would have been embarrassing to a useful ally.

In a somewhat contradictory tone, however, the FBI also thought that Hemingway's foray into intelligence gathering was useless. Perhaps they meant that not only was he poking around in places where he shouldn't but that the intelligence he did gather about possible fifth columnists was irrelevant or unhelpful. As agent Edward Tamm noted in one memo in Hemingway's file, "I

---

[*] Interestingly, in that same year of 1940 the Cubans wrote and adopted a new constitution that was remarkable for its liberalism.

don't care what his contacts are or what his background is—I see no reason why we should make any effort to avoid exposing him for the phony that he is."[9] Tamm's boss no doubt approved of the sentiment, for Hoover took a dim view of Hemingway personally and of Ambassador Braden's scheme to use him for counterintelligence: "Certainly Hemingway is the last man, in my estimation, to be used in any such capacity. His judgment is not of the best, and if his sobriety is the same as it was some years ago, that is certainly questionable."[10] The comment about his sobriety is fair enough; Hemingway was well-known to be a heavy drinker, and of course that theoretically is a security risk for anyone in the intelligence business. But the risk is that an agent who drinks too much may compromise secret information, whereas ironically the Bureau's view was that Hemingway's operation never turned up anything of value to begin with, so there was nothing to be compromised. It would seem hard to be a "phony" and a legitimate security risk at the same time.

In his later years Hemingway worried obsessively about the FBI, and to some extent his worries were justified. True, his paranoia at the end of his life was out of control, but given the large dossier on him, how much of his worry was the result of governmental scrutiny and how much was the result of his imagination? The Freedom of Information Act, which allows access to certain government files, was not passed until well after Hemingway's death. If he knew or suspected the FBI had a file on him, he could easily brood about it and magnify its importance; his ego would most likely lead him to overestimate the file's function and content. Although over a hundred pages long, the file really has little of significance in it, for nothing Hemingway ever did could even remotely qualify him as a dangerous political activist.* But he had no way of knowing the

---

* Throughout the intensely politicized thirties, Hemingway was criticized by his peers for not taking a more aggressive political stance, and that criticism might in part have driven him to produce *To Have and Have Not*—a novel that he later admitted was a failure.

file lacked substance. And while he had every right to resent this sort of official snooping, there might never have been a file on him if he had not volunteered for amateur counterintelligence work in Cuba—that's when it all began. His earlier activities in Spain would probably have been noticed in some reports, but that would most likely have been the extent of it. This is speculation, but it comes from reading through his entire file.*

The Crook Factory was not a success. During its short run it turned up little or nothing of value to the war effort. The FBI was right about that. The entire episode has a decided air of comic opera. You have a shadowy crowd of locals wandering around in the Havana nights asking questions and coming to the finca to report, annoying Martha with their drinking and odd hours, with Hemingway self-importantly relishing the role of leader and someone who was in the know: "He had come to like it. It was part of being an insider but it was a very corrupting business."[11] Perhaps he was imagining himself as Philip Rawlings from *The Fifth Column* doing interesting and dangerous things while his beautiful blond "girl" stood by and watched with breathless admiration: "Philip's marvelous. He does go about with dreadful people though. Why does he, I wonder?"†

Needless to say, the real blonde took a different view, and if Martha was ever breathless, it was with rage over the constant atmosphere of boozy, mock intrigue. Less than a year after granting it his blessing, the ambassador revised his own view and shut

---

* While having a "file" on you may seem a sinister Orwellian predicament, that is not necessarily the case. For example, the late football player Walter Payton has a file, too, but this is because he received death threats upon being given a humanitarian award. In this case the file was designed to protect rather than harass the subject. J. Edgar Hoover, however, is well-known to have maintained files on numerous political enemies and apparently was not reluctant to use what he knew. Thus if Hemingway erred on the side of paranoia, he had some justification.

† Edmund Wilson in his review of the play called it a "small boy's fantasy."[12]

down the operation (this coincided with FDR's order consolidating counterespionage work under the FBI): "As of April, 1943 . . . Hemingway's activities as an undercover informant for the American ambassador were terminated. This resulted from general dissatisfaction over the reports submitted."[13]

*   *   *

The greatest dangers to liberty lurk in insidious encroachment by men of zeal, well meaning but without understanding.

Louis Brandeis, Supreme Court justice, 1916–39[14]

Viewed objectively, this entire episode with the FBI does not reflect especially well on the methods of J. Edgar Hoover and his Bureau. Hemingway was not the only writer who aroused their interest. They maintained files on dozens of writers and artists, especially those who had any connection to the Spanish Civil War or leftist politics in this country, and the whole period is an example of how unsupervised power and a political agenda can get out of hand and trample on the civil liberties of citizens who are not guilty of anything other than speaking their minds. But reading the files, you also sense that Hoover's information gathering was a waste of resources during a time of national emergency. True, the FBI did do a good job of preventing potential sabotage from German agents. But the amount of time spent thinking and writing about Hemingway and other writers was not only unnecessary but also based on an almost comic lack of understanding of their potential influence, much less their actual ideas.

Of course, some writers swallowed and tried to promote the Communist Party line. Dashiell Hammett was a member of the party, and his longtime mistress, Lillian Hellman, was a dedicated fellow traveler. But their political influence was so limited as to be almost nonexistent. (If there are subtle communist messages in *The Maltese Falcon,* they are elusive.) When radical ideas of any stripe—political or religious—are given a forum in the marketplace of ideas, they are more likely to be sent off to the dustbin of indifference or risibility than if they are somehow suppressed and their authors made martyrs. Many, if not most, of the left-leaning artists of the day were in large measure political naifs who were unable to distinguish between ends and means, i.e., unable to separate their sympathy for the common man (and their contempt for the middle class) from political policies that would, if instituted, subjugate the people they were trying to assist and merely substitute a new class of rulers for the older and often less coercive governments. Those few who were able to go through the intellectual and moral contortions required to maintain solidarity with the Communist and, more specifically, the Stalinist line were simply dishonest. (One thinks again of Lillian Hellman and Mary McCarthy's famous description of her.)* Few had the clear sight or the courage to tell the truth (and then suffer the attacks of their former colleagues) that George Orwell or John Dos Passos had. But were any of these writers really worthy of FBI attention? Some perhaps. But not many.

As for Hemingway, a few hours spent reading *For Whom the Bell Tolls* might have saved the taxpayers some expense and given FBI agents extra time to go after the genuine enemies. Or they might have read a review of the book by Mike Gold, columnist for the *Daily Worker,* which assailed the novel as "limited, narrow . . . mutilated by his class egotism . . . and the poverty of his mind."[15] In short, the most visible American Communist propaganda organ didn't like the book or its author very much. The book didn't have the right political message as far as Gold was concerned—a criticism Hemingway would have swatted away and forgotten: "All you can be sure about in a political-minded

---

* "Every word she [Hellman] writes is a lie, including *and* and *the.*"

writer is that if his work should last you will have to skip the politics when you read it."[16]

Another review, this time in the Havana newspaper *Hoy,* a Communist organ, too, said about *For Whom the Bell Tolls* on April 25, 1943:

> Here is the literate Hemingway, author of a slanderous book which is a rehashing of others of his, this time directed against the Communist Party and against the Spanish people. Here is the portrait of a revolutionary tourist. His destiny will be the destiny of all traitors, of all provocateurs who maneuver openly or in cover against the Communist Party, against the people, against history. And against good literature.[17]

Surely this sort of thing should have raised serious doubts in the FBI about Hemingway's communist credentials or supposed sympathies. Perhaps it did to a degree, although agents continued to send reports on his activities in Cuba, keeping the director up-to-date on his patrolling.

For a variety of reasons, Hemingway's antics with the Crook Factory were probably not his finest hour and provided ammunition for those, like FBI agent Tamm, who viewed him as a "phony"—a view to which Martha tended, at least later in her life, and perhaps at the time, too.

On the other hand, it did seem like a good idea at the beginning. After all, Falangists *were* on the island; Hemingway *was* well connected with all sorts of "dreadful people," for he loved the company of jai-alai players (many of whom were Basques and veterans of the Spanish war), fishermen, small-time crooks, and assorted Cuban versions of Damon Runyon characters—the sorts of people who hear things. And if Hemingway got some minor psychological gratification from being the leader of this motley gang, it doesn't necessarily mean it was a bad idea. It just didn't work out.

~~~

Chapter Six

THE WANDERING ANGLER

There is for every man some one scene, some one adventure, some one picture, that is the image of his secret life, for wisdom first speaks in images.

W. B. Yeats

No novelist has more than a few stories to tell. They are the myths of life which each novelist creates for himself.

Anthony Powell

O N May 2, 1942, Hemingway read in the *Havana Post* the account of the sinking of the *Federal* by *U507*.[1] That story alone would have been sufficient to prove the existence of the threat, regardless of how extensively the subsequent sinkings were reported. Hemingway was also friendly with the first secretary of the American embassy, Robert Joyce, and with the newly appointed ambassador, Spruille Braden, from whom he no doubt got unofficial information about what had suddenly erupted in the Gulf and to whom he had expressed willingness to volunteer his boat. The idea of using private boats and yachts for patrolling did not originate with Hemingway. The *New York Times* reported on June 28, 1942, that some twelve hundred boats were in use in some capacity all along the eastern and Gulf of Mexico coasts. But Cuba, although an ally, was a foreign country, and Hemingway needed to work through the U.S. embassy to get legal authorization to go on an armed hunt for U-boats from a base in Cuba. He couldn't simply raise the black flag and wander off, because the essence of the mission was reconnaissance and communication, and only secondarily combat, but in either case Hemingway would need equipment and weapons and reporting procedures, which required cooperation between the embassy, the Cuban government, and the U.S. Navy command responsible for the Gulf, whose headquarters were in Key West, Florida.

The important point, however, is that Hemingway was at least partially informed of the serious nature of the U-boat threat, both through newspaper stories—though censorship restricted that to a large degree—and through his private channels at the embassy.

This was no game. And he knew it.

So it's fair to ask, just what were Hemingway's motives for this venture? Why did he want to do it?

The most obvious motive was to do some service for his country. As he says in the introduction to *Men at War,* "Once we have a war there is only one thing to do. It must be won." Moreover, the enemies were the same Nazis who had fought with Franco and the rebel generals only three years before. Hemingway's novel of that war, *For Whom the Bell Tolls,* had recently been published, in October 1940, and the sad and bitter memories of Republican Spain's despair and defeat would have been sharpened by the writing of the book. Here was a chance to exact a measure of revenge and to continue the war against fascism in a different venue, while answering the call of his own country at a time of quite desperate need. The same June 28 *New York Times* article that described the twelve hundred volunteer boats already in service also said, "It is hoped that upward of 1,000 additional small boats may be added to the auxiliary. . . . Boats found to be qualified will be equipped with radio, armament and suitable anti-submarine devices as rapidly as possible."[2]

German intelligence agents could read the newspaper, too, so articles such as this increased the risk for all the volunteer U-boat hunters, since it's reasonable to assume that the agents would have passed this information back to Dönitz's headquarters. This is a classic example of the tension in a free society between the public's right to know, the military's legitimate need for operational secrecy, and the media's responsibility to inform. In World War II the media were generally cooperative, and censorship was in place. Still, articles like this, which may have been designed to boost civilian morale by showing that *something* was being done about the U-boats, did increase the risks of ventures such as Hemingway's by making the U-boats all that much more wary and less likely to take a harmless-looking fishing boat at face value. That wariness would render Hemingway's planned attack tactics that much more impracticable. Hemingway must have known that, too.

Additionally, a fascinating element of espionage was attached to the whole antisubmarine business. It was widely believed and reported in the United States and Cuba that one of a U-boat's missions was to land spies and saboteurs, and this was in fact the case, though this activity was far less extensive than the nervous and suspicious public feared at the time. In actual fact, there were four German saboteurs landed by U-boats off Long Island, and another four off Jacksonville, Florida, in June of 1942. (After landing the four on Long Island, *U202* returned to base, pausing to sink the Argentine freighter *Rio Tercero*.)[3] The saboteurs were hastily rounded up by the FBI and the Coast Guard, and six were summarily tried and executed, and the other two imprisoned—leniency in return for cooperation. But the story gave credence to the idea that espionage and U-boats went hand in hand and naturally appealed to Hemingway's appetite for shady doings in warfare—an appetite that was sharpened during his stays in Spain during the Civil War and reflected in his play *The Fifth Column*. (In *For Whom the Bell Tolls*, Robert Jordan was essentially a saboteur.) Additionally, the complicated coastline of Cuba with its myriad mangrove islands and hidden inlets seemed an ideal spot for landing saboteurs or for hiding fuel and supply dumps for the U-boats. When he examined his charts and maps, Hemingway probably experienced a frisson of excitement as he considered what might be going on—not only at sea but also along the uninhabited coast. Searching out these hidden bases was an ideal assignment for a small boat with a shallow draft. A well-camouflaged enemy supply dump might avoid notice from the air, but it could be located and eliminated by a crew from a converted sportfishing boat.

In this light, Hemingway's desire to acquire small arms and grenades made a great deal of sense. Who could say what might be lurking at the end of some narrow, uncharted channel through the mangroves? Having a grenade or two at hand, along with a well-oiled Thompson, would be very comforting. The final scene of *Islands in the Stream* indicates clearly what Hemingway was considering as a possibility, for the firefight in which Thomas Hudson is killed is precisely what could have happened to Hemingway and his crew if they had stumbled on a hidden German supply dump on an obscure mangrove island: "There were no birds at all and since the tide was high he knew that the birds had to be in the mangroves. The ship was entering the narrow river now and Thomas Hudson, bareheaded and barefooted and only wearing a pair of khaki shorts, felt as naked as a man can feel."[4]

Anyone who has poked the nose of his ship into the shallow waters around islands where the enemy may lie understands this feeling of nakedness and knows that what Hemingway intended to do as part of his mission was not nothing.

* * *

But what else was driving him? Hemingway could not have regarded his U-boat hunting on a purely literal level. A creative artist does not disengage his imagination when he is not working. The same images and habits of mind, the same tendencies to look for meaning, the same ways of thinking and imagining are simply applied to the current reality—perhaps inescapably. To Hemingway the U-boats must have been both real and symbolic. Metaphorically they were the close cousins of the sharks in *The Old Man and the Sea*—sinister forms appearing suddenly to turn a calm sea into a scene of bloody carnage. Looking for them was therefore both a useful service and a kind of quest with its own meaning and significance related to, but independent of, its military value. These are not the sorts of things an artist, or anyone for that matter, can say about himself without sounding a little self-important or absurd (not that Hemingway always, or even usually, avoided such traps). But they are the sorts of things an artist can think when he is alone on the bridge of his boat looking for gray shapes or periscopes in the distance. And they are the kinds of thoughts that he can then convert into his art.

Nor was this a death wish, despite Hemingway's habit of going on and on about the subject in his conversations. A quest is not a search for death. It may turn out that way, but that is not the object. However, the long odds against success in this venture (that is, long odds if he tangled with a U-boat) may have appealed to Hemingway, some of whose heroes took grim satisfaction in facing impossible odds without flinching. Perhaps Hemingway, like T. E. Lawrence—another individualist with complex motivations—believed "there could be no honor in a sure success, but much might be wrested from a sure defeat."[5] We know that Hemingway had long ago dismissed such words as *honor*, especially in military grandstanding of the kind that led to the insane butchery of World War I:

I was always embarrassed by the words sacred, glorious, and sacrifice. . . . We had heard them, sometimes standing in the rain almost out of earshot, so that only the shouted words came through, and had read them, on proclamations that were slapped up by billposters over other proclamations, now for a long time, and I had seen nothing sacred, and the things that were glorious had no glory and the sacrifices were like the stockyards at Chicago if nothing was done with the meat except to bury it. There were many words that you could not stand to hear and finally only the names of places had dignity. Certain numbers were the same way and certain dates and these with the names of the places were all you could say and have them mean anything. Abstract words such as glory, honor, courage, or hallow were obscene beside the concrete names of villages, the numbers of roads, the names of rivers, the numbers of regiments and the dates.[6]

Hemingway had his own notion of what we think of as honor—a resistance to the inevitable defeat, a rejection of the unavoidable. To repeat: "And each man retained now, better than any citation or decoration, the knowledge of just how he would act when everything looked lost."[7] Or: "We were all cooked. The thing was not to recognize it."[8]

This is the celebrated "grace under pressure," but the idea meant more than just facing down hopelessness and certain defeat. It applied as well to the U-boat patrols even though—or perhaps especially because—nothing was at all certain about a patrol. You could not be sure that anything would happen, much less that you would have to confront an inevitable defeat. The image of a U-boat suddenly surfacing from what had been an apparently empty sea is an apposite metaphor. You are looking for something that could appear at any time anywhere—or never appear at all. This requires a different form of fortitude, one that is consistent with the idea of a quest. A quest is a search for something, not a confrontation. Confrontation may be the climax of the story, but searching is the heart of the matter, staying with it in the face of persistent failure or disappointment. After all, the Old Man fished eighty-four days in a row, catching nothing.

In short, the great attraction of hunting U-boats was the opportunity it gave Hemingway to be the hero of his own life, to become one of his characters. The sea hunt was much more important and significant to Hemingway as man and writer than it was to the war effort, although it was a legitimate contribution, no larger than some but no smaller than most.[*] If he could catch a few fish along the way and have a few laughs and a few drinks with the crew, who were also his friends and admirers, so much the better.

If Frederic Henry had made a separate peace in *A Farewell to Arms,* perhaps Hemingway thought of this new venture as making a separate war.

* * *

It is usually a mistake to look to fictional characters to gain biographical information about the author. For example, Hemingway was nowhere near Caporetto[†] during the disastrous retreat, although you might think he was, given the vividness of the portrayal in *A Farewell to Arms.* However, a writer's imagination and ideas are obviously on display in his fiction: that is the whole point. "The

---

[*] The vast majority of military personnel in World War II never saw an enemy, never fired or heard a shot fired in anger, and dealt mostly with routine operations—patrols, supply problems, training, and so on.

[†] Caporetto was a crushing defeat for the Italians, who were facing the Austrians in the northern theater of war. In October 1917 the Austrians, Hungarians, and Germans broke through the Italian lines. Italian casualties were nearly three hundred thousand men, most of them captured. The Italians re-formed along the Piave River, only thirty kilometers north of Venice, and halted further Austrian advances.

only writing that was any good was what you made up, what you imagined."[9]

So it's possible to look at a writer's work and in particular his characters, especially his heroes, and from them gain some understanding of the writer's imagination and state of mind, which, in turn, gives some indication of why the man himself acted the way he did. If we want to know why Hemingway went U-boat hunting—why beyond the mere desire to serve—we can look to the heroes of his fiction.

If you took all of Hemingway's major heroes—Nick Adams, Jake Barnes, Frederic Henry, Robert Jordan, the Old Man, and Thomas Hudson—and combined them into one fictional biography, you would see a kind of progression, a series of stages through which the character, that is, the Hemingway Hero, developed.

The first stage exists mostly in the hero's memory, for it was a time of innocence, a kind of youthful paradise. We associate this phase mostly with the outdoors, a place that the hero is always trying to come back to, a place, too, with innocent friendships and camaraderie of the kind that Hemingway as an adult was constantly trying to re-create. In one sense his whole crew aboard *Pilar* was in part an attempt to put together kindred spirits who would not only take orders from Hemingway the leader but also join wholeheartedly and unreservedly in Hemingway's enthusiasm of the moment, whether fishing, eating, or poking around in the mangroves for fifth columnists and spies.

This first stage is what Jake Barnes is looking for when he escapes from the delirium of the fiesta and goes into the mountains to fish the Irati with his best friend. It is also what Nick Adams was looking for when he returned to the Big Two Hearted River, although in Nick's case he was going back alone to try to recapture the way he used to feel, if only temporarily. "Nick's heart tightened as the trout moved. He felt all the old feeling." As his name obviously suggests, he is originally from that Eden, though now wounded, nicked, by the experience he has had since leaving or losing that paradise of youth—the place and "the old feeling" that he remembers . . . and longs for.

And he returns to the same feeling in the short story "Now I Lay Me":

"Some nights too I made up streams, and some of them were very exciting, and it was like being awake and dreaming."

And then:

"I lay in the dark with my eyes open and thought of all the girls I had ever known and what kind of wives they would make. It was very interesting to think about and for a while it killed off trout fishing and interfered with my prayers. Finally, though, I went back to trout fishing, because I found that I could remember all the streams and there was always something new about them."

Fishing is a continuing metaphor for Hemingway; it is also a means of escaping back to the time of innocence, a time before the world intruded violently. It is both a practical activity as well as an exercise of the imagination—"like being awake and dreaming." Nick Adams, Hemingway's surrogate, wades in rivers to wash away the sins of his world, or at least the memories of them. The concentrated act of angling for trout purges his mind of nightmarish thoughts and cleanses his imagination and sensibilities and returns him to a state of, if not grace, innocence: "Nick felt happy. He felt he had left everything behind, the need for thinking, the need for writing, other needs. It was all back of him."[10]

The second stage is more obvious: the young man who has gone into the world and been damaged by his experience—Nick in "A Way You'll Never Be" and Frederic Henry at the opening of *A Farewell to Arms*—the youthful soldier who has lost his illusions and has settled into the round of whoring and drinking and priest baiting like the others in his unit. This, too, is Robert Jordan at the beginning of his journey, a professional now with no particular faith except his antifascism; he is not really for anything, just against the fascists. These young men at this stage are, to borrow Graham Greene's phrase, "burnt out cases." They are men who lie awake in the night: "I can't sleep without a light of some sort. That's all I have now."[11] War is both the event that triggers this fall from innocence and the most glaring metaphor for the universe's fundamental lack of design or purpose. All the proud strategies of the generals are so much papering over the abyss, as in the grand attack at Caporetto that dissolves into the chaos of defeat and retreat, or the scene in *For Whom the Bell Tolls* in which Golz watches the start of the attack that he now knows will fail and says, "No. Rien à faire. Rien." Nothing to do. Nothing. War is the hero's window into nothingness, and the wounds the hero receives are literal and figurative simultaneously.

But then Henry finds Catherine and Jordan finds Maria; they fall in love and move into a third phase of their development— a time of suddenly discovered meaning; a romantic relationship sweeps away the cynicism and nihilism of their earlier lives and creates a reason for being, answers the questions they had no answers for before. Love allows Frederic Henry to move away from a world that has no intrinsic purpose or direction and to create significance in his small and separate world—the world of a snowbound Swiss cabin, where the days are filled with skiing and the nights with wine and good food and then a warm bed and physical passion— all of this far away from the mud and madness in the trenches. Robert Jordan finds the same sort of completion with Maria: "But in the night he woke and held her tight as though she were all of life and it was being taken from him." He knows what the younger Frederic Henry perhaps does not know: that it is too good to last.

For intense romantic love—as represented by what Maria calls La Gloria—cannot endure; it is by definition transitory, like the sexual passion that is both a symbol and an integral part of this stage of being. The realities of the world inevitably intrude, often violently, randomly, senselessly, and the hero is left alone—Frederic Henry walking away in the rain, Robert Jordan wounded and lying in wait for the fascist cavalry, Jake Barnes disabled and permanently separated from Brett, Santiago alone in a skiff far out in the Gulf. This is the last and most permanent stage of the hero, the place and the time where he stares at defeat and decides what to do about it. "A man can be beaten but not defeated," says the Old Man. Yes, but only if the man makes an effort of will to deny defeat, despite the evidence of his eyes and his experience—like the bullfighter in "The Undefeated" who maintains his dignity as pillows rain down on him, thrown by the irritated spectators who are disgusted by the old matador's repeated failures to kill his bull.

This is the existential hero—the man who must create his own meaning out of a world in which none is provided, in which nada is the operating principle, a world that seems to be doing its best to destroy what little meaning a man can find, and to destroy it not maliciously, but indifferently, which seems somehow all the more appalling, for it is all so formless and random. This menace is often characterized in Hemingway's writing as "they"—an anonymous danger, like the sharks that attack the Old Man's great fish. The hero must live in this world with the full knowledge of its dangerous, even chaotic indifference. The Old Man fights the sharks, knowing he will lose. Robert Jordan, at the end, waits for the fascist cavalry, knowing he is doomed.

Some lines from Stephen Crane apply here: "The man said to the Universe, 'Sir, I exist,' and the Universe replied, 'Yes, but that does not create in me a sense of obligation.'"[*] Crane wrote these lines well before existentialism became a popular way of looking at things, and it may well be critical overanalysis to ascribe existentialist ideas to Hemingway's heroes. Both Crane and Hemingway

[*] Hemingway was well familiar with Crane, the author of *The Red Badge of Courage*. Hemingway included that work in his *Men at War* edition.

simply looked at the world in an attempt to find some sort of order and meaning and saw . . . nothing—nothing beyond what they could create. And unlike Crane's Universe, Hemingway's never bothered to answer, only to act, or rather, lurch, randomly, indifferently, and with disastrous results usually.

So the generic Hemingway Hero goes through four stages of development—innocence, disillusion, romantic fulfillment, and, finally, isolated endurance. The individual heroes of the stories and novels may exist at one of these levels or pass through several, as does Robert Jordan—albeit his stay at the final level is brief, whereas Jake Barnes is there permanently and Frederic Henry is only just beginning the final stage as he walks away from the hospital.

There's another, somewhat different, but related way of looking at the hero and his travails. Albert Camus's book *The Myth of Sisyphus* mirrors this same sort of heroic problem. Sisyphus has annoyed the gods through various acts of hubris and defiance and is therefore condemned to push a great rock to the top of a hill, only to see it roll back down, at which point he must walk down and start again, endlessly, throughout eternity. At the end Camus says we must consider Sisyphus happy, because he is enduring in the face of an absurd situation and that is about as well as anyone can do. This myth mirrors the arc of the Hemingway Hero—he starts fresh at the bottom, then struggles through disillusion to reach a pinnacle, romantic love for the briefest moment, only to see the whole thing plunge down into the abyss where he must then follow and repeat the process. Robert Jordan says much the same thing as he muses:

"It is a vast wheel, set at angle, and each time it goes around and then is back to where it starts. One side is higher than the other and the sweep it makes lifts you back and down to where you started. There are no prizes either and no one would choose to ride this wheel. You ride it each time and make the turn with no intention ever to have mounted. There is only one turn; one large, elliptical, rising and falling turn and you arc back where you have started."*

You climb the heights from disillusion to romantic love, then, having lost it, plunge down again, like Sisyphus' rock. But having loved—and necessarily lost—you have learned something; you are not the same callow burned-out case, but someone who has seen what the universe has to offer and endured in spite of it. Until the fascist cavalry arrive, that is.

While Hemingway's view of the hero is certainly an expression of postwar modernism, it also has distinct overtones of Romanticism and the Romantic poets, especially in his emphasis on the transitory nature of love. The Hemingway Hero at the final stage of development seems very like the knight-at-arms in "La Belle Dame sans Merci"—alone and palely loitering and wondering where the girl has gone off to. And what is it exactly that Keats envied about the lovers on the Grecian urn? That they are frozen at the moment of greatest desire and will therefore never experience the sense of loss that must inevitably follow consummation. As Hemingway's friend Scott Fitzgerald said in *This Side of Paradise,* "The sentimental person thinks things will last—the romantic person has a desperate confidence that they won't."

Despite their experience of inevitable loss, Hemingway's heroes in this last stage of their development are not rendered inert by their visions but remain active in spite of everything, or perhaps *because of* everything. The Old Man continues to fish despite the eighty-four days of failure, and we know he will continue to fish when he wakes the next morning after his ordeal with the great

---

* Renaissance philosophers and theologians would have nodded their heads at this passage, for Fortune's Wheel was a common symbol; someone caught on it was there because he had made worldly choices that separated him from God. Hemingway's characters have no God to become separated from and are trapped on the wheel "with no intention ever to have mounted."

fish and the sharks. Jake Barnes will probably go on rescuing Brett, knowing it will only lead to continuing despair. They are alone, but not "palely loitering."

So if the Keats analogy doesn't seem precisely appropriate, another poem, by W. B. Yeats, almost exactly mirrors the several stages the Hemingway Hero passes through. A sometime poet himself, Hemingway admired Yeats: "As for Yeats, he and Ezra [Pound] and Anonymous are my favorite poets. If Yeats hasn't written swell poems, then nobody else ever had or ever will."[12] Presumably Hemingway knew of this particular poem, called "The Song of the Wandering Aengus":

I went out to the hazel wood
Because a fire was in my head,
And cut and peeled a hazel wand
And hooked a berry to a thread,
And when white moths were on the wing
And moth-like stars were flickering out,
I dropped the berry in a stream
And caught a little silver trout.

When I had laid it on the floor
I went to blow the fire aflame,
But something rustled on the floor
And someone called me by my name:
It had become a glimmering girl
With apple blossom in her hair
Who called me by my name and ran
And faded through the brightening air.

Though I am old with wandering,
Through hollow lands and hilly lands,
I will find out where she has gone

And kiss her lips and take her hands,
And walk among long dappled grass
And pluck till time and times are done,
The silver apples of the moon,
The golden apples of the sun.

Yeats took this story from an old Irish myth, yet it seems such an appropriate synthesis of the Hemingway Hero. At the beginning the poet, Aengus (who is a kind of Irish god of youth and love and poetry), is unsettled about something—has a fire in his head—so he goes out into nature to fish, hoping to soothe away whatever is bothering him. He catches a trout that changes into a glimmering girl with apple blossoms in her hair (a reference, probably, to the Celtic myth of the Isle of Apples, a place of everlasting life—not unlike Eden before the Fall). She calls him by his name, then vanishes, leaving him bereft—just as Catherine leaves Frederic, or Maria disappears on horseback, calling to Roberto as she rides away. Aengus vows to find her again, but the poem ends with the hero alone and on the verge of what seems to be a hopeless quest.*

The imagery would strongly have appealed to Hemingway—the trout stream and the hazel woods are a place of refuge and remembrance for the disturbed hero, who is looking for some relief through fishing and simply being in nature; the woman who appears gives him a glimpse of romantic fulfillment and meaning before disappearing; the search begins and looks very much as if it will be never ending. Joyce would have called seeing the girl an epiphany, for the image of her gives direction to the hero's life from then on.

I believe Hemingway had this sort of imagery permanently

---

* In the original Irish myth, Aengus does find her again, and the two are turned into swans and live, presumably, happily ever after.

fixed in his imagination—the desire to be in nature to relieve whatever was troubling him, and especially to be fishing, which was always his best release. And I believe he had in him the constant longing for that dream woman, a longing that took many different shapes during his life, some of whom he married and some of whom he merely longed for (Agnes, Adriana), but all of whom, because of their reality, inevitably fell short of this romantic image. As Yeats said, "There is for every man some one scene, some one adventure, some one picture, that is the image of his secret life, for wisdom first speaks in images."

In Hemingway's case, marriage was never the solution, for the dream vision can never successfully morph into a wife. A man with Hemingway's imagination must inevitably look outside to have some sort of vision to fix on, and the woman who is in the kitchen supervising dinner becomes disqualified as a muse—at least over the long term. No doubt this dichotomy between image and reality was a source of some of the friction that existed between Hemingway and all of his wives, but no doubt, too, his muse in whatever form she was taking was a powerful stimulus to his writing, for "the best writing is certainly when you're in love."[13]

Although the prototypical hero of his fiction moves through four fairly well-defined phases, presumably these four stages were always simultaneously present in Hemingway the man and writer. These states of mind alternated depending on the situation. He was the wandering Aengus looking for relief in nature, dreaming of a glimmering girl, finding her and losing and longing for her afterward and enduring the loneliness that was both a metaphor and a condition of life.

So the search for something, the quest, was a continuing theme in his art and in his life and even in his recreations. Small wonder, then, that the idea of looking for U-boats appealed to him. It was one piece of the whole.

* * *

I think we are far too concerned with our own navels.

Martha Gellhorn[14]

Someone with little or no sympathy for this sort of romantic imagery would probably say it's nothing more than an adolescent fantasy or, worse, that most boring of clichés, the male midlife crisis, although in Hemingway's case it seemed to begin in his teens and go on for as long as he lived, so it can hardly be called midlife. But for the skeptic the essential point remains—the man was a dreamer and longed for other women. That is hardly unique. The utterly common George Babbitt, human repository for all the bourgeois values that Martha detested, has the same longings and dreams the same dream, more or less, as Aengus: "He stumbled into the admission that he wanted the fairy girl—in the flesh." Then Babbitt inevitably falls into a genuine midlife crisis, starts drinking, and has a nearly disastrous affair with a woman who hardly fits the image of his dreams and is in fact very much "of the people." In short, he makes a thorough fool of himself and learns the great difference between the dream vision and a human variant.

Not surprisingly, this was more or less Martha's version of Hemingway's romantic nature: "I can't think why one of us [the wives], specially Mary, didn't shoot the bloody man. If you ever think you married the world's worst shit, you're wrong. I did. . . . E.H. must have slept with four women, his wives, and maybe a fifth during Pauline's reign. If any others they must have been whores which he'd deny to his last breath. In fact I think that's true and accounts for his being such a ghastly lover—wham bam thank you maam, or maybe just wham bam. No experience. Two virgin wives before me and me not about to raise my voice in complaint because I imagined it was all my fault, not getting anywhere. The great sex talker and writer must, in fact, have been terrified of women. Interesting."[15]

Martha wrote this in 1983—almost forty years after the end of her marriage. Clearly time did not and probably could not dull her edge. She excuses herself from any responsibility for any deficiencies in the bedroom, although she was self-admittedly a failure in this business with every man in the long line of her lovers both before and after Hemingway. Martha is simply not a reliable reporter—not on this subject, particularly. Of course, no one who is looking back on a failed relationship can be expected to be completely objective. And it does not matter that he and Martha lived a life as querulous as a pair of ill-tempered swans; what matters is how he used romantic imagery to define his art and his life. Whether Hemingway was an adept or inept lover is not the point so much as that he was a romantic in his imagination and applied the imagery of the questing hero to his writing and to his life. Looking for U-boats was essentially an expression of the imagination, the same restless mind-set that drove his writing: "I will find out where she has gone." Not surprisingly one of the results of this quest was *Islands in the Stream,* the only one of his posthumously published works, aside from *A Moveable Feast,* that ranks with his better writing. And the last third of the book is the story of a search for the crew of a U-boat.

Martha didn't think much of any of this; to her the patrols were little more than parties with his cronies, parties from which she was excluded, not that she wanted to join in. You can see her point to some extent, but you also realize that by nature she tended to be dismissive and contemptuous. Also, clearly, some of this was self-protection at a time when their relationship was beginning to show signs of strain:

I hated his toughness, because I know it for what it is; the brave do not have to be cruel. The brave can be gentle. The toughness is a pose to get away with being nasty, and ungenerous (it allows you to mock everyone and everything). In Spain he was not tough; he was kind. He was never kind to me, even there, because I was the woman he wanted which meant the woman he intended absolutely to own, crush, eat alive. But he was good to soldiers, to poor people.[16]

Arguments between them became more frequent, and Hemingway once shouted at her, "I'll show you, you conceited bitch. They'll be reading my stuff when the worms have finished with you."[17] This sounds like something out of *Who's Afraid of Virginia Woolf?* and looking back after their breakup, Martha could well feel justified in saying, "I honestly thought Ernest would drive me mad with cruelty."[18]

Not that there weren't good days, too. During the same period she wrote to Hemingway from Florida, apparently suffering as much from separation as from constant contact, "Oh please write to me. I need a big hugalug. Always, your mopey wife."[19]

But by the middle of 1942 the happiness at being in the sunlight of Cuba had worn off, and Martha was getting bored playing lady of the finca, bored, frankly, with the day-to-day requirements of being married: "I like living alone, I do not enjoy shared daily life, and think marriage the original anti-aphrodisiac. I like excitement from men, all kinds there are; and you can't get that Sunday through next Monday."[20] Ironically, this is probably the same sort of feeling that Hemingway had. She was also fed up with watching Hemingway go off with his pals, resentful of her subordinate position, dismissive of the value and danger of the patrols. If she heard about the *Gertrude* incident, it probably didn't bother her greatly—just a few onions, after all. The war in the Gulf seemed to be a sideshow. So her attitude about Hemingway's patrolling plans was colored by a number of personal and professional frustrations that had nothing really to do with whether the patrols were useful or merely another example of Hemingway's self-dramatization, another of his "fakes."

Her spirits received a lift when she got an assignment from *Collier's* to travel around the Caribbean for two months to gather material about the various locations and their readiness for war. If she spotted a U-boat of her own, so much the better; the irony would have been delicious to her—though what on earth she intended to do about the information is a mystery. They—the U-boats—certainly were around; on July 13, *U84* torpedoed and sank the merchant ship *Andrew Jackson* a few miles off Havana. On July 16, the day *U166* blasted the *Gertrude* into so much flotsam, Martha was writing to her editor at *Collier's* to thank him for arranging the assignment and closed by saying, "My articles are always to be signed Martha Gellhorn, always. That is what I always was, and am and always will be: you can't grow a name on to yourself."[21] Whether she spotted a U-boat or not, this trip would be a chance not only to do some work but also to get away from Hemingway for a good long while—a hiatus that would allow the happier and warmer feelings to build again, which they did. So much so that she would be able to write to him from Haiti on July 23, only seven days after the *Gertrude* was sunk, addressing him as "Bug dearest" and signing herself "Mrs. Bug." So Martha's attitudes about her husband's U-boat hunting need to be considered within the context of their parabolic relationship and her own professional frustrations and ambitions. She was a writer and wanted to be where the action was; fiction did not satisfy her creative urges the way it did for Hemingway; she did not have that sort of imagination. She needed to see in order to write: "What the hell does it matter all this learning about oneself? You learn by doing, not by sitting looking at your own innards. You are what you do; you learn by listening, *hearing,* feeling, for others, putting yourself in the place and lives of others."[22]

He plumbed the images in his imagination; she looked outward to find subjects to write about: "I have to see before I can imagine."[23] They approached the business of writing—and living—very, very differently.

* * *

Martha left on her fact-finding mission in the middle of July 1942. She was in high spirits as she went off on her own two-month adventure. She went to Puerto Rico and spent some days flying antisubmarine patrols in B17s. From there she went to Tortola and hired a potato boat, manned by five local men, to cruise the Caribbean for her stories. She was intrepid to the point of foolhardiness. In some ways it was a reprise of her trip with Hemingway to China in 1941, just after they were married. They went to report on the war there. She flew harrowing missions over the mountains in airplanes better suited to museums and seemed to love all of the adventure and to hate the squalor of Asia and especially the appalling smells—things that did not bother Hemingway in the least. He had a talent for making himself comfortable in any sort of surroundings, whereas she, with an abiding fastidiousness, did not.[*]

The Caribbean trip did her good, for it allowed her freedom and the chance to work, although she did not see any U-boats or much in the way of damage—aside from the shipwrecked mariners who had been rescued and brought to Puerto Rico—and it was only later, "thirty four years late,"[24] that she found out how bad things really were just then in her home waters. Perhaps at that point she began to appreciate Hemingway's own small contribution and realize it was worthwhile. Perhaps the realization caused some chagrin.

This trip, with its enforced separation from Hemingway, helped

---

[*] They interviewed Chiang Kai-shek during this trip—and also Chou En-lai, an incident that raised some eyebrows in the State Department and the FBI.

them both, though both complained of loneliness. When you are feeling free and productive, it is a little easier to remember the good times. And when the woman who is also your wife is gone, it is a little easier for her image to merge with that other, more enduring image that you carry around in your head.

Chapter Seven

~~~

FATHERS AND SONS

I was watching the man at the table. His name was Luis Delgado and the last time I had seen him had been in 1933 shooting pigeons at San Sebastian and I remembered standing with him up on top of the stand watching the final big shoot. We had a bet, more than I could afford to lose that year, and when he paid coming down the stairs, I remembered how pleasant he was and how he made it seem like a great privilege to pay. Then I remembered our standing at the bar having a Martini, and I had that wonderful inner feeling of relief that comes when you have bet yourself out of a bad hole and I was wondering how badly the bet had hit him. I had shot rottenly all week and he had shot beautifully but drawn almost impossible birds and he had bet on himself steadily.

"The Denunciation"

I
N Hemingway's story "The Denunciation" Luis Delgado is a Fascist pilot who has come back to Chicote's in Madrid, disguised in a Loyalist uniform and therefore legally a spy—though one senses that nothing sinister is going on and that the uniform is mere camouflage to allow Delgado to come back to a place he had enjoyed before the war and perhaps also to enjoy the bravado of a dangerous act. The narrator, an American whom the

waiters call Enrique, remembers him as a friend from the old days of pigeon shooting—"He is a Fascist and for him to come here, no matter what his reasons, is very foolish. But he was always very brave and very foolish." A waiter who also remembers Delgado asks Enrique whether he should denounce Delgado, and eventually Enrique gives the waiter the number to call. Enrique then leaves as the police arrive, only later to call a friend in counterintelligence to ask him not to reveal that the waiter was the informant and to take on the guilt himself, so that Delgado, who had been a good client at Chicote's and presumably happy there, would not "be disillusioned or bitter about the waiters there before he died." Besides, Enrique and Delgado "had been friends," and "any small acts of kindness you can do in life are worth doing." This wonderful line is full of irony, yet is sincere, too, for Delgado in addition to being "very brave" also "used to be a marvelous pigeon shot." In Hemingway's world that meant something.

* * *

Isn't fishing lovely though? I would hate to die, ever, because every year I have a better time fishing and shooting. I like them as much as when I was sixteen. . . . If you don't know how to enjoy life, if it should be only one life we have, you are a disgrace and don't deserve to have it.

Hemingway letter to Hadley, July 23, 1942[1]

Hemingway was never one to neglect his pleasures. Pigeon shooting was one of them, especially in the summer of '42.

This is how you shoot live pigeons—you stand on a mark, perhaps twenty or so yards away from a line of traps, which are nothing more than boxes big enough to hold a pigeon and a spring device. There may be only one trap or five or sometimes more arranged in a semicircle in front of you. Beyond the traps, maybe another twenty yards, is a fence, also in a semicircle. You are holding a shotgun and when you are ready you shout "Pull!" and a club employee will spring one of the traps—you don't know which one—and out will fly a pigeon, motivated by the spring he has been sitting on while awaiting his destiny, unsuspectingly. The bird can fly in any direction: toward you suddenly, straight up, away at a severe angle, straight away—anywhere and at any altitude. Occasionally a bird will pop out of the trap and decide not to fly and merely land awkwardly and begin to strut, pigeon fashion, while assessing the situation. At this point one of the club boys will throw a ball or a stone at it so that the bird finally takes wing. Most of the time, though, the pigeons come darting out of the traps and fly off at excellent speed.

The object is to shoot the bird and drop it before it can get over the semicircular fence on the outer edge of the shooting area. If you kill the bird but its momentum carries it over the fence, it is the same as a miss.

Unsurprisingly, live-pigeon shooting is frowned on in many parts of the world today, although it is still legal in some places in the United States. These shoots are discreetly conducted so as not to alert infuriated bird fanciers, who would otherwise show up carrying signs. Live-pigeon shooting used to be popular in Europe, and an urban legend claims that the pigeons who speckle tourists in St. Mark's Square and other European plazas are descendants of birds who escaped the live-pigeon rings.[*]

The game was popular wherever there were men with money who liked a little wagering on the side, for live-pigeon shooting generally carried with it side bets, sometimes in the form of Cal-

---

[*] People may wonder why live birds are necessary when clay targets, "clay pigeons," offer a humane substitute. Many shooters do of course shoot clays today, as they did then. But live birds offer more difficult shots because they fly in 360 degrees at any angle of climb, whereas clay pigeons thrown from a spring trap do not offer nearly as many different shots.

cuttas in which various club members had a convivial lunch and afterward bid for shooters they fancied, with the winning shooter sharing the total pot with the one who bought him. This could run into serious money. Monte Carlo used to be one of the hot spots for pigeon shooting, until Princess Grace arrived and put a stop to it.

The game was a combination of behaviors that are often disapproved of—festive lunches with plenty of alcohol, killing inedible birds, and gambling.* It was popular in certain circles of Cuba—at the Club del Cazadores del Cerro. Hemingway was a member there and a regular shooter. So was Martha:

> I split the rest of my time between trying to write (which is the soundest occupation I know) and trying to shoot 20 out of 20 live pigeons, flying like hell bats with a big norther driving them. We have a measly little international championship on live pigeons, down here in a few days, and I am going to enter, mainly because I am the *fille du régiment* of the shooters, being the only female on the island who hangs around the club, shooting as solemnly as the oldest shoot-fools in the place. They all make loud sad sounds when I miss and rush out and shake my hands and say that I made a shot of surpassing beauty when I bring down the birds. It is all very jolly.[2]

No doubt it was very jolly. It's not hard to imagine the impact Martha made there, succeeding at a traditionally male sport and charming the members with her attitude and her looks. Hemingway would have basked in her success, since he took credit for teaching her to shoot. (After their breakup he said, "I hate to lose anyone who can look so lovely and who we taught to shoot and

---

*A shooter who drank too much at lunch, though, was both a fool and most likely a loser. As for the inedible birds, perhaps in Cuba they were given to peasants who were not too fastidious.

Ernest Hemingway, a writer at the top of his game, on the patio
at Finca Vigia.

Martha Gellhorn at Finca Vigia.

Hemingway poolside, working under the arbor.

Gregory, Patrick, and Martha at Finca Vigia.

Ernest and Martha in New York. Martha is wearing the fox coat she acquired in Madrid during the civil war there.

An earlier photo of Hemingway and son Jack (Bumby) that is rife with symbols: a half-empty glass, a fishing rod, a boat, a Thompson submachine gun. The gun is unloaded (it has no ammunition magazine, and the breech appears to be open), so the situation is not as dangerous as it might appear.

Martha, awarding a shooting trophy to Winston Guest at the Club de Cazadores del Cerro.

Hemingway and his son Gregory (Gigi) at the Club de Cazadores del Cerro.

The *Pilar* under way in Havana Harbor. Hemingway is at his usual station on the flying bridge, to the left.

Hemingway at the helm, a happy man.

The *Pilar* in close quarters, most likely searching *cayos* for secret enemy supply dumps. This was probably photographed from a military patrol plane.

The *Pilar* alongside a merchant vessel. The comparison emphasizes the *Pilar*'s relatively small size for the task Hemingway had set for her and her crew.

The *U166* in transit through the Kiel Canal (between the Baltic and the North Seas) on her way to her homeport in Lorient, France. From the rear, the conning tower is exposed, suggesting that Hemingway's plans of attack might have succeeded—if he could have gotten close enough. *(Photograph courtesy of the PAST Foundation.)*

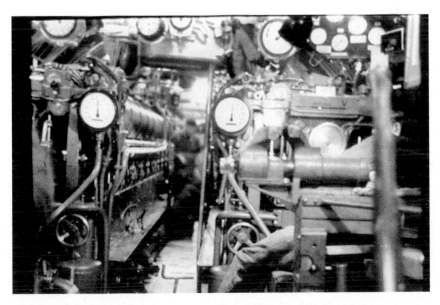

The *U166* engine room, showing the huge diesels used for surface running. *(Photograph courtesy of the PAST Foundation.)*

The passageway inside *U166*. Claustrophobics need not apply for submarine service. *(Photograph courtesy of the PAST Foundation.)*

U166 under way. The skipper, Hans-Gunther Kuhlmann, is the officer in the white hat perched on the conning tower rail. From this angle, a U-boat with its 105 mm deck gun looks more than a little imposing—an iron and steel weapon of mechanized, modern war. This is the enemy Hemingway intended to take on, in the *Pilar*. *(Photograph courtesy of the PAST Foundation.)*

write so well"[3]—a remark that would no doubt have infuriated Martha, especially the part about the writing.) But Hemingway did love to teach friends and family things that he enjoyed and knew about, wing shooting being just one of many subjects that fascinated him.

Hemingway was a good wing shot. Those not familiar with the business might be interested to learn that this is mostly a matter of instinctive hand-eye coordination and reflexes. Shooting a shotgun (and you only use a shotgun on flying birds, live or clay) is not aiming, as in sighting down a barrel, but rather pointing, as in directing your left hand (which is holding the barrels) toward the target, pulling the stock to your cheek and firing when the gun reaches your shoulder and as your left hand continues pointing at the moving bird. You forget the gun is there and concentrate on the target, and when you pull the trigger, a stream of pellets emerges—their lethal range at most sixty yards. Beyond that, the pellets lose energy, and although they will fly as far as two hundred yards, they won't penetrate a bird's feathers. Shots that bring down a bird beyond sixty yards are more or less just luck, because of the diminished energy and because the grouping of the pellets, which was initially compact, has dispersed, leaving large gaps through which a bird can easily, albeit frantically, fly.

This contrasts with rifle shooting, in which a single bullet passes through a rifled barrel (which generates spin to create a true trajectory) and travels lethally perhaps as far as a thousand yards. In this form of shooting the rifleman stares down the barrel, through sights or a scope, at a target that is most likely stationary, lines up the sights and the target, perhaps takes a breath, then squeezes the trigger. Through various writings and commentaries we sometimes get the impression that Hemingway may not have been quite so good a shot with a rifle as he was with a shotgun. Whatever the truth of that, the point remains that these are two radically different forms of sport.

The most difficult shooting of all, though, is shooting a rifle at dangerous game that is charging. Now the two sets of skills must somehow be coordinated—the instinctive shot at a fast-moving target combined with the need to place a single projectile precisely. The novelty of the situation is enhanced because the animal charging is just as bent on your destruction as you are on its—and is probably better equipped, both physically and mentally, to do the job:

> When a buff comes he comes with his head high and thrust straight out. The boss of the horns covers any sort of brain shot. The only shot is straight into the nose. The only other shot is into his chest or, if you're to one side, into the neck or the shoulders. After they've been hit once they take a hell of a lot of killing.[4]

In June of 1942 Hemingway's three sons, Jack (nicknamed Bumby), Patrick, and Gregory, arrived in Havana for a lengthy visit. Jack was Hemingway's son from his first marriage, while the other two boys—Patrick and Gregory, known as Gigi—were the result of his second. All three boys had met and spent time with Martha in Sun Valley, and all three seemed to like her and enjoy her company, in part because of her easygoing way with salty language. But while Martha seemed to be perfectly comfortable around the boys, she was getting restless about the war and her own work, so she was off on her Caribbean scouting trip not long after the boys arrived. She would be away for several months.

In July, Hemingway wrote a long letter to his first wife, Hadley, now married to Paul Mowrer:

> Gigi is fine this summer. He is a better boy all the time. He is shooting marvelously and so is Patrick. The Local shooting club gave Gigi a gold medal engraved: "To Gigi as a token

of admiration from his fellow shooters, Club de Cazadores del Cerro." At nine years old he beat 24 grown men, all good shots and many of them very fine shots, shooting live pigeons. He is useing [*sic*] a .410* against men useing 12 gauge. And live pigeon shooting isn't just a trick like skeet. You have to kill them dead inside a certain distance. Patrick right now is outshooting Gigi but he docs it so modestly and quietly and with no form or style that nobody notices it except the old timers and the book makers but Gigi is known in the papers as el joven fenómeno Americano and day before yesterday an article called him "el popularissimo Gigi." So now we say go down to the post office and get the mail popularissimo or time for bed, popularissimo. But inside himself he is very happy to be the popularissimo and he shoots like a little angel. Bumby shoots pigeons beautifully too. And they must all shoot pretty well because the shooting critics wrote that there aren't four shots in Cuba that can beat the combination of Bumby, Papa, and the two boys. Gigi killed twenty one straight the other day. Patrick shot 19 out of twenty two shoots running. I have an average of 92 x 100 for the season. We shoot in the championship of Cuba on Sunday.

This really is good shooting, and in Gigi's case, remarkable.

Toward the end of the letter, though, the tone changes and reflects a combination of loneliness and nostalgia for the lost days in Paris when they were happy with each other and before Pauline had come along and he had the "bad luck" to be in love with two women at the same time:

---

* A .410 is the smallest gauge (barrel dimension) of all shotguns and therefore uses a cartridge containing fewer pellets than the larger 12 gauge, so that although the gun is lighter and easier for a small boy to handle, it takes even greater skill to hit a bird because of the limited number of pellets.

"But the good luck is to have had all the wonderful things and times we had. Imagine if we had been born at a time when we could never have had Paris when we were young. Do you remember the races out at Enghien and the first time we went to Pamplona by ourselves and the wonderful boat the Leopoldina and Cortina D'Ampezzo and the Black Forest? Last night I couldn't sleep and so I just remembered all the things we'd ever done and all the songs,

A feather kitty's talent lies,
In scratching out each other's eyes.
A feather kitty never dies.
Oh immortality."

He closes the letter:

"Goodbye Miss Katherine Kat. I love you very much. It is all right to do so because it hasn't anything to do with you and that great Paul; it is just untransferable feeling for early and best Gods. But will never mention it if bad. Thought you might just be interested to know. Your friend Taty. Ernest Hemingway."[5]

Perhaps this is the sort of thing Hemingway thought about during those lonely, quiet hours on the flying bridge of *Pilar*. A sailor's life is one of separations and long hours alone on watch with little to do except remember the good times and the times you regret. Hemingway had a large measure of both. The letter foreshadows *A Moveable Feast,* which might just as easily have been titled *The Early and Best Gods.*

In late summer Hemingway wrote another letter, this one to his editor (and Martha's), Maxwell Perkins:

"[Martha] is at present navigating the Caribbean in a thirty foot sloop with a 4x5 cabin with a 4'5" head room accompanied by three faithful negro followers. I understand that if she is lost at sea *Col-*

lier's will pay double for her last article. I expect they will also want me to write a Tribute to their intrepid correspondent. Tell Charley [Scribner] he can start now writing a piece of it. That way we can always have it in the morgue and not so much time will be lost."[6]

The ironic tone suggests quite clearly Hemingway's loneliness and bitterness about the extended nature of Martha's ramblings. But at least the boys were there (although Jack left early for Dartmouth).

On July 28, less than two weeks after the *Gertrude* had been sunk[*] and only two days before the *Robert E. Lee* would be torpedoed and sunk, Hemingway took Patrick and Gregory (along with his regular crew) with him in *Pilar* to investigate the rumors of a secret supply dump near Matanzas, a port city east of Havana. Perhaps the Crook Factory operatives supplied the information. Hemingway and his crew had to travel some sixty miles along the north shore where the water was deep enough to accommodate even the wariest of U-boat captains.

What was Hemingway thinking when he took his sons along? His biographer Carlos Baker suggests that Hemingway was a fan of Frederick Marryat's adventure novels, and since young boys often served as cabin boys or indeed midshipmen in those days of Nelson's navy, Hemingway saw no reason his own boys should not have a similar experience.

Perhaps. But it seems somehow oddly inconsistent with his awareness of how the universe worked: "That is what you did. You died. You did not know what it was about. You never had time to learn. They threw you in and told you the rules and the first time

---

[*] The *New York Times* article regarding the *Gertrude* appeared that same day, July 28, so it's possible but unlikely Hemingway saw it. But it's reasonable to speculate that he had heard about the incident from fishermen and/or the embassy staff. Further, he most certainly knew of the sinking of the *Federal* by *U507,* since that was reported on May 2. In other words, he was aware of the possibility of encountering a U-boat.

they caught you off base they killed you."[7] Maybe he thought that by taking them along he would be able to teach them how not to get caught off base.

Or maybe he thought there wasn't all that much danger, for *Pilar* had not yet received her outfit of weapons or electronic gear. If a U-boat did appear and send over a boarding party, there would be no real evidence of Hemingway's actual purpose. Even so, he would be depending on the U-boat captain's sporting nature—rather a thin reed to rely on. Perhaps he assumed that a U-boat would not risk surfacing during the day, not that close to Havana. But this was still early in the war when defenses were poorly organized and equipped, so the danger to U-boats was minimal, and they knew it. And, after all, Hemingway's tactical concept was based at least in part on luring U-boats to the surface by posing as a harmless fishing boat—which in this particular case was precisely what *Pilar* was.

But the trip was uneventful, and when they arrived off the coast near Matanzas, they spotted a cave that looked suspiciously like a place a fifth columnist would use to hide provisions—close to the shore so that a U-boat's inflatable raft could make a quick run to the beach to pick up fresh food. Hemingway decided to anchor and go ashore to investigate.

The mouth of the cave was big enough at first to accommodate the men, but as they moved farther in, the cave became narrower and narrower—too narrow for an adult. So Hemingway sent Patrick and Gregory through the constricted passageway to check out the rear of the cave.[8] They found nothing.

Here again, it seems strange that Hemingway would send his sons into the unknown, and potentially into harm's way. Perhaps he could tell from the surroundings that there was no real danger, and he merely wanted to give the boys a kind of Tom Sawyer adventure to remember. But he must at the very least have put his immense imagination on hold for those moments as he watched his children disappear into the gloom. Fifth columnists and spies on the island were holed up in just such places, where they not only provided supplies but also watched ship traffic and radioed the information to U-boats. (Indeed, two German spies were arrested and tried in Havana that following September; one was sentenced to death.)[9] Even if no spies were lurking, a cave has no rational design. Who could say what sort of pitfalls, literally, might lie beyond the constriction—and beyond the ability of the adults to do anything about it?

Furthermore, the situation was not all that different from the climactic scene in *Islands in the Stream*—Thomas Hudson is guiding his armed fishing boat through the mangrove islands when he is ambushed by the crew of a German U-boat. In the firefight Hudson is killed, although his crew manages to kill the Germans with grenades and an explosive fire extinguisher. In short, both Hemingway and Thomas Hudson were investigating a place where an enemy could be waiting in ambush. Hemingway therefore obviously could, and ultimately did, imagine something going very wrong. In *Islands* all three of Thomas Hudson's sons are killed, two in an accident, the other in combat. So it's clear that Hemingway not only imagined such a disaster but also tried to neutralize this most hideous of all nightmares by writing about it: "If he wrote it he could get rid of it. He had gotten rid of many things by writing them."[10] Fortunately, this turned out to be nothing more than a grand lark for the boys.

Perhaps Hemingway took them along solely to spend as much time with them as possible; sometimes the simplest explanations are the best. Or maybe he was also trying to give them an experience to help "make men" out of them, especially Gregory, for something about Gregory was worrisome even then. That phrase in Hemingway's letter to Hadley—Gigi is a "better boy all the time"—suggests at least an element of prior dissatisfaction and doubt, as does this passage in *Islands in the Stream*:

He was a devil, too, and deviled both his older brothers, and he had a dark side to him that nobody except Thomas Hudson could ever understand. . . . He was a boy born to be quite wicked who was being very good and he carried his wickedness around with him transmuted into a sort of teasing gaiety. But he was a bad boy and the others knew it and he knew it. He was just being good while his badness grew inside him.

The various memoirs of the Hemingway family members have since revealed that Gregory was a troubled boy who grew into a troubled man and struggled all his life with sexual identity and mental stability. Perhaps Hemingway sensed some of this even before the evidence became undeniable. Perhaps taking the boy pigeon shooting and fishing and patrolling was Hemingway's attempt to exorcise whatever "badness" he sensed in Gigi. But then what about Patrick? Frankly, the whole episode of the cave is puzzling. For the risks were real. The cave is as apt a metaphor as the U-boat for Hemingway's separate war, for there was no way of knowing what, if anything, lay inside.

However, nothing happened, and *Pilar* returned safely to her home port. Hemingway's luck was holding. Certainly he had a fine adventure to share with his boys:

I've been very happy with women. Desperately happy. Unbearably happy. So happy that I could not believe it; that it was like being drunk or crazy. But never as happy as with my children when we were all happy together.[11]

In Anthony Trollope's *Orley Farm,* he describes the happiest period of a man's life to be when he can still walk his ten miles a day and his children have not yet disappointed him. Perhaps

Hemingway sensed that that time in his own life was coming to an end. Perhaps that was part of the reason for his nostalgic letter to Hadley.

* * *

Hemingway liked people who were good at things, especially if they were good at things that interested him. It didn't matter if it was fishing or boat handling or jai alai or soldiering or writing or pigeon shooting or bullfighting or painting—to master a particular skill and display it artfully was something he admired and respected. It accounts to some extent for his eclectic collection of friends and cronies, not only in Cuba during the war, but throughout his life. It also explains his contempt for artistic poseurs and for bureaucrats and most politicians whose stock in trade was compromise, manipulation, or bluster, rather than direct and effective action. Sometimes his own highly competitive nature got in the way of his relationships, even the good ones, but that very competitiveness, unattractive though it could be, was necessary in learning to be good at something and then practicing the art at a high level. Anyone who achieves excellence in anything has competitive drive; most just do a better job of masking it than Hemingway did. As he said in a letter to Charles Scribner, "Am a man without any ambition, except to be champion of the world. . . . Know this sounds like bragging but Jeezoo Chrise you have to have confidence to be champion and that is the only thing I ever wished to be."[12]

Doing something well, especially something difficult, was the principal element of his ethical code: "I only know that what is moral is what you feel good after." At first glance this may seem like nothing more than a conventional belief in conscience, but there was more to it than that, for Hemingway's code of conduct was akin to the classical-Greek idea that excellence is virtue—not *a* virtue, but virtue itself. A man creates his own morality and therefore happiness when his actions approach the ideal, especially in his work: "Writing is something that you can never do as well as it can be done. It is a perpetual challenge and it is more difficult than anything else I have ever done—so I do it. And it makes me happy when I do it well."[13] This standard applies when facing any worthwhile or challenging task. In "The Short Happy Life of Francis Macomber," Macomber achieves happiness, albeit briefly, because he has at last behaved well in a testing situation; he has done the right thing.

Hemingway's code had nothing to do with the conventional morality or the "noble moral tone" so favored by his mother, which he detested. A man performed as well as he could and did it for his own sake, not for the approval of the herd. The only opinions that mattered were those of comrades-in-arms, people who understood the nature of the challenge and could therefore appreciate the quality of your response.

"It makes me happy when I do it well"—Hemingway might also have been talking about his seamanship and his command of the crew. Seamanship and leadership are two related but separate sets of skills—neither is easy and both require seriousness of purpose and knowledge. The U-boat patrols gave Hemingway the chance to exercise both. They were as satisfying, or nearly so, as his artistic work, and both repaid the effort by supplying new grist for his knowledge mill, for every day at sea, and every day in command, brings new challenges, some greater than others, but all interesting, if taken seriously, as Hemingway certainly did.

Hemingway reveled in being in charge—in any situation—but he also seemed to inspire loyalty among the men who sailed with him. Perhaps he chose them simply because they were loyal to him, for plenty of others would not have put up with his style. But when a commander is inefficient or abrasive, even strong initial loyalties quickly degenerate into dissatisfaction. *Pilar* was a small boat, and such close quarters intensify minor irritations and resentments. But Hemingway's men stayed with him throughout the many patrols, and clearly they shared a mutual affection. His leadership skills must have been appropriate and well adjusted for the men he chose to take with him and for the missions they undertook.

Certain passages in *Islands in the Stream* are almost meditations on leadership. In a scene toward the end Thomas Hudson is on the bridge talking with one of his Spanish crewmen, Ara, a man he respects. Hudson is barely holding himself together emotionally as he and his men search for the fleeing crew of a sunken German submarine. Hudson is, like Frederic Henry at the end, or Jake Barnes, or the Old Man, at the final stage of the hero's development, enduring not only the loss of his three sons but also the only woman who mattered: "My own [trouble] is different because I only really loved one woman and I lost her."[14]

Knowing Hudson well and understanding his ordeal, Ara worries that Hudson's command judgment might be clouded:

> "We will get them or we will drive them into other people's hands," Ara said. "What difference does it make? We have our pride but we have another pride people know nothing of."
>
> "That is what I had forgotten," Thomas Hudson said.
>
> "It is a pride without vanity," Ara said. "Failure is its brother and shit is its sister and death is its wife."
>
> "It must be a big pride."
>
> "It is," Ara said. "You must not forget it, Tom, and you must not destroy yourself. Everyone in the ship has that pride, including Peters. Although I do not like Peters."
>
> "Thanks for telling me," Thomas Hudson said. "I feel fuck-all discouraged about things sometimes."
>
> "Tom," Ara said. "All a man has is pride. Sometimes you

have it so much it is a sin. We have all done things for pride that we knew were impossible. We didn't care. But a man must implement his pride with intelligence and care. Now that you have ceased to be careful of yourself, I must ask you to be, please. For us and for the ship."

"Who is us?"

"All of us."[15]

A good officer listens to such things from a man who knows what he is talking about. Leadership is much more than giving orders.

* * *

Winston Guest was good at some things, too. Hemingway's second-in-command, Guest was the son of an American mother and an English father, Frederick Guest, who was first cousin to Winston Churchill, and in fact Churchill was Winston's godfather. Guest went to school in England and America and enjoyed a massive trust fund established by his mother's family. But he did not rest on his wealth, not completely, for he graduated from Columbia Law School, so we can assume he had some intellectual ability as well as some professional ambition.

In addition to being wealthy, Guest was also a fine athlete. At six feet four he excelled in polo, a rich man's sport, but he was no dilettante, for he was a "ten goal" player. That is as good as it gets.[*]

Hemingway got to know him when they were both hunting big game in Africa in the thirties. In the summer of 1942 Guest

---

[*] When two teams play a handicapped match, the goal handicaps of each team's players are added and compared against the other team's total. The team with the lower total receives bonus goals figured by a mildly complicated formula. Thus the higher the handicap, the better the player. The highest possible rating is ten goals.

came to visit Hemingway in Cuba and quickly signed up to be a member of *Pilar*'s U-boat hunting crew. He was thirty-six and, like Hemingway, seemingly beyond the age of active military service, although he had been trying, so far without success, to volunteer.

Guest soon acquired the nickname Wolfie because the Hemingway boys thought he resembled Lon Chaney in the 1941 movie *The Wolf Man*. Guest may not have appreciated the name, but he was easygoing and devoted to Hemingway and not likely to raise a fuss about it.

"Ernest reveled in Winston Guest's admiration and secretly called him 'the ideal subaltern.' He was so well disciplined, said Ernest, that if he said, 'Wolfie, jump out of this airplane; I know you have no parachute but one will be provided on the way down,' Wolfie would merely say 'Yes, papa,' and go diving through the door."[16]

Papa. Hemingway had recently taken to referring to himself that way, and the people around him picked it up. It has a whiff of affectation, a not-so-subtle indication of just who was in charge in any situation, social or military, and it seems especially odd because Hemingway at this time was only forty-three. (*Papa* is also Italian for "pope"; perhaps Hemingway secretly enjoyed the double entendre.)

Hemingway seemed to have an ambivalent attitude toward the rich. He liked being around wealthy people, especially if, like Wolfie, they were content to remain in Hemingway's rather large shadow. When he was younger, he was also attracted, for example, to Gerald and Sara Murphy, models for Fitzgerald's *Tender Is the Night*—attracted to their elegant lifestyle. There is nothing peculiar about that, though, for the Murphys were famously charming and hospitable. Hemingway was not quite so immune to the wealthy and wellborn as he made out to be in, say, "The Snows of Kilimanjaro" when he writes, "He remembered poor Julian and his romantic awe of them and how he had started a story once that began, 'The very rich are different from you and me.' And how someone had said to Julian, 'Yes, they have more money.'"* Yet an element of reverse snobbery also seemed to be at work here, as though Hemingway enjoyed the obvious contrast between his own fame and success—entirely of his own making—and the scanty achievements of people who were simply lucky in their ancestry. Looking back on his early years in France in *A Moveable Feast,* he would disdainfully dismiss the Murphys' "fiesta concept of life." In this he reflected the middle-class values of his upbringing— a respect for hard work and individual achievement combined with outward contempt for, and inward envy of, the merely fortunate—an irony that would no doubt annoy him, if and when he thought about it. He would angrily have rejected any suggestion that his values even slightly coincided with those of his invincibly conventional mother—about whom he never seemed to have a good word, and from whom he never seemed to receive one that was free from noble pieties or criticism. (She said about *The Sun Also Rises,* "Every page fills me with a sick loathing.")[18] But in his attitude toward the rich, he seems not all that different from his difficult mother and her Main Street values.

After the war Winston Guest and Hemingway remained good friends. Guest did not suffer the fate of so many of Hemingway's friends, most likely because he did not challenge Hemingway, and because they had a shared wartime experience. Hemingway was Guest's best man in 1947 when he married Lucy Douglas Cochrane, aka CeeZee, a stunning former Ziegfeld girl whose other principal achievement to that point had been to pose in the nude for Diego Rivera. The painting hung above the bar in the Hotel Reforma in Mexico City until Winston bought it and retired

---

* "Poor Julian" was "Scott Fitzgerald" in the originally published version of the story. Fitzgerald did not appreciate the mention and said so in a letter to Hemingway: "Riches have never fascinated me, unless combined with the greatest charm or distinction."[17]

it for good. CeeZee went on to become a much photographed society hostess and fashion cynosure; Winston was apparently content to stay in the background, second-in-command once again.

The rest of *Pilar*'s crew reflected Hemingway's appreciation of specific abilities. Juan Dunabeitia was a Basque seaman of such prowess that he was nicknamed Sinbad the Sailor. Gregorio Fuentes was Hemingway's much valued first mate and cook: "He would rather keep a ship clean and paint and varnish than he would fish. But I know too that he would rather fish than eat or sleep . . . his seamanship has saved Pilar in three hurricanes. So far, knocking on wood, we have never had to put in a claim on the all-risk insurance."[19] Paxtchi Ibarlucia was an expert jai-alai player and frequent guest at Hemingway's home. Don Saxon was a Marine sergeant, an expert with small arms and their maintenance, who would also operate the radio—no mean talent in those days. Saxon had been recruited from the U.S. embassy by Colonel Thomason—further indication that the operation had official blessing. These were the core of his crew; other friends joined him on occasion—notably, Fernando Mesa, an exile from Catalonia, and Roberto Herrera, a Spanish Cuban whose brother had been a Loyalist surgeon in the Civil War.[20]

The summer passed and Hemingway's sons went home. The crew was in place, each man willing to take orders from Papa. And Papa had finally "secured from the Ambassador a promise that his crew members will be recognized as war casualties for purposes of indemnification in the event any loss of life results from this operation."[21] The operation had its code name, Friendless, after one of Hemingway's legion of cats at the finca. All that was needed now to start serious patrolling were weapons, some time to train in using them, and the installation of electronics that would give *Pilar* her far-ranging eyes and ears.

Chapter Eight

≈≈≈

"AND FADED THROUGH THE BRIGHTENING AIR"

We had to improvise rapidly and on a large scale. We took over all pleasure craft that could be used and sent them out with makeshift armament and untrained crews. We employed for patrol purposes aircraft that could not carry bombs, and planes flown from school fields by student pilots. We armed our merchant ships as rapidly as possible. We employed fishing boats as volunteer lookouts.

Admiral King memo to General Marshall, June 19, 1942[1]

Truth is the most valuable thing we have. Let us economize it.

Mark Twain

ALMOST all of the volunteer patrol boats, which came to be known as the Hooligan Navy, operated off the U.S. Atlantic and Gulf coasts. Some of the boats had armament, including the twin .50-caliber machine guns that Hemingway coveted, as well as a few ash-can-type depth charges that could be rolled off the stern. But the crew of *Pilar* would have to content themselves with smaller arms, submachine guns, and grenades, although biographers suggest that Hemingway got hold of a bazooka—a handheld rocket-firing weapon that could damage a U-boat's conning tower or deck armament. Although the early-war models were accurate only at short ranges, at most 150 yards, Hemingway planned to get a lot closer than that.* Nor would Hemingway have the satisfaction of being a member of a select club of citizen-sailors in Cuba, for he seems to have been the only such volunteer operating in Cuban waters. Whether that pleased him or not is open to question. Years after the war he wrote to his old friend Chink Dorman-O'Gowan that eleven Q-ships were operating from Cuba and that he was the only civilian to command one, and that seven of the ships (boats really) were lost because of poor security. Further, he said that only four of his nine-man crew were still alive, implying (though not stating) that the others had been killed in combat.[2] None of this appears to be true, although he may have been confusing Cuban-navy patrol boats with Q-ships. But certainly none of his crew was killed or even injured. Marine sergeant Don Saxon suffered from a foot disease that caused anyone near him to suffer as well, but that was the extent of the crew's maladies.

No doubt Martha would describe Hemingway's letters to Chink as "apochryphying," and with good reason. Old warriors are sometimes tempted to look back on their service and exaggerate its importance or degree of peril, but few would go to this level of fabrication. This kind of thing bothers and puzzles Hemingway's admirers. Why embroider legitimate service? Maybe he was just trying out a story, perhaps with a few daiquiris as fuel. It would not be the first time, though. His service in World War I as a volunteer Red Cross ambulance driver somehow evolved through retelling into service with the Arditi, an elite Italian infantry unit.[3] Apparently, seeing frontline action and being blown up and wounded while distributing chocolate was not enough; it had to be done in the more glamorous uniform of a fighting unit. But that first set of

---

* Hemingway biographers Carlos Baker and Michael Reynolds both mention this bazooka. Yet it doesn't seem to figure in Hemingway's training sessions or in his planned tactics as he explained them to Colonel Thomason.

fabrications is to some extent understandable in a boy not yet nineteen. Quite possibly Hemingway felt some disdain or resentment from the Italian troops he worked with. Soldiers in the front lines tend to feel contempt for the rear echelons and staff people—not that most wouldn't change places in an instant. Hemingway would have been understandably sensitive to any slights, real or implied, for a mortar shell makes no class distinctions, as he was quick to learn. As long as he was in the forward areas, he was running the same risks as everyone else. So it's not hard to understand his temptation to embellish the story once he returned home, where there was no one to contradict his version of the truth. After all, he had the wounds to show for it. Still, it seems out of character for a man who would write to Maxwell Perkins, "My idea of a career is never to write a phony line, never fake, never cheat, never be sucked in by the y.m.c.a. movements of the moment."*[4]

Hemingway was clearly well aware of what he was doing and saying, for he referred to this sort of storytelling several times in his fiction:

"His lies were quite unimportant lies and consisted in attributing to himself things other men had seen, done or heard of, and stating as facts certain apocryphal incidents familiar to all soldiers."[5] Or: "The Austrians were sons of bitches. How many had I killed? I had not killed any but I was anxious to please—and I said I had killed plenty."[6]

Hemingway's tendency to exaggerate, to use a polite term, would become worse as he grew older. In a May 1950 letter to Dorman-O'Gowan he baldly states, "I have it completely accurate and straight now that have killed 122 (armeds not counting possible or necessary shootings)."[7] Presumably he was talking about the period of his service as a war correspondent in Europe in 1944.

---

* Hemingway often used *YMCA* as shorthand for the pious moralizing he so thoroughly detested.

War correspondents are noncombatants and face legal difficulties if caught using weapons. In fact Hemingway was summoned before a U.S. Army inquiry about reports he was carrying arms as a correspondent in France. Although the charge had some merit, he escaped any serious consequences when the inspector general dismissed the case. But no evidence supports his claim of having killed 122 of the enemy. This sort of story gave rise to Hemingway's occasionally well-deserved reputation as a blowhard. Few combat soldiers have ever personally killed so many of the enemy.* Even fewer would be proud of the tally. Fewer still would talk about it.

Hemingway's story sounds like something that would come from a genuine war lover, such as George Patton. But Hemingway said he didn't feel that way at all about war. As he wrote to Martha, "You have a fine time at wars and love them maybe [and are] happiest at them. . . . But by God I hate them."[8]

Consider the conversation between Robert Jordan and Anselmo, the thoughtful, elderly Spanish partisan:

"You have killed?" Robert Jordan asked in the intimacy of the dark and of their day together.

"Yes. Several times. But not with pleasure. To me it is a sin to kill a man. Even Fascists whom we must kill. . . . No. I am against all killing."

"Yet you have killed."

"Yes. And will again. But if I live later, I will try to live in such a way, doing no harm to anyone, that it will be forgiven."

"By whom?"

"Who knows? Since we do not have God here anymore, neither His Son nor the Holy Ghost, who forgives? I do not know."[9]

---

* Self-effacing Audie Murphy, America's most decorated soldier in World War II, was credited with killing 240 of the enemy in campaigns from North Africa, Sicily, Italy, and Germany; his memoir was called *To Hell and Back*.

Hemingway's admirers may be excused for thinking that this is a truer statement of his actual beliefs than a few lines in a letter designed to impress a friend who was also a professional soldier. Certainly the passage is beautifully written, unlike the slapdash prose of his letter to Chink. Hemingway wrote many letters throughout his lifetime, often to warm up before settling down to the hard job of fiction. Whereas he revised and revised his fiction so that it would be "true," he did not pay nearly as much attention to crafting his letters. They were often just long-distance conversations.

Hemingway also wrote to Dorman-O'Gowan about his patrols in *Pilar*: "We preyed on everything neutral that was doing any good for Germany and on Miss Submarine."[10] Not only was this untrue, but the blustering language cheapens the service that he and his crew did actually perform. They certainly did not "prey" on neutrals. As a lightly armed, thirty-eight-foot fishing boat, they could hardly do much if any damage to merchant shipping. As for the term *Miss Submarine,* it sounds like something out of The Boys' Book of Sea Adventures.

However, this was in a personal letter to a close friend, and they may have had a private language of sorts—certain code words and inside jokes—so that the important information was between the lines. Or the statement may simply have been the kind of thing that a man makes just to give a friend the opportunity to grin and say something obscene in return—a kind of locker-room badinage. Still, it makes one wonder.

But a great difference exists between this sort of apochryphying about his own life and creatively using his actual experience in his fiction. No one should confuse the hero of *A Farewell to Arms* with the young Hemingway in Italy. They had similar experiences, but they are not the same person: "When you first start writing stories in the first person if the stories are made so real that people believe them the people reading them nearly always think the stories happened to you. That is natural because while you were making them up you had to make them happen to the person who was telling them."[11]

His story is not his characters' story. But it's disturbing when the reverse happens and their stories in some way become his. Perhaps when he looked back on his life, the whole truth was just not as interesting to him—or good enough for him. It should have been, but apparently it wasn't. Or perhaps he felt it wasn't good enough for the people he was trying to impress, though why he should bother is another question.

This sort of thing made Martha furious as she watched him telling stories to his friends and hangers-on at the finca—men she called "grown-up well-off semi-illiterate pigeon shooting and fishing pals" who listened to his stories "spellbound."[12] Although her own standards of objective truth could be a little lax, she objected as much to Hemingway's braggadocian style of storytelling as to the exaggerations themselves. She had begun to think that the demands his massive ego placed on other people, herself most of all, were no longer being counterbalanced by his artistic talents. The cost-benefit ratio was slipping out of equilibrium. If other elements of their relationship had been more settled, maybe she would have overlooked his outsize need for adulation in response to his stories. But their relationship was straining at the seams, with only a small margin for error on either side: "He wasn't present except in the flesh. He needed me to run his house and to copulate on (I use the adverb advisedly, not with but on) and to provide exercise in the way of a daily tennis game. There wasn't any fun or communication, none. When I thought I'd go mad from loneliness and boredom, I slipped off to war."[13]

From Hemingway's perspective, his stories and exaggerations were only talk, and maybe he expected people to understand that they were nothing much at all. He said in an interview with Robert Manning of the *Atlantic,* "When I talk, incidentally, it's just talk. But when I write, I mean it for good."[14] That may be an overly generous interpretation of his apochryphying, but it's consistent with his lifelong priorities. Writing was what mattered. When the work was finished for the day, relaxation began and generally included both cold drinks and tall stories, none of which had lasting importance to him. Perhaps he expected his listeners to be able to sort through and discard the most outrageous stories. His well-known fondness for Mark Twain and for *Huckleberry Finn* in particular might provide a clue to his attitude about storytelling: "That book was made by Mr. Mark Twain, and he told the truth, mainly. There was things which he stretched, but mainly he told the truth." What was good enough for Mark Twain was most likely good enough for Hemingway.

Many of Hemingway's most egregious claims and statements came in interviews. He did not like giving interviews and quite understandably resented the interruptions to his work or his recreation, so that he was apt to treat them as necessary evils to be dispensed with as soon as possible. Throwaway lines and exaggerations born of the need to perform and to get things over with are not surprising. When responding to George Plimpton about some remark Hemingway had long ago forgotten, he said, "It sounds silly and violent enough for me to have said it to avoid having to bite on the nail and make a sensible statement."[15]

Hemingway also had a certain shyness—or perhaps intense privacy—that, combined with his underappreciated sense of humor, often led to strange interviews, such as the Lillian Ross *New Yorker* "Portrait" in which he sounds like a cross between "The Battler" and Tonto. In that interview he was plainly drinking steadily and heavily throughout, perhaps to calm himself in a mildly stressful situation, or perhaps because he simply wanted to. But heavy drinking rarely brought out the best, or the truth, in him. He was not unique in that, but in an era when everyone drank a lot, he drank more. A small slip of paper—about the size of a hotel-nightstand notepad, in a file in the Hemingway Collection at the JFK Library—reads, "You are drunk and when you are drunk you are a bore. I love you very much and it's time to stop." The note is signed "M.W." Presumably this is Mary Welsh[*] and presumably she wrote it during the early days of their affair in London. It's easy to imagine her scribbling this and sliding it across the table to him in some London pub after an hour or so of listening to him hold court. Being a journalist, she got right to the point.

Still, a difference exists between off-the-cuff, deflective statements made in interviews and alcohol-fueled exaggerations, and the claims he made while writing letters to his closest friends, such as Dorman-O'Gowan. So there is no avoiding the fact that Hemingway now and then "economized on the truth," to adapt Mark Twain's phrase. Amateur psychologists would say he felt he had to live up to the image he himself had created. If so, it was a dangerous tactic. A navigator who ignores his bearings and simply says, "This is where I am, because this is where I would like to be" will soon find himself aground, or worse.

Mark Twain also said, "Everyone is a moon, and has a dark side which he never shows to anybody." That's probably true for most people, but in Hemingway's case, especially when it came to his public apochryphying, Twain was wrong—Hemingway was more likely to display his dark side and keep his bright side hidden.

*   *   *

Although Hemingway did have an offensive plan in the event he found a U-boat, his real potential value, aside from ferreting out any hidden supply dumps or fifth-column radio installations, would be in spotting a U-boat and then calling for help. On patrol he and his crew expected to spend most of their time scanning the sea for surfaced U-boats or perhaps for a periscope cutting a

---

[*] Mary became the fourth Mrs. Hemingway.

diminutive wave in a flat calm. This involved long hours of concentration and was not glamorous or heroic, but it had to be done. The boredom and fatigue that came with the need to search for something that never seemed to be there were the lot of all the airmen and sailors who looked for U-boats. Hemingway and his crew would be no different.

They would have no radar or sonar to help them out. But *Pilar* did have HFDF, or "huff duff," a high-frequency direction finder. As mentioned before, this electronic device picked up transmissions from the U-boats—both between each other and back to Admiral Dönitz's headquarters. (The Germans never seemed to catch on that they were being spotted because of these transmissions.)

The major HFDF installations were onshore, all along the U.S. eastern seaboard. They had great range and the ability to fix the position of a U-boat by taking bearings on a single transmission from several different HFDF locations, in much the same way that a navigator takes bearings on several different landmarks—or stars—to fix his position on the chart. Where the lines of the different bearings cross on the chart, there lies the ship. Where the lines of the different HFDF bearings crossed, there lay the U-boat. But unlike radar, which could track the physical shape of a surfaced U-boat and follow her course and speed, HFDF was more like a snapshot than a moving picture, unless the U-boat continued to transmit as she traveled. Plotting the transmission therefore only gave subsequent attackers a general idea of where the U-boat was—assuming the U-boat was not hove to on the surface, perhaps for repairs or for refueling from a "milch cow"— because as soon as the German stopped transmitting, the contact was lost, and the U-boat could disappear. HFDF was most effective in identifying and plotting wolf packs in the Atlantic because German commanders talked back and forth as they gathered to attack a convoy. A lone wolf in the Gulf of Mexico, though, had no reason to transmit often—just back to headquarters regularly, as required, and perhaps to a comrade in the area or a fifth columnist onshore.

Unlike shore-based HFDF, shipborne huff duff did not have great range. *Pilar*'s installation had a range of thirty miles, at most, and if the sea was at all choppy, the system didn't work well. Still, it was sophisticated and expensive equipment, and Hemingway was required to sign a receipt for it as well as for the radio that he would need to send back information on U-boat sightings. The total cost of the gear he signed for was somewhere around $32,000*—a significant sum—and it was so bulky that it took up all the space in *Pilar*'s toilet, or head. The crew would therefore have to use the over-the-side technique when the time came— a minor inconvenience during a daytime patrol, but something more than that when the boat stayed at sea for several days or more. The huff duff also required an antenna with a distinctive basket arrangement at the top—something a U-boat commander might wonder about as he inspected what otherwise seemed to be a harmless fishing boat. Most likely the antenna was portable and was raised only when the huff duff was in use. Obviously, *Pilar*'s huff duff was capable of giving only a single bearing, but that bearing alone would provide a rough course to the target, and given that the range was thirty miles, a single bearing might well allow *Pilar* to get close to the target within a couple of hours. (Of course, if the U-boat was cruising on the surface, rather than basking, as the boats sometimes did, *Pilar* would have to adjust her course as the bearing to the U-boat changed—assuming the U-boat cooperated by continuing to transmit now and then and thereby revealed her location.) But certainly, once Hemingway radioed in the bearing to the Navy, the bombers or patrol vessels would have a vector to the general location of the U-boat. The Navy and Air

---

* Roughly $417,500 in 2009 dollars; Hemingway was therefore undertaking substantial financial risk.

Corps planes were being equipped with radar, so when they got a general idea of a U-boat's location, they could zero in on it fairly quickly. During the early days of the anti-U-boat war the planes used rather primitive "meter wave" radar, which the Germans could detect with their onboard sensing equipment. When they noticed a signal, they would immediately dive. But soon the Allied planes were equipped with the newly developed microwave radar, and the German sensing devices were unable to detect the incoming radar waves. The planes could thus locate and attack before the U-boats could make an emergency dive. The element of surprise that microwave radar allowed was vital because U-boat commanders were deathly afraid of attacks from the air and submerged whenever they saw aircraft of any kind, at any distance—even private planes. But a fast attack plane carrying bombs and depth charges and vectored unerringly by undetectable radar could be on top of them before they could completely disappear below the surface—or even clear the bridge for an emergency dive. With any cloud cover at all to hide the airplane until the last possible moment, the U-boat would most likely be doomed.

Navy and Coast Guard vessels were equipped not only with radar but also with sonar, which could track a submerged U-boat. In several cases in the Gulf, U-boats were sunk as a result of a coordinated attack between aircraft that damaged the frantically diving U-boat and patrol craft that finished her off after locating her on sonar and then dropping a pattern of depth charges. (In June of 1942, after sinking an American tanker just five miles off Cuba's northern coast, *U157* suffered through two days of aerial tracking and attacks only to be finally destroyed by depth charges from the Coast Guard cutter *Thetis*.)

Navy and Coast Guard vessels and planes were constantly patrolling specific sectors and thus in many cases could quickly arrive at a contact. At the start of the war, few of these aircraft and few surface patrol craft were available—hence the need for the Hooligan Navy. But in time both air and sea patrols were beefed up and equipped with microwave radar, and by the end of 1943 the war against the U-boats in the western waters was essentially won. Airborne microwave radar was, in Admiral Dönitz's view, the single most important factor in the destruction of his U-boat fleet and therefore the loss of the war. But a long time passed between *Pilar*'s first fully equipped patrol in November of 1942 and the end of the U-boat battle—more than a year—and during that time many more ships would be sunk. Plenty of work remained. After the war Admiral Dönitz said that January through March of 1943 was the height of success for his U-boats: "The number of U-boats was constantly increasing and losses were slight."[16] In the autumn of 1942, Dönitz had shifted much of his attention from the Gulf to the Caribbean, but he fully intended to return to the Gulf. So Hemingway was beginning his fully equipped patrols at a time when the situation was still dangerous.

Pilar's military two-way radio was battery-operated, like the HFDF; she did not have a generator strong enough to run either one. The radio, too, was a bulky item in those days of vacuum tubes. Both the radio and the HFDF would have been clear evidence of *Pilar*'s clandestine business if a U-boat commander ever decided to send a boarding party in search of fresh food. Furthermore, the HFDF installation would have been too unwieldy to dismantle and throw over the side before a U-boat could discover them. The very presence of this equipment, therefore, was a risk. Since the Germans did not know about HFDF, they might not identify the unusual antenna, but they would certainly have realized that such a thing did not belong on a pleasure craft. That would have aroused their curiosity as much as the prospect of fresh fish. Once they came across and discovered the electronics, *Pilar* and, probably, her crew were as good as finished. The Germans didn't need justification to sink any kind of vessel. Indeed, they needed to find reasons not to. In this light Hemingway's plans to attack seem a little more understandable, albeit fatalistic.*

Perhaps to minimize the risks of being boarded, Hemingway decided to pose as a scientific vessel engaged in fishing research, and to this end he used a canvas sign on the flying bridge that identified *Pilar*'s mission for the American Museum of Natural History. That might defuse a U-boat's suspicions about the HFDF antenna when it was in place. After all, before the war he had hosted a quasi-scientific mission/fishing trip for some museum scientists, so he would have had a ready-made story to tell if questioned. Maybe the sign would reassure a wary captain, who might then allow *Pilar* to get within grenade range, and while that seems unlikely, displaying the sign was at least worth a try.

Pilar was also fitted with a blinkered searchlight for use in poking her nose in narrow channels between dark islands, although a searchlight makes an admirable target. More likely, it was designed for signaling to friendly aircraft and vessels—flashing a recognition signal to forestall friendly fire. *Pilar*'s recognition signal was the letter *V.* Dot dot dot dash. (The well-known first four notes of Beethoven's Fifth.) A list of the Morse-code alphabet is in the back of the log Hemingway kept for these patrols, which suggests that, aside from Saxon, no one aboard was all that conversant with blinker signaling, for a competent signalman needs no primer. This assigned recognition signal is further proof of the official sanction of Hemingway's patrols, for it would have been useless unless all

---

* Hemingway was not alone in considering extreme tactics. In May 1942 another Hooligan, the *Jay-Tee,* a thirty-eight-foot cabin cruiser out of Ft. Lauderdale, tried to attack *U333,* which it had spotted on the surface. *U333* submerged and the *Jay-Tee* followed and found itself being lifted out of the water when the U-boat resurfaced. The *Jay-Tee* was totally unarmed and carried a crew of two elderly fishermen. The *Jay-Tee* returned safely with some paint scrapings to prove her adventure. *U333* was never aware of the incident and merely submerged again when she felt some unusual bumps when she tried to surface.[17]

the aircraft and patrol craft in the district were notified that a flashing *V* indicated *Pilar*, a specific, friendly vessel. Hemingway was part of a large Gulf- and Caribbean-wide system, with an assigned role, no greater and no less potentially useful than any of the other thousands involved in fighting the U-boats. Hunting and killing U-boats was generally a cooperative effort requiring coordination of both visual and electronic surveillance as well as effective communication among a number of military assets, air and sea.

The Cuban coastline was divided between two overall commands. From the western tip eastward for about one-third of the island, on both northern and southern coasts, it was part of the Gulf Sea Frontier, based in Key West. This was a rather tenuous headquarters location because then as now Key West was connected to the other keys and the mainland by a single bridge—an easy target for a U-boat's 105 mm deck gun. Why it was never shelled is something of a mystery. In fact, U-boats never shelled any U.S. coastal city or installation. They could have easily enough. The lights of the cities would have made it a simple matter. And there would be no need to worry about picking a military target—a few shots fired into downtown Miami would have been a major propaganda coup, if nothing else. The 105 had a range of about eight miles, so a U-boat could have shelled a city with relative impunity, especially at night. The only explanation is a captain's reluctance to stay too long on the surface near the U.S. coastline, since it takes time to secure a gun and recover the gun crew before submerging, and the danger of aircraft, especially those equipped with radar, was ever present. Admiral Dönitz explained:

> A U-boat needs one minute for the crew to come in through the hatch before it can submerge at all. An airplane flies on the average 6,000 meters in one minute. The U-boat, therefore, in order to be able to submerge at all—and not to be bombed while it is still on the surface—must sight the aircraft from a

distance of at least 6,000 meters. But that also is not sufficient, for even if the U-boat has submerged it still has not reached a safe depth. The U-boat, therefore, must sight the airplane even earlier, namely, at the extreme boundary of the field of vision. Therefore, it is an absolute condition of success that the U-boat is in a state of constant alert, that above all it proceeds at maximum speed, because the greater the speed the faster the U-boat submerges; and, secondly, that as few men as possible are on the tower so that they can come into the U-boat as quickly as possible which means that there should be no men on the upper deck at all.[18]

A U-boat did fire on an oil refinery in Aruba, however, which indicates that shore bombardment was at least a consideration in Dönitz's overall tactical concept.

The Gulf Sea Frontier was responsible for anti-U-boat warfare from the coast of Florida throughout all of the Gulf of Mexico. The Caribbean Sea Frontier looked after the eastern two-thirds of Cuba's northern and southern coasts and most of the area south to the South American border.[*] Its headquarters were in San Juan, Puerto Rico, but the command was rather decentralized so that the operations in the eastern half of Cuba, both north and south coasts, were directed from Guantánamo Bay.

Hemingway's first patrols would, therefore, report to the Gulf Sea Frontier via Havana, whereas his last patrols, which were concentrated in the eastern half of the island, would be controlled from Guantánamo. Four naval air stations were in Cuba—two in each of the frontiers. An air station was in the Miami area also, so that the Straits of Florida as well as the Crooked Island Pas-

---

[*] Technically, the term *Caribbean* only applies to the waters south of Cuba and Puerto Rico, this despite the tendency of tourists and travel agents to call the whole region by that name, including the Gulf of Mexico. The Bahamas are actually part of the Atlantic.

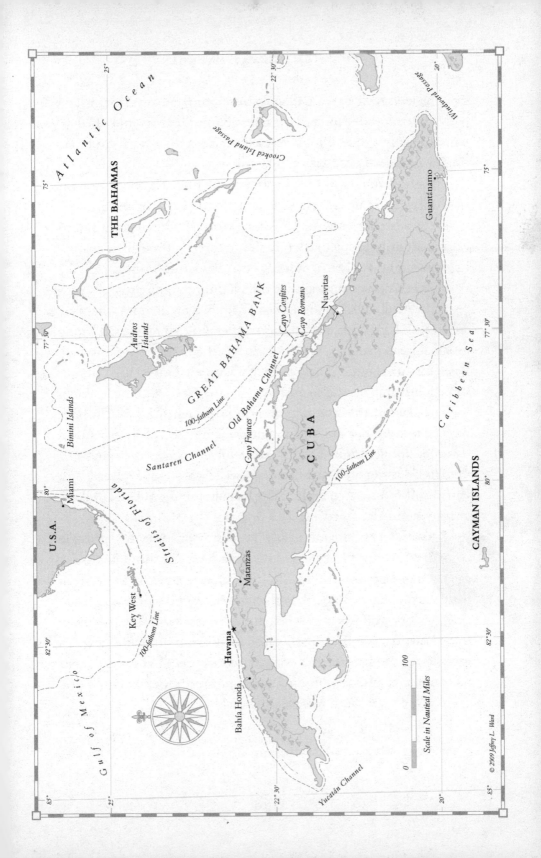

sage through the eastern Bahamas were ultimately under constant patrol by fixed-wing aircraft as well as blimps. Miami and Guantánamo were equipped with both kinds of aircraft, as was San Julián on the western tip of Cuba.

Panama was the third Sea Frontier. The U.S. Navy was responsible for protecting the Atlantic and Pacific ends of the Panama Canal, while the Army dealt ashore with a difficult local political and security problem. Before the outbreak of war the Panamanian president was Dr. Arnulfo Arias, a Francoist sympathizer; the Falange had offices throughout the country issuing pro-Axis propaganda. Also, Panama and fascist Spain had an obvious linguistic and cultural connection. A number of enemy agents were lurking in Panama; their target for sabotage was the absolutely vital canal. The entrances to the canal offered rich opportunities not only for torpedoing ships but also for laying mines—a common mission for U-boats off the Americas. Passing through the canal in both directions were not only merchant ships but also U.S. and Allied warships, for the United States was involved in a "two-ocean war."

Arias was deposed just before Pearl Harbor and replaced by a Panamanian more amenable to democracy, but the Falange and the enemy agents remained.

A glance at the map on page 69 will show that one possible course for a U-boat traveling to the canal area was through the Yucatán Channel by way of the Straits of Florida and Cuba's western tip. This is a longer route than through the Windward Passage, for example, but it allows the U-boat the greatest possible opportunity to find targets in the Gulf as well as the Caribbean. Hemingway's initially assigned patrol area was just northwest of Havana, where he could spot U-boats heading west and north for the Gulf ports or west and then south toward the canal.

* * *

> *Watch officers responsible for the maintenance of the log must appreciate the importance of their undertaking. They must ensure that all entries are complete, accurate, clear, concise and expressed in standard naval phraseology. Taken together, the entries should constitute a true and understandable historical and legal record of the ship.*
>
> Watch Officer's Guide

Apparently Hemingway never read the *Watch Officer's Guide,* for the log of *Pilar* is a mess. First of all, it was written in the 1941 Warner's Calendar of Medical History, even though it covers the patrols of *Pilar* in 1942. The dates and days of the entries do not therefore correspond to the printed dates on the calendar. Here and there Hemingway wrote down the actual date of an entry; other times he did not. Page after page deals with tallies from poker games—who owes how much to whom: "P owes E 2.00." Paxtchi owes Ernest? References appear to the war news from Guadalcanal, site of a bloody campaign fought in the Solomon Islands between August 1942 and February 1943. Then, strangely, there is the notation "Mr. Josie died today." Josie was Joe Russell, Hemingway's old fishing companion from Key West. More important, he was a drinking buddy and fast friend of the kind Hemingway admired most—a tough man who knew his business, a man with no pretenses or affectations, a man whose respect Hemingway valued. But Russell had died the year before—in June 1941. Perhaps the entry marks the anniversary of Russell's death, or perhaps it was a leftover notation. For those who knew about his fondness for Russell, Hemingway's terse notation does not mask his emotion. It is only the tip of the iceberg again.

Other notations are careful records of fuel use, wind and weather, engine performance, as well as fishing reports: "Caught

7 white marlin, 6 dolphin, 8 albacore in June." The number of fish caught does not seem excessive, not does it validate Martha's claim that the whole thing was a grand fishing trip at government expense. *Pilar* was posing as a fishing boat doing scientific research, and when she was on patrol, she would have her outriggers set and baited and would travel at trolling speed as part of the *ruse de guerre*. Besides, the fish were welcome additions to their diet. If the men enjoyed themselves catching them, well, so be it. Even in war sailors are lighthearted much of the time, as long as the weather is good and the food plentiful. And unlike in the regular Navy, Hemingway and his crew had plenty of alcohol on board.* Besides, *Pilar* was patrolling an assigned sector, which meant that Hemingway could not simply fish as he pleased, following the clues of the seabirds and flying fish. He had to stay on station.

Hemingway was also careful about expenses, noting in the log, "Win [Guest, presumably] brought 12 live chickens @ .75, 2 live turkeys @ 2.50, 1 pig @ 8.00, 400 eggs @ 3[cents]." Guest was the designated supply officer, it seems, assigned to running into town periodically to stock up. Gregorio was the cook, responsible for converting the livestock into table fare. While the list may suggest that *Pilar* was a floating barnyard, she was actually going in and out on relatively short trips, sometimes for only a day, so the livestock was probably slaughtered as needed onshore and packed in ice for cruises of more than a day or so. Although Hemingway did not keep a record of these short cruises, we can deduce their duration by remembering *Pilar*'s fuel capacity was three hundred gallons, and that she used three gallons an hour at trolling speed (five knots) and four gallons at cruising speed (eight knots, approximately). Since they were posing as fishermen, they would have

---

* U.S. Navy ships do not permit alcohol on board, unlike the ships of the Royal Navy. It was outlawed in 1913 by Secretary of the Navy Josephus Daniels, who suggested coffee as a better choice, hence the name *joe* for coffee ever since. Or so the story goes.

run most of the time at trolling speed once they reached their patrol sector, which means their absolute maximum range would be one hundred hours. But they would most likely have used cruising speed to get to their sector, so practically speaking, *Pilar* could stay out for something like three days before having to come in for fuel.*

Despite his care in noting gambling debts and fuel use and such matters, Hemingway's log would have got him thrown out of the regular Navy, for the dates are obscure, the position rarely noted, course and speed mentioned only rarely; in short, the log, which is supposed to be a legal record of all important information, is haphazard and eccentric. Some scholars have suggested that this was a clever ploy on Hemingway's part—a way of masking the true mission—in case he was boarded by enemies. But this seems unlikely, since the simplest thing in the world would have been to throw the log over the side in a weighted bag while the enemy was paddling over in their inflatable boat. More likely, the log was simply Hemingway's personal notebook and nothing more. But because of the log's gaps and omissions, there's no way to know exactly how many of these short patrols Hemingway and his crew undertook.

In the summer and early autumn of '42 Hemingway's patrols were more or less informal runs, like the one he made to investigate the suspicious cave in Matanzas in July, because he did not as yet have his electronics installed and would not until November. Nor did he seem to have any specific orders or assignments from the Navy. But here and there in his log some entries indicate he took seriously even these informal patrols: "Heavily loaded schoo-

---

* Hemingway could have carried extra drums of fuel, and did do so later in the war on his long patrols to the eastern end of Cuba. But it seems unlikely that he did so on these earlier, short patrols, since he was close enough to Havana to return easily enough; further, the extra drums of inflammable fuel would have made the cramped *Pilar* even more uncomfortable for the crew.

ner in lee of Alacranes with outboard dinghy. Checked all coves, creeks, passes, cays from past Punta Purgatoro [*sic*] to brulata end of Alacranes."

Finally in late November the gear and weapons were on board, and he was ready for his first official patrol. His assigned area was off Bahía Honda, which is forty-three miles west of Havana—a good vantage point to watch for U-boats traveling the Straits of Florida on their way either to or from the Panama Canal or the Gulf ports.

The December 9 log entry states, "Waited at Bahia Honda for ice. (Win spent 40.00, EH spent 10.00) Ran out 16 miles—prepard [*sic*]—cruised to [illegible] Medano—practiced—[illegible] [illegible] best yet. Cut box to pieces—P[illegible] good throws—Win 2 excellent—2 good—2 erratic—tried to throw too hard."

This was a small-arms training exercise. Someone was apparently firing the Thompson at a box thrown overboard as a target. "P[illegible]" was probably Paxtchi, who along with Winston Guest was practicing with grenades. Hemingway, with his typical need to coach others in anything related to weaponry, cannot resist logging a critique of his subordinates' techniques and performances.

On that same day, they spotted the passenger liner *Marqués de Comillas*. Her position was eighty-three degrees, twenty-five minutes west, and twenty-two degrees, fifty-six minutes north, which is just off the coast, west of Havana and north of Bahía Honda. She was presumably inbound to Havana, probably from Veracruz, and in a position with plenty of water beneath her keel despite being close to the coast.

The SS *Marqués de Comillas* was an oceangoing liner of the Spanish Compañía Transatlántica. Described in various accounts as "luxurious, but not ostentatious," she featured a single stack and some enclosed weather decks for more comfortable promenading; she cut a reasonably fine figure. Built in 1928, she was 9,922 tons, which is almost twice as big as the ill-fated *Robert E. Lee,* which

U166 had sent to the bottom. Her regular ports of call were Barcelona, Cádiz, New York, Havana, and Veracruz. Being a passenger liner, she naturally had numerous cabins in which shadowy characters en route to Cuba or Mexico by way of Spain could remain out of sight until they disembarked, either officially or unofficially. Being of Spanish registry, she seemed to travel these dangerous waters with impunity and was a vessel of interest to the counterintelligence authorities in Cuba.

The longest entry in Hemingway's log records the sighting of this ship. It runs for eleven pages, and his handwriting gets less and less legible as it goes along, suggesting either that Hemingway was getting tired as he re-created the events of the day or that cocktail hour had begun and proceeded at its usual efficient pace. (Ironically, the entry starts opposite a page listing liver diseases in the Warner's Calendar of Medical History that he was using for his log.) Here is the entry, complete with all his punctuation mistakes, odd spellings, and abbreviations:

1130 sighted ship proceeding E hull down in 15 min noticed she was proceeding very rapidly with much smoke.

12 She was approaching our position and behind Colorado reef abeam Cayo Medano de Corigua. At this time we could see her white super strut clearly—could see the four Sp flags painted on the star side of her hull. As she approached our posi which was clearly marked by the sandy shoreline of the cay—a prominent peak directly to the southward the ship was identified as the Marques de Comillas, slackened speed appreciably. It took her almost 15-20 minutes from time she was abeam until she regained her speed—15-20 minutes slow and *no* smoke.

While she was still proceeding slowly we sighted at sea NNW from our pos op Medano what appeared to be a gray painted vessel with a tow of some kind.

From the top of the flying bridge at a height of approx 15 ft above the water with 10 power glasses, the object looked like a large Coast Guard cutter towing an oil tanker—except there was no visible bridge on the supposed tow—nor was there any funnels visible on the presumed cutter (or corvette).

While we were examining this ship which appeared to be 6–8[*] miles away. The vessel which we had identified as the Marques de C continued to proceed slowly at the angle from which we were observing—

Studying the object through glasses I was convinced that it was a tow and we proceeded to sea at once at 1215 to investigate.

We proceeded toward the object on a NNW course at a fishing speed of 7 knots with the lines out to simulate fishing.

At the same time we served out sub-mach & frag.[†]

Outside the reef while still on a NNW course the vessel was proceeding directly toward us. We were rapidly shortening our distance from the vessel when she turned due W swinging broadside to us at 3 miles distance. When by the silhouette of her conning tower & her forward structure she appeared to be a large sub.

Her color as far as we could be sure of was gray & showed gray at all times. At this time her after structure did not show at all. At the moment that we were headed for her a large piena [barracuda] hit one of the outrigger baits and while the [anti-submarine] team was perfecting their installation on the lee

---

[*] Remembering the formula for distance to the horizon: fifteen feet for *Pilar*'s flying bridge plus another six feet for Hemingway standing and looking through the glasses equals twenty-one feet, the square root of which is roughly 4.6, times 1.3 equals roughly six miles. So Hemingway's guess on the range is a good one, since the object he saw would have shown itself somewhat above the horizon, albeit hull down.

[†] Submachine guns and grenades. *Pilar* was going to "general quarters," i.e., battle stations. No mention of a bazooka, though.

side—away from observation of the supposed sub we proceeded on a parrallel course to that of the "sub" attempting to close with her unostentatiously while we "fought" the piena very obviously from the flying bridge. We slacked off line to the fish & we ran fast and this showed to simulate a hard fight with the fish.

At the same time we attempted to close the distance bet us & the "sub" which was proceeding WNW direction.

At 125 the sub speeded up from the course she had held & on which we were converging & drew steadily away from us We attempted to follow her for a short distance but she was making too much speed for us to draw up with her at all.

Thinking then that the M de C might have dropped some object which the "sub" due to our presence, <u>if it were an enemy sub</u>, had been unable to recover we then covered the ground of the course of the M de C searching for any such object—we found nothing.

If this were a US sub the incident is of no significance.

If this were an Axis sub the following alternatives are presented;

1) Communication could have been delivered to the sub in case the 2 ships had a rendezvous off Medano de Casigua.

2) It would have been possible due to the ships encountering each other at the hour of the noon day meal, for Axis agents to have been put overboard during the time the passengers were in the dining saloon, without such operation being any more noticed than the picking up or dropping off of a pilot under the same circumstances if there were any rendezvous between 2 ships instead of this merely having been observation of two neutral ships by an Arm [American] patrol vessel. Point selected was ideal for such purpose as it is opposite a part of the Cuban coast where there is no possible observation of the coast from shore & and where there is a clearly defined mt

range & a sandy beached cay with coco-palms, which giving a bearing against the peak for as much as fifteen miles out to sea.

At 140 the "sub" (supposed) having disappeared over the horizon still continuing on her NNW course we proceeded to Habana at a distance of about 12 miles from the coast. in order to take advantage of the eastward set of the current & by widening the distance from the coast to take advantage of any opportunity for contact with subs. if such should be present.

Hemingway and his crew were reasonably sure that they had seen a U-boat. They could not be sure if the U-boat had transferred people to or from the *Marqués de Comillas,* but they were fairly certain that something of that nature had occurred because of the way the liner had slowed almost to a stop while the submarine was nearby. The range made it impossible to be certain it was a U-boat because a submarine lies low in the water—only the conning tower and the weather deck are completely above the surface, and at a range of six miles the curvature of the earth comes into play, further lowering the profile. Also, the gray color of the U-boat blends in with the sea and atmosphere (after all, that's why they're painted that color), so it was difficult for Hemingway and his men to be sure. But it was a legitimate possibility, and when they spotted this possible U-boat, they headed straight for her,[*] Hemingway at the helm, while the other men armed themselves (on the side not visible to the U-boat) with their grenades and machine guns. As far as they could tell, they were going into combat. It was not their fault that the U-boat turned away nor that the U-boat's speed was so much greater than *Pilar*'s and that she disappeared heading north-northwest, in the direction of the U.S. Gulf ports. Whether Hemingway and the others were disappointed is

---

[*] Lord Nelson would have approved: "No captain can do very wrong if he places his ship alongside that of the enemy."

another matter; but they had thought it was a U-boat and they had tried to put their planned tactics into operation.

They were sure enough about the contact to radio the embassy in Havana. The embassy in turn radioed the Key West headquarters of the Gulf Sea Frontier, which then contacted the Havana FBI and asked them to meet the *Marqués de Comillas* when she docked and to inspect the crew and passengers. Key West may also have vectored aircraft to the general location of the U-boat; if so, they found nothing. But that means little, for the U-boat would almost certainly have submerged after taking on the agents from the *Marqués de Comillas*.

The message from Key West came to Agent Leddy—the skeptical FBI man who still harbored some resentment about being called a Gestapo agent.[*]

A subsequent FBI memorandum reviews what happened:

Hemingway reported sighting a contact between a submarine and the Spanish steamer SS Marques de Comillas at high noon on December 9, 1942 off the Cuban coast. Hemingway was ostensibly fishing with Winston Guest and four Spaniards as crew members. [Next sentence censored] The report was referred to the Legal Attache. [Censored] The Legal Attache's [i.e., Agent Leddy] investigation consisted of interview[s], with Cuban police cooperation, of forty crew members and some fifty passengers of the vessel, most of the latter known anti-Fascists repatriated from Spain. None of the persons interviewed would admit sighting a submarine as Hemingway had from his 36 foot launch [*sic*]. The negative results of this

---

[*] This was a silly overreaction on Leddy's part, for *gestapo* was widely used to describe any authority—and used jokingly. In his memoir of service with a Highland regiment, George MacDonald Fraser humorously describes the British military police as "the gestapo." See *McAuslan in the Rough*. Further, the U.S. Navy's Bureau of Ships had a "Gestapo Board" (nicknamed, that is) to oversee civilian contractors.

inquiry were reported. Thereupon Hemingway submitted a memorandum stating that it would be a tragedy if the submarine were carrying saboteurs possibly let off the steamship at this point on a mission to the United States and that the Legal Attache discounted Hemingway's report because it had not come from an FBI agent, thereby permitting the saboteurs to land in the United States without advance notice.[19]

The next day Hemingway wrote a somewhat more coherent report of the contact, citing three possibilities:

1) Communication could have been delivered to the submarine, in case the two ships had a rendezvous off Medano de Casigua.
2) Any objects which were aboard the Marques de Comillas, which Axis agents wished to transship, could have been delivered to the submarine.
3) It would have been possible, due to the ships encountering each other at the hour of the noon day meal, for Axis agents to have been put overboard during that time that passengers were in the dining saloon, without such an operation being any more noticed, if the men were lowered from a hatch close to the waterline, than would be the picking up or dropping off of a pilot under the same circumstances. The time that the Marques de Comillas slowed down affords the possibility for the completion of such an operation.

Hemingway and his crew were thoroughly disgusted with the lack of results and felt the FBI had mishandled the operation and that Axis agents were even then on their way to U.S. shores. As Winston Guest wrote later:

We got our glasses out and you could see it was a submarine. I think a 740 class. But it speeded up and went directly on the course north-northwest. That was the submarine that ended up at New Orleans. I think they landed three men at the mouth of the Mississippi River. Ernest made a report back in Havana which they thought incredible. But two days later they called him and said he was completely right, and that several tankers had sighted it on the same course.[20]

This seems a little odd since the U-boat would probably have been submerged. But maybe the tankers spotted her just after she left the *Marqués* and just before she submerged. Or maybe they saw her periscope. We can be reasonably sure it was not a U.S. submarine since you would assume headquarters at Key West would have known about it. As for the confirmation of the sighting, Guest certainly did not get the information from the FBI, for they stuck to their version of events and used the incident to try to place a wedge between Hemingway and the ambassador: "Any information which you may have relating to the unreliability of Ernest Hemingway as an informant may be discreetly brought to the attention of the ambassador."[21] (Note that Hoover wrote this memo just a week after the reported U-boat sighting.)

Maybe Wolfie heard about the confirmation from Hemingway himself, perhaps over drinks at the Floridita. If so, remembering Hemingway's habit of occasionally economizing with the truth, it's fair to wonder, just what was it that "faded through the brightening air"?*

In *Islands in the Stream* the main characters discuss an incident

---

* Admiral Dönitz's tactics were generally to shift the focus of attack from one area to another, both to avoid losses and to keep the Allies off-balance. Accordingly, no U-boats were sent to the Gulf from early September 1942 until the start of the new year. But he also habitually left behind a lone wolf here and there, to take on targets of opportunity. That no ships were torpedoed in the Gulf during that time does not necessarily mean that Hemingway's sighting was a mirage—especially if, as Guest suggests, the U-boat's mission was to land saboteurs. However, if saboteurs were landed, they were not apprehended, nor did they seem to accomplish their mission, whatever it was. They could have been spies, though, sent to observe shipping.

that is obviously derived from the *Marqués de Camillas* sighting; it has the color of something drawn from reality, something that Hemingway remembered vividly. The incident serves no essential purpose in advancing the story. Instead, it seems like a scene Hemingway felt was too good to waste. Possibly, too, he wanted to give himself and his crew the credit in fiction that was denied them in reality.

"OK, Tom," George said. "If I see any really big submarines do you want me to tell you?"

"If you see one as big as you saw that one time keep it to yourself."

"I dream about her at nights," George said.

"Don't talk about her," Willie said. "I just ate breakfast."

"When we closed I could feel my *cojones* going up like an elevator," Ara said. "How did you really feel, Tom?"

"Scared."

"I saw her come up," Ara said. "And the next thing I heard Henry say, 'She's an aircraft carrier, Tom.'"

"That's what she looked like," Henry said. "I can't help it. I'd say the same thing again."

"She spoiled my life," Willie said. "I've never been the same since. For a nickel I'd have never gone to sea again."[22]

So did they really see a U-boat? In one sense it hardly matters, for the important point is they believed they did, and they acted accordingly. They went full speed ahead toward the target, got out their weapons, and prepared to put their plan of attack into action. The emotion they felt was real enough, and they mastered it well. Whether the U-boat was real is another question, but to borrow a line from Jake Barnes, "Isn't it pretty to think so?"

Chapter Nine

~~~

IN ANOTHER COUNTRY

I don't know what's happening. I sit here. Sit and sit and sit. It's enough to drive anyone crazy. It's like being in a beautiful jail.

   Liana[1]

They were aground in a patch of mud and sandy bottom that should have been marked with a stake, and the tide was still falling.

   Islands in the Stream[2]

ABOUT the time that Hemingway and his crew were chasing what they believed to be a U-boat, Martha, at home at the finca, began work on a novel that would eventually be called *Liana*. It is the story of a beautiful mulatto woman who marries a wealthy, older man on the French Caribbean island called St. Boniface (modeled most likely on St. Barts or St. Martin in the days before they became fashionable). The marriage is not happy, and Liana falls in love with her French tutor. Their affair ends badly when the tutor returns to France to rejoin the war, and her husband, who has learned of the affair, starts to build Liana a separate house where she can live out what looks to be a lonely life. She decides to commit suicide, cuts her wrists, changes her mind, but too late. The story is reminiscent of *Madame Bovary*, although

Martha treats her female main character with a little less ironic detachment than Flaubert had for the romantically besotted Emma Bovary.

The three main characters reflect to some degree Martha's conflicting attitudes about life and work at the Finca Vigia. Liana's emotional isolation, her husband's insularity and contentment with island life, and her lover's impatience with the slow pace and his growing desire to get back into the war—all seem to be facets of Martha's always complex and often shifting perspective.

Liana is a good novel and owes few if any stylistic debts to Hemingway, though for the next six months he read the developing book and offered advice. While Martha's mood alternated between creative satisfaction and dark doubts about the quality of the book, the writing of it gave her an outlet for her energies and also allowed her to use some of the background material—Hemingway's well-known "how the weather was"*—that she had absorbed on her Caribbean adventure a few months before.

While she apparently learned enough about island life to create a credible novel, her ostensible reason for going was to write an article for *Collier's* on the war in the Caribbean. She flew from Cuba to San Juan and from there went by motorboat to Tortola, where she hired the potato boat and the five (not three) locals who took her to Anguilla, St. Martin's, St. Barts, and Saba, where her not-so-faithful retainers abandoned her, whereupon she hired another boat and went to Antigua. From there she flew via Pan Am clipper to Suriname, where she investigated the bauxite mines and explored a jungle river. Suriname seemed to be a backwater where a handful of American soldiers suffered the miserable weather and

---

* "All good books are alike in that they are truer than if they had really happened and after you are finished reading one you will feel that all that happened to you and afterwards it all belongs to you; the good and the bad, the ecstasy, the remorse and sorrow, the people and the places and how the weather was."[3]

kept an eye on the bauxite mines. Shallow-draft ships that could clear the bar at Paramaribo took the bauxite to Trinidad for re-loading on larger ships to be convoyed north. Trinidad at the time became one of the busiest ports in the world—a starting point for a regular Trinidad–Aruba–Key West convoy. With such tempting targets, U-boats were never far away, although the increasing effi-ciency of convoys with their screens of warships and aircraft made attacking them more and more dangerous.

While Martha hoped to see a U-boat and thereby trump her husband, the only experience of war she got from her trip was secondhand—from talking to the wretched survivors of a U-boat attack or to military men scattered throughout these island out-posts of empire—U.S., British, Dutch, and French. Always in-trepid, she had traveled miles and miles at sea in a small boat and had seen nothing—even crossing the Anegada Passage, which was a prime route for U-boats coming from France and heading for the oil refineries of Venezuela, Aruba, and Curaçao. When she re-turned to Cuba and began her novel she had only a limited and vicarious understanding of how bad things were. The novel would have almost nothing to do with the war and would instead focus on the internal lives of the three characters: "I am entranced by the furious miseries people make for themselves in their own heads."[4]

Her experiences during those few months may have contrib-uted to her impatient dismissal of Hemingway's patrols. After all, she had been out there, too. Also, the role of the Hooligan Navy in general—all up and down the Atlantic coast and in the Gulf—was not widely publicized by the War Department for fear of alerting the Germans and thereby putting the volunteers at greater risk. So it's not difficult to understand Martha's point of view, that the real war was in Europe and the Caribbean and Gulf were mere sideshows, for she had no evidence or information that would lead her to any other conclusion. Press censorship contributed to her assessment, since the extent of the horrific toll on shipping was not reported.* If her relationship with Hemingway had been less difficult, she might have been more supportive. But here, as in the past, the only thing that seemed to strengthen her feelings *for* him was absence *from* him. Her attitude about the patrols, which he quite understandably considered useful, further strained their marriage, because when he returned, he naturally wanted some significant time in bed with her, followed by time spent relaxing in a congenial setting, such as the Floridita Bar. A wife might put up with a little of this, but a wife who does not think the patrols were either useful or arduous, much less dangerous, is not likely to have much patience for a sailor's traditional notion of shore leave. Martha thought the patrols were just one more excuse to go drinking, although she should have understood by this time that Hemingway needed no such excuses and would please himself on that score. But husbands who go out drinking enjoy it less when they know they'll return to looks of disapproval or temperance lectures. Each succeeding daiquiri fuels growing resentment over the anticipated confrontation. Hemingway's drinking was the cause of more than a few arguments:

> Dorothy: And I'm glad it's daylight. Now get out of here. You conceited, conceited drunkard. You ridiculous, puffed-up, posing braggart. You commodity, you. Did it ever occur to you that you're a commodity, too? A commodity one shouldn't pay too high a price for?

---

* If Martha was ignorant of the extent of the U-boat threat, it's fair to wonder how much Hemingway really knew. The simplest explanation is that his contacts with the embassy and the military attachés there, as well as their receptivity to his patrol proposals and subsequent assignment of patrol areas, gave him a greater understanding of the seriousness of the threat. Why he did not or could not communicate that to Martha is another question. Either he did not try hard or she dismissed his assessment as typical Hemingway exaggeration. Or perhaps the information he was given was classified.

Philip (Laughing): No. But I see it the way you put it.

Dorothy: Well, you are. You're a perfectly vicious commodity. Never home. Out all night. Dirty, muddy, disorderly.[5]

Hemingway wrote this scene for *The Fifth Column* in Madrid during the civil war. But apparently he had the ability to see into the future. Most likely, the scene had been played a few times in Madrid, too.

It's easy to think that Hemingway and Martha were both self-absorbed artists who looked at life very differently. She traveled the world at war with apparent immunity from anything other than discomfort; he had been blown up and wounded while still a boy and viewed the indifferent and unpredictable universe with doubt and suspicion, if not fear; she carried with her the confidence of the intrepid and unimaginative[*]; he carried with him the nightmares of the front lines and his sleep-destroying brush with death. He was essentially a romantic; she was not; he was consistent in his priorities and disciplined and focused at his work; she was uncertain and vacillated between creative joy and grave doubts, which caused periods of inactivity that he found inexcusable; he was lonely without her, or someone; she needed time to be alone. She was the most independent and yet the neediest of his four wives—depending on her feelings of the moment; and of all her many lovers, both before and after Hemingway, much the same could be said of him. They may have loved each other, and at times they sincerely did, but they also looked at each other across a gulf of "furious miseries." They did experience periods of genuine affection and domestic peace, and of some creative cooperation, so the easy interpretation of their relationship, as with any relationship, may not do either of them full justice.

---

[*]While it may seem strange to call a novelist "unimaginative," we should remember that she herself said she had to see before she could imagine.

When Hemingway returned from the *Marqués de Comillas* patrol, he dismissed his crew for the Christmas holidays and looked forward to having his sons join him again and to a few weeks of pigeon shooting, jai alai, and cockfighting, followed by late-night camaraderie and laughs with the crew and assorted cronies at the Floridita. There, his special daiquiris, the Papa Doble, were made of two and a half ounces of rum mixed with lime and grapefruit juices and a few drops of maraschino and blended with shaved ice. These would come in Falstaffian numbers, as new records were set and then surpassed.

Soon after Hemingway returned and the boys arrived, Martha packed up the first few chapters of her new novel and headed for the States to visit her mother in St. Louis, either escaping or merely fulfilling a daughter's responsibility. But as Hemingway said about her later, she did "exactly what she wants to do willfully as any spoiled child. And always for the noblest motives."[6]

* * *

Those damn .357's are hard to get now because the draft-dodging FBI's have to use them to hunt down draftdodgers.

Islands in the Stream[7]

The new year brought a new brush with the FBI. Although Hemingway had stepped back from the Crook Factory to concentrate on his patrols, he somehow got involved with a mysterious box that one of his shadowy friends had discovered at a local bar. It's easy to imagine this character arriving at the finca in the dead of night with stage whispers of "Ernesto! Here is something you must see!" This kind of thing infuriated the light-sleeping Martha, when she was there, even as it aroused Hemingway's imagination and played upon his fascination with the underworld of spies and fifth columnists.

The box was carefully and securely wrapped and, according to FBI documents, was "left by a suspect at the Bar Basque under conditions suggesting that the box contained espionage information."[8] No doubt feeling pleased that this kind of discovery would help to justify his counterintelligence operation, Hemingway turned the unopened package over to the embassy, which gave it to the legal attaché, that is, the FBI agent, who "made private arrangements for opening the box."[9]

Afterward the FBI man, perhaps suppressing a smirk, returned the contents to Hemingway: an inexpensive edition of *The Life of Saint Teresa*.

Saint Teresa is, among other things, the patron of headache sufferers. It's doubtful that the FBI or Hemingway recognized that irony, and it stretches credulity to think that the FBI removed useful intelligence information from the box and substituted Saint Teresa's biography as a humorous gibe at Hemingway's well-known drinking prowess and subsequent hangovers. The joke is far too subtle. But Hemingway did accuse the FBI of removing valuable information and substituting "something worthless." The prickly FBI man resented the accusation, and Hemingway backed off: "When this statement was challenged by the Assistant Legal Attaché, Hemingway said he was only joking but that he thought something was funny about the whole business of the box."[10] Hemingway was right about that, though not in the sense he meant it. This incident merely bolstered the FBI's claim that "something worthless" was actually a good description of Hemingway's Crook Factory.

A few weeks later Hemingway was again embroiled with the FBI, which had sent a new agent to Cuba, Ed Knoblaugh, a former journalist whom Hemingway had met in Spain during the civil war. Hemingway immediately objected to Knoblaugh's assignment because in Hemingway's view Knoblaugh had pro-fascist sentiments that were revealed in his book about the Spanish war, called *Correspondent in Spain*. To Hemingway, putting this man in charge of investigating Cuban Falangists and local Spanish fascists would almost certainly result in a less than serious effort to root out the enemy. Hemingway's memo to the ambassador detailed the charges, but the FBI defended their man, and Ambassador Braden dismissed the problem as nothing to worry about. But the incident was noticed and reported in the FBI file on Hemingway as further proof of his enmity toward the Bureau.

During these first few weeks of the new year *Pilar* was being refitted for more patrol duty. Boats, especially wooden boats, are always in need of some maintenance, and most maintenance is expensive, whether in parts or labor or both. Aside from Marine sergeant Saxon, most of Hemingway's crew were volunteers, but his first mate, Gregorio Fuentes, was an employee of long standing and needed to be paid. All of this maintenance money was coming out of Hemingway's pocket.* True, he did receive a government HFDF and radio, but the operating expenses, aside from fuel, were his to bear, and his crew needed to be fed and supplied. Moreover, despite the success of *For Whom the Bell Tolls,* Hemingway was not a wealthy man. As he wrote in his nostalgic letter to Hadley the previous summer, "Had to borrow 12,000 bucks to pay my 103,000 income tax last year.† I have to pay that back and get enough ahead so I will not be wiped out and broke when come back [*sic*] from war."[11]

He also bitterly resented paying alimony to Pauline: "Pauline's

---

* It's possible some money was available from the embassy. The Octocer 8, 1942, FBI document that discusses the allotment of fuel has a phrase censored that may relate to additional payments. Even so, a few hundred dollars at best would not go far in maintaining a boat like *Pilar*. This operation was separate from the Crook Factory subsidies. Winston Guest no doubt contributed something, too.

† Approximately $1,344,000 in 2009 dollars—a staggering sum that reflects his success as well as the high income tax rates of the time and explains his remark that if someone asked him what he did during the war, he would answer, "I paid for it."

blood money keeps me broke between books. But that was what she really wanted it for so that it would be impossible for me to write. Once she had me ruined she could simply ask her family for any amount of money or income she needed. She is now behaveing [*sic*] abominably about the children; really wickedly. I think perhaps she is off her rocker as women often are at such times. But women who are that way continue to do their damage for years."[12] Hemingway, in that letter to Max Perkins in May 1943, asked him to deposit $2,000 as a loan against future royalties. Hemingway was not the first man to resent alimony payments, but his resentment was intensified because Pauline's family was wealthy. Interestingly, Hemingway's description of Pauline mirrors his unchanging opinion of Zelda Fitzgerald, who, in Hemingway's view, constantly tried to ruin her husband to keep him from writing. This idea of women ruining men—whether from spite or jealousy or bitchiness or insanity or some combination of all—appears quite often in his work, most notably and dramatically in "The Short Happy Life of Francis Macomber." His observations and, later, his unhappy experiences may well be the source of his lifelong affection and nostalgia for his first wife, Hadley, a "healthy" woman who had offered only support and understanding during the early years of struggle, years that were happy in spite of the difficulties of getting started artistically. Hemingway must have spent more than a few nights on patrol on the flying bridge of *Pilar* wondering what life might have been like if he had stayed with Hadley and simply had affairs with the other women who caught his eye. Of course, staying married and having affairs is easier to contemplate than to carry off, as he learned. One also feels that, despite his European experience, he still carried with him some vestige of his mother's conventional morality that required physical passion to be sanctified by marriage. Martha Gellhorn would have been quite content to keep their relationship as it had been from the start. She had few qualms about living with him when he was married and would have had even fewer about living with him after he was divorced from Pauline. As she wrote much later, she thought "marriage the original anti-aphrodisiac."[13] But he insisted on legalizing the relationship. Aside from feeling the tug of a vestigial Middle American morality, perhaps he also felt he could control her more effectively that way. He should have known better by then.

Speaking of money and Martha: "Marty knows nothing about money, she saves terrifically on pennies and lets large sums go without a thought. She has a brave child's attitude toward it but she doesn't know that when you get older you have to have a steady something to live on between books—books get further apart as you get older if you write only good books."[14]

During this period of the war, Hemingway was worried about money. Even so, he did no writing, though the opportunity was there, and even though, as mentioned before, he was acutely aware that "the time to work is shorter all the time and if you waste it you feel you have committed a sin for which there is no forgiveness."[15] Time and money—two things he always felt he was short of. Yet he volunteered for the both thankless and potentially dangerous task of searching for U-boats.

* * *

On February 8, 1943, *U155,* a Type IX boat, left Lorient heading for the Gulf of Mexico. The boat was commanded by Adolf Piening, one of the aces of the German navy. The preceding November he had attacked an Atlantic convoy and sunk HMS *Avenger,* a British escort carrier. One torpedo hit amidships, setting off explosions in the carrier's bomb-storage compartments, and the ship sank in two minutes. There were 12 survivors out of a crew of 550. In that same attack Piening sank another British warship and damaged an American cargo ship. Piening was also famous for developing the

Piening Route, which hugged the French and then Spanish coast before setting off across the Atlantic. The course was designed to avoid the most dangerous part of the passage to the Americas—the trip across the Bay of Biscay. Allied aircraft scored many kills against U-boats that tried to run straight across the bay. Piening's route was longer but safer because it took his boat out of the range of Allied aircraft sooner. A dangerous and clever man was on his way to the Gulf.

The week before Piening got under way, another U-boat, *U183*, left Lorient also bound for the Gulf. *U183* was commanded by Henrich Shafer. He had not been as successful as Piening, but he had at least one Allied merchantman on his score sheet. Unlike Piening, who would enter the Caribbean via the Windward Passage, Shafer most likely used the Anegada Passage—the same waters that Martha had navigated in her hired potato boat. Both U-boats would then travel along the southern coast of Cuba, then turn north through the Yucatán Channel to enter the Gulf.

About this time Hemingway returned to his patrols. His assigned area was the same as before—off Bahía Honda. He was ordered to pay particular attention to the movements of the *Marqués de Comillas*, which indicates that not everyone shared the FBI's skepticism about Hemingway's earlier report. These relatively short patrols allowed him to return to his home port at Cojimar after a few days at sea. Even short patrols were fatiguing, though, because of the constant need to keep watch over an apparently empty sea. Boredom and daydreams are a lookout's greatest enemies. No action had taken place in the Gulf for months now because Dönitz had shifted his attention to the Caribbean. But things changed on March 11 when *U183*, newly arrived from the Caribbean, torpedoed and sank the *Olantha,* a Honduran merchantman steaming alone. The attack occurred just off the western tip of Cuba, off Cape San Antonio, a little over one hundred miles from Hemingway's patrol area. Apparently content with this victory, Shafer turned around and headed back along the southern coast of Cuba, passed through the Windward Passage, and returned safely to Lorient. The boat's patrol lasted 104 days, and she was no doubt in need of repairs and resupply.

But Piening in *U155* was still in the area. On April 2 Piening sighted the Norwegian steamer *Lysefjord* traveling alone. The position was almost precisely in the center of Hemingway's patrol area—just north of Bahía Honda. Piening torpedoed the Norwegian and sent her to the bottom, killing four of the crew. Eleven of the survivors managed to lower a lifeboat, and after rowing fourteen hours, they landed at the Gobernadora Lighthouse on the Colorados, the barrier reef just outside Bahía Honda.

The next day Piening sank the *Gulfstate,* a tanker steaming alone off the Florida Keys. That set off a furious attempt by the Gulf Sea Frontier headquarters to find the U-boat. Air and sea patrols were launched, but Piening eluded everyone and headed home by way of the Florida Straits. From start to finish his patrol lasted eighty-two days; Piening had sailed around Cuba and returned via the Gulf Stream—unlike Hemingway's marlin, swimming with the current.

Both U-boats had been at sea for significant periods, yet between them they accounted for only three ships. This may have been bad luck. But their lack of significant success also indicates that the system of grouping merchant ships into convoys and protecting them with screens of warships and aircraft was beginning to be effective. The three ships the U-boats sank were traveling alone. Piening had shown that he was not shy about attacking warships. The Royal Navy escort carrier he'd sunk the previous November had specifically been designed to travel with convoys to provide air cover for the entire length of the transit, thereby solving earlier problems when convoys sailed beyond the range of land-based aircraft. But Piening also survived the war, something 75 percent of his comrades, including Henrich Shafer, did not do.

So he was probably a prudent as well as a skillful commander, and if he sighted any armed convoys on his way into the Gulf, he may have decided to pass them by and hope to come across unescorted merchantmen, as he did.

Both boats went home with unfired torpedoes. The "Happy Time" for the U-boats was over.

But what of Hemingway during this period? The *Lysefjord* had gone down virtually in the center of Hemingway's assigned patrol area. Had *Pilar* been on station, the survivors might at least have been saved from having to row for fourteen hours to reach Bahía Honda; *Pilar* could have towed their lifeboat without difficulty. There might even have been the opportunity to attack the U-boat, if the Germans used their preferred method of attack and surfaced to fire their torpedoes. But it was not to be. Hemingway had returned to port for resupply the day before the attack on the *Lysefjord*. He undoubtedly heard reports of this attack, though, through his contacts at the embassy, so his disappointment would have been intensified. His luck as a hunter was worse even than Piening's or Shafer's.

*   *   *

> *You and I weren't born to die very easy (knock on wood). . . .*
> *I have decided (again knocking on wood) now to live a long*
> *time and have plenty of fun and I hope that some of it will be*
> *with us together. It is the best fun I have.*
>
> Hemingway, letter to Philip Percival, May 25, 1956

When Robert Jordan first meets Pilar, she asks to see his hand, as though to decipher the future and especially the outcome of their plan to blow up the bridge. She peers at it a moment, then drops it, saying nothing. Jordan asks her what she saw:

"Nothing," she told him. "I saw nothing in it."

"Yes, you did. I am only curious. I do not believe in such things."

But he did. Or at least Hemingway did, a little. Certainly he believed in luck and in its evil twin, which was a lurking menace always to be deflected or propitiated with a touch on wood, just to be on the safe side—menace in the form of the amorphous "they," as in "They killed you in the end. You could count on that. Stay around and they would kill you."[16] It is probably significant that Hemingway's spiritual homelands, the places he was drawn to most—Spain, Italy, France, and of course Cuba—were all Catholic countries, places where a sense of mysticism seemed intertwined with everyday life in a way that he had never experienced at home as a boy in the Middle American Congregationalism of his parents, and especially of his mother. Bourgeois morality, the YMCA, the confident assurance of salvation through good work and character—all these were missing in the more ancient rituals and images of the Catholic Church. The clean, well-painted Protestant churches of the Midwest were worlds and ages away from the dark, incense-scented European cathedrals with their images of saints and martyrs casting pity and terror into the hearts of the congregation. Even the worshippers reinforced a sense of mystery and dread, for unlike the well-dressed Norman Rockwell congregations back home, these were mostly old women whose heads were covered in dark scarves, kneeling stiffly and summoning the saints to intercede for them and protect them from the always present evil. They prayed and made the sign of the cross to keep this evil away—old women in black who reminded everyone else of the tragedy of life and the fact that heaven was not guaranteed. None of this made sense to the heirs of the Puritans, whose relationship with God needed no intercession, no grotesque imagery, no Gothic architecture, no absolution requested of some strangely celibate and unnatural priest, no church hierarchy whose dictates must be followed no matter how strange or irrational. But it seemed to make sense to Hemingway, perhaps because it was so different from what he had known as a boy, and certainly because he loved the people and the countries in which this older, more mystical form of belief combined with a structured ritual that appealed to his emotions and to his aesthetic sense.

This same sort of feeling attracted him to bullfighting, with its elaborate ritual, its ornate imagery, its roots in ancient pagan rites, and its inevitable tragedy that is structured as carefully as a drama, but involves actual death. The feelings that the bullfight aroused, when it was a good fight, were similar to the feelings that the deeper mysteries of the Catholic Church created for him— appreciation of carefully constructed and well-orchestrated emotion. He was trying to create this kind of emotion in his writing: "After a book I am emotionally exhausted. If you are not you have not transferred the emotion completely to the reader."[17]

People who have seen bullfights understand that most fights do not approach these levels of emotive perfection; most turn out to be rather straightforward scenes of bloody cruelty. But when it does happen, then "something rare" is created, something transcendent that has to be seen to be appreciated. Similarly, prayer is often nothing more than going through the motions. But now and then, under the inspiration of ritual and imagery, music and liturgy, it can be something rare, too. Hemingway was looking for these moments, and Catholicism appealed to him because of them. As an artist, he appreciated artistry. As a romantic, he appreciated a moment in which everything comes together perfectly, before inevitably flying apart—in bullfighting, the celebrated "moment of truth" when matador and bull are merged; in love, the moment of "La Gloria"; in prayer, the moment when it seems possible there is a God listening.

Hemingway converted to Catholicism in the late twenties, and he and Pauline were married in a Catholic as well as a civil ceremony in Paris in 1927. Since he was a divorced man, this required a few canonical contortions, but nothing too out of the ordinary. Unlike most converts, though, he was not an enthusiast. His allegiance to the Church as an institution was tenuous at best and suffered considerably during the Spanish Civil War, when the Catholic Church officially supported the fascist rebellion and subsequent Francoist government. Just as he was not and could not be a Communist because he "hated tyranny" and was an irreducible, unreconstructible individualist who was immune to any dogma, so he could not give himself over to an institution that was siding against the peasants and Republicans in Spain. His religion, such as it was, was more a collection of emotional and aesthetic instincts than a conventional faith. He would have understood John Henry Newman, another famous convert, who said, "From shadows and symbols into the truth."

In spite of, or perhaps because of, his unorthodox faith, Hemingway also generally carried some kind of good-luck charm in his pocket. "For luck you carried a horse chestnut and a rabbit's foot in your right pocket. The fur had been worn off the rabbit's foot long ago and the bones and the sinews were polished by wear. The claws scratched in the lining of your pocket and you knew your luck was still there."[18] Some might call it being superstitious; others would call it hedging your bets, which is, after all, eminently practical—a version of Pascal's Wager.* Lucky pieces and his own unique brand of faith were two aspects of Hemingway's multifaceted response to the unpredictable universe. In *A Farewell to Arms* when Frederic Henry is about to return to the front, Catherine Barkley gives him a St. Anthony's medal. Surprised, he asks her:

---

* On belief in the existence of God, Pascal said the decision was essentially a wager in which if you believe and "you win, you gain all; if you lose, you lose nothing." Similarly, if you believe a lucky piece works and you're right, you gain; but if you're wrong, you're no worse off.

"You're not a Catholic, are you?"

"No. But they say a St. Anthony's very useful."[19]

Chestnuts and St. Anthony's medals—talismans designed to summon good fortune and, more important, to keep bad luck at bay while shoring up a sometimes shaky sense of well-being. While it's true the St. Anthony's medal disappeared when Henry was wounded, Henry did survive. (There is a mild irony here since St. Anthony is the patron of lost things.) Stuffy old Ralph Waldo Emerson, noted Unitarian, said, "Shallow men believe in luck." Maybe so. But Emerson had never been blown up by a trench mortar—and lived to tell about it or, worse, lived to remember it in the middle of the night.

* * *

Perhaps a change of scene would bring *Pilar* a change of fortune. In May 1943 she was assigned to a new area off Cuba's central north coast. Her base would be a small island called Confites, roughly three hundred miles east of her former patrol. This meant Hemingway would be shifting to the Caribbean Sea Frontier and would report to the U.S. base at Guantánamo.

It would appear that *Pilar* was going to a dangerous place. On May 13, *U176* arrived through the Crooked Island Passage and sank two freighters—the *Mambi,* a Cuban vessel, and the *Nickeliner,* a U.S. cargo carrier. The action happened in the Old Bahama Channel just off Nuevitas, in the middle of what would be Hemingway's assigned area. After sinking her two targets *U176* continued west along the channel, and on May 15 she was spotted by a U.S. aircraft, which contacted Cuban-navy patrol boat *CS13,* commanded by Captain Rameriz Delgado. The Cubans attacked with depth charges, setting off four explosions in the U-boat that sent her to the bottom with all hands.

But once again *Pilar* missed out on the action, for she did not leave Havana until May 20, 1943, for her weeklong voyage to her new patrol grounds.

A little more than a third of Cuba's northern coast is sheltered by a line of barrier islands, some large and reasonably habitable, others little more than mangrove islands fit for nothing but wading birds and mosquitoes. Collectively these barrier islands are called *cayos,* the Spanish origin of our word *keys,* and like the Florida Keys these islands tend to be flat and somewhat featureless (although the larger *cayos* have greater variety). Altogether they are a maze of structures surrounded by flats and shoals, and while it is not difficult to navigate the main channels that run between the Cuban north shore and the line of *cayos,* it is something else to try to poke into and around these islands and to navigate through the narrow channels between them, channels that are sometimes marked by local fishermen with stakes and sometimes left unmarked. Periodically, existing channels are swept away by hurricanes and new channels are carved. The bottoms here are sand and mud and marl—a limestone composite—and thick grass that looks like gorse.

This was no country for a U-boat, but it was excellent country for clandestine radios, whose operators could watch from the north ends of their little *cayos* to plot the shipping in the Great Bahama Channel and send messages to waiting U-boats. It was also good country for supply bases, for most of the *cayos* were deserted and close to the hundred-fathom line, where the shallow water drops off into a deep channel. A small supply boat, hidden during the day, could easily run out to a rendezvous with a U-boat after the light had faded.

Cayo Confites was on the eastern edge of the *cayos* and on the very edge of the hundred-fathom line of the Great Bahama Channel, the only water deep enough for a U-boat to operate safely. So Confites made an excellent base for Hemingway's patrols in the channel and also a good starting place for checking out the myriad small keys to the west and south of his base.

It took Hemingway and his crew nine days or so to make the trip from Havana. He carried extra drums of fuel and water, for it would be some time before he could tap his new supply base at Nuevitas. At first he traveled in the deep water of the channel, but when he reached Cayo Frances, he turned into the Bahía Buena Vista, a navigable stretch of water between the *cayos* and the mainland. He motored along slowly for two days, scouting the *cayos* for any unusual activity, then turned north again and passed through the difficult stretch between Cayo Coco and Cayo Romano, running aground a number of times, backing off the soft bottom or in some cases waiting for the tide to come and lift him off. Back into open water, he made the last day's run to Confites, where he met a bored Cuban officer and his two enlisted radiomen. This would be home for the next six weeks.[20]

Hemingway describes his arrival at Confites in *Islands in the Stream*:

> The sun was behind him and it was easy to find the first big pass through the reef and then, skirting the shoals and the big coral heads, to come up on the leeward shelter. There was a sandy half moon of beach and the island was covered with dry grass on this side and was rocky and flat on its windward end. The water was clear and green over the sand and Thomas Hudson came in close to the center of the beach and anchored with his bow almost against the shore.[21]

The daily patrols out of Confites started early and ended late, with Hemingway typically standing bridge watch the entire time, steering *Pilar* while his crew divided the compass into sections and spent the hours squinting through binoculars, looking for periscopes. Saxon no doubt tried listening for signals on the HFDF, but it does not appear that this equipment worked consistently or well. They never did pick up a useful signal from the HFDF, although their radio was occasionally able to intercept German transmissions that they believed came from "way up with the wolf packs."[22] Since U-boats operated individually in the Gulf, not in wolf packs, these intercepted transmissions apparently came from the Atlantic during times when the atmospheric conditions were favorable, and the various U-boats in the wolf pack were chattering back and forth as they gathered for an attack. It's also possible, though, that these transmissions were from lone wolves in the Gulf making their periodic reports back to U-boat headquarters.

When *Pilar* came in at night, the tired crew would wash down the boat, polish the brightwork to keep corrosion at bay, and get her ready for the next day's patrol, while Don Saxon radioed coded reports of the day's activities and received instructions for the next day and Gregorio prepared dinner, usually fresh fish seasoned with lime juice. After dinner there'd be a poker game. Once a week a supply boat from Nuevitas would arrive, bringing ice and food and a few bottles of whiskey and gin and the mail, including the latest pages of *Liana* that Martha had sent for Hemingway's comment. Now and then Winston Guest would run over to Nuevitas to augment their supplies.

On June 8, U.S. aircraft based on Cayo Frances dropped bombs and depth charges on a suspected U-boat in deep water just off Cayo Fragoso, which was close to Confites. The attack resulted in an oil slick and some debris on the surface of the water and so was reported as a probable kill. It wasn't, though. On that same day Hemingway and his crew went ashore on two small *cayos*—Cayo Chico and Cayo Megano Grande.[23] Their assignment was to check for clandestine radios or supply dumps. Hemingway would have approached these islands warily, scanning with his binoculars before getting too close. Probably the outer edges of the islands were covered with mangroves, a salt-water-loving plant that grows in a tangle of exposed roots and thick green foliage, making it impossible to see through it into the interiors of the islands. To check an island thoroughly the men would have to go ashore in their dinghy, for the water close to the islands would be too shallow for *Pilar*'s roughly four-foot draft. The men would be alert to the birds as they approached the mangroves, for if the birds acted strangely, or if there were no birds at all, that might signal something unusual on the *cayo*. They would have taken the "ninos" and some "frags." The ninos were the Thompson submachine guns, so called by the Basques in the crew because they rested in sheepskin cases that hung like cradles on the flying bridge. The frags were grenades. The men would have struggled to push through the mangroves to get to the interior, and if the wind was stiff, mosquitoes would not have been a problem, but if there was no wind, the mosquitoes would have descended on the men in swarms: "To say they came in clouds, he thought, was not a metaphor. They truly came in clouds and they could bleed a man to death."[24] Thrashing through this thick tangle, sweating and swatting insects, stumbling over mangrove roots, Hemingway may well have smiled grimly at the memory of Martha and her easy dismissal of this whole business as an excuse to go fishing. Or he might not have had time for that sort of thinking, for there was no telling what lay beyond the mangroves, and each man could well be excused for wondering if, just a few yards away, there were people waiting with their own ninos.

But there weren't. Both islands were deserted.

On June 18, Patrick and Gregory arrived on Confites; they were fetched by the ever-accommodating Winston Guest. But this time they joined in few if any of the patrols, for the quarters aboard *Pilar* were cramped with just the regular crew aboard. And perhaps because of the bombings the week before, Hemingway felt that the possibility of encounters with U-boats was serious.

Hemingway and his crew set out each day, following the assignments delivered the night before by radio, and scanning the apparently empty sea with its garland of equally empty *cayos*. It went on this way day after day.

Conditions on Confites were barely tolerable, supplies were only adequate, and as the weeks went by, *Pilar* began to suffer from overuse. Frequent groundings had damaged a prop and driveshaft, and the normal wear and tear that all boat engines experience was threatening to develop into something serious. Hemingway no doubt watched *Pilar* gradually deteriorating and probably began to wonder whether it was worth it. A man so attuned to symbols and imagery could not have escaped the obvious comparison between himself and his boat. As he watched the bright colors of his boat gradually fading from the brutal sunlight and from salt air and spray, he was ruefully aware that he and his men were gradually wearing down, too, from a combination of long hours, close quarters, and tropical weather.

The climate at that time of year was so humid that their damp clothes clung to their skin, and the humidity, combined with the salt air and salt water they bathed in, meant that they could never feel quite clean. On the beach the air smelled heavily of the sea and any sea grasses thrown up onshore as well as any marine life that had washed up and rotted. The sunlight beating down seemed to have actual weight. The insects were ever present and always voracious, unless the offshore breeze was strong enough to keep them at bay. At sea there was some relief from the heat and the insects, but not the sun, which glared off the surface of the water, so that the men were being burned from below as well as above, even as they squinted into the glare looking for contacts. Hemingway stood his watches without any covering on the flying bridge, wearing a long-billed fishing hat, sometimes, and a pair of shorts. His full beard protected his face from the sun, but only partially. The men in the crew suffered equally in the cramped quarters of what was, after all, a small boat, a boat that rolled and pitched even in a gentle sea, so that at the end of a long day their muscles were tired from the unconscious but constant need to shift their weight to maintain balance. In Hemingway's case the fatigue would have been excessive, for he was standing his watch on a leg that had been shattered and rebuilt, a leg that from time to time after his wounding had oozed fragments of metal and must even now have ached from the ordeal of long hours at his wheel. And for all of the men there was always the lurking possibility of encountering a U-boat, and the controlled but constant tension that awareness aroused gradually drained away each man's energy throughout the day, so that when evening came, they were far more tired than they would have been had they merely been fishing. Small wonder that Hemingway and his crew looked forward to the evening's coolness and a glass or two of gin with ice, if any ice was left in *Pilar*'s icebox. And any gin.

Still, they went out every day. But they found no signs of U-boats.

The U-boats were around, though. On July 18, *U134* was traveling at night on the surface in the Florida Straits and was spotted on radar by Navy blimp *K74*. It was bright moonlight. Seeing no one on the weather decks, the blimp commander decided to attack. The stately blimp started her bombing run and passed over the U-boat, but the bomb release malfunctioned just as the Germans suddenly materialized on deck and opened fire with their antiaircraft machine guns. To the German gunners it must have seemed like a slow-motion antiaircraft exercise with an unmissable target. They shot the blimp down after she tried a second bombing run and suffered the same malfunctions. Nine of the ten crewmen were rescued the next day, and the tenth, the ill-fated bombardier, was killed by sharks. The following day *U134* was spotted by aircraft, bombed, and severely damaged. The attack was reported as a probable kill, but *U134* escaped, only to be bombed again and sunk in the Atlantic on her way back to Lorient.

Similarly, *U527* was in the Gulf from May until July, but like her colleagues, she was finding the opportunities harder and harder to come by and the risks ever greater. She fired one spread of torpedoes at a fast-moving, zigzagging merchantman. All four missed, and that was the extent of *U527*'s action. She, too, was attacked and sunk on her way home by aircraft off the USS *Bogue*.

And what of *Pilar*? After six weeks and more of frustration and discomfort and yet dedicated and disciplined service, she and her tired crew were recalled to Havana. She arrived there, limping badly, on July 18—the night the blimp was shot down in the Florida Straits, just off the coast of Cuba.

Hemingway did not know it at the time, but *Pilar* was returning from her last patrol.

* * *

For the next several months Hemingway oversaw the repairs on *Pilar* and waited for his next assignment. But nothing came. This was a frustrating period. Martha was trying to convert him to her notion of where the real war was and to convince him to go to Europe. Waiting for orders, he was in no mood to begin any kind of creative project. When he was writing, interruptions of any kind were intolerable. Perhaps this was also a fallow period creatively, although he must have started making at least mental notes on what would become *Islands in the Stream,* the last third of which would heavily rely on his experiences hunting U-boats. Most of the action takes place in the same waters he had been sailing during his trip to and around Confites.

One of the many things that Martha did not understand— perhaps because Hemingway did not take the time or trouble to explain—was his reluctance to go to Europe as a war correspondent. To Hemingway journalism was essentially a press-box job, a notch above spectating.[25] It was something he had done as a young man, something he had essentially grown beyond. Europe was in the midst of a total war that was being waged by steel machines, not wooden boats like *Pilar,* and those covering it were part of an equally complex machine designed to write propaganda as well as the news, while they simultaneously scrambled among themselves for column inches, bylines, and professional advancement. Asking Hemingway to leave his post of independent command—a post of direct action against the enemy—to become a journalist was like asking a privateer to leave the sea to become a maritime-insurance agent working on commission. Skippering *Pilar* among the flats and mangrove islands or out along the hundred-fathom line was in many ways analogous to writing fiction—you started with what you knew and what you were learning as you went along, then imagined your way from there to create something that had value, even if it was only a report that said, "No contacts." There is artistry to seamanship as well as to fiction, both satisfying in similar ways. Maybe the patrols of *Pilar* were quixotic, but that was part of their appeal—that and the sense of doing something unique and useful and of being in command. True, like all sea captains he followed orders from headquarters, but once he was under way, he could savor the exhilarating and sobering knowledge that he alone was responsible for his vessel and his crew. No other feeling is quite like it. It was action and artistry combined. It was also fun, most of it, especially when there was enough gin.

Martha apparently did not understand the romantic appeal the patrols had for Hemingway's imagination. Or if she did, she had little sympathy for it. One of Hemingway's favorite writers was Frederick Marryat, an actual British sea captain in the age of fighting sail, a man who had fought in the Napoleonic Wars and served with Lord Cochrane[*] and who retired to become a renowned novelist, the progenitor of C. S. Forrester and Patrick O'Brian, among

---

[*] The model for Captain Jack Aubrey in Patrick O'Brian's estimable series. Marryat's novels are extremely well written and compare favorably with any modern sea stories.

others. Certainly Hemingway could identify with Marryat—a fighting sailor and a writer. How different, really, were the standard tactics of Marryat's navy—broadside exchanges followed by boarding parties armed with pistols and cutlasses—from Hemingway's own plans to run alongside a U-boat, fire machine guns, and throw grenades? The difference is only in the nature of the weapons—and of the enemy, for in Hemingway's case it would be wood against steel.

Looking at it that way, perhaps it's not so surprising that Hemingway did not or could not explain any of this to Martha. Probably he understood that she would regard it as melodramatic swashbuckling and playacting—something similar to his boastful storytelling that she disliked so much. But to him the patrols were, at least in part, an echo of an earlier time. And maybe that sheds a slightly different light on his letter to Chink O'Gorman-Smith in which he talked of preying on enemy shipping and "Miss Submarine." He *would have* done it if the opportunity presented itself, for he thought of himself as a privateer in the Marryat tradition. And that's what privateers did. The distance between "would have" and "did" was not very great to someone with his imagination. As usual Hemingway, as an artist, viewed this reality on several different levels at once—unlike Martha, who tended to see things as they were literally, through her journalist's eye. The patrols were a privateering adventure as well as a romantic quest, and of course they were also an exercise in realism, a genuine attempt to serve and fight.

Some may wonder about this notion that Hemingway was a romantic, since his prose was so uniquely unadorned and seemed such a clear reflection of postwar modernism. But there is a difference between the way an artist approaches and interprets the world, and the style he uses to present his findings. Hemingway's subjects and his style may appear to be realistic, but his imagination is the primary engine behind his art. A romantic approaches the universe with his imagination first; it is the primary organ of interpretation and creation. All other faculties—observation, reason, emotion—are subordinate to it and serve it. His art emerges from the imagination, which after all is a word derived from *image, imagery.*[*] This definition of romanticism is not the same as romantic love and sexual passion, although they figure importantly in the equation and in his art, as fuel for the imagination. As he said to the *Paris Review,* "But the best writing is certainly when you are in love. If it is all the same to you, I would rather not expound on that." Just as meaning is conveyed in images, so the value of existence is created in moments—the moment of truth, of passion, of courage in the face of danger. Yet the tragedy of life is that these moments quickly fade. You cannot stand on a pinnacle for long. But these moments are life's affirmation, and they leave their mark, whether in the form of pride or melancholy or wistful nostalgia.

For a realist, or a journalist, observation and reason drive the creative process, and imagination merely adds color here and there, if at all; facts, not images, are the conveyors of truth.

Knowing all this, Hemingway, not surprisingly, had scant interest in going off to a war where he would have to leave behind not only his adventures, his friends, his beloved boat, but also his fundamental way of being and working, his independence—all to become a cog in a massive machine grinding out censored war information, facts and quasi-facts.

But in the end, he would have no choice, for the war in the Gulf had changed. And because it had changed, the patrols of *Pilar* were over.

---

[*] Also, *imago,* which is "an idealized image of another person or the self."

* * *

The Hooligan Navy ceased to be on 1 October, 1943.

Morison[26]

Why were there no new orders? Perhaps because of a residual and behind-the-scenes antagonism from the FBI, but nothing in Hemingway's file suggests the Bureau was responsible for his being "sent ashore." No, the real reason is that Hemingway and all the other members of the Hooligan Navy based up and down the Atlantic coast were no longer needed. The war against the U-boats was being won worldwide because of a number of factors—first and foremost, the development of aircraft with radar and the gradual building up of air assets throughout the various sea frontiers. Also, the convoy system was now well organized so that merchant ships could travel escorted by warships armed with depth charges, radar, and sonar, and in some cases by escort carriers that could launch attacking aircraft at the merest suggestion of a sonar or radar contact. Further, the Navy was getting better and better at tactics, both through training and experience, and new antisubmarine vessels—destroyers, Coast Guard cutters, and patrol craft—were being created in massive numbers,* even as new merchant vessels such as Liberty ships were coming off assembly lines in unheard of numbers and at undreamed of speeds (almost one a day), faster than the U-boats could sink them. Further still, the bombing of German factories that produced parts for U-boats was beginning to have an effect, and although attempted bombings of the heavily constructed U-boat pens in France were less successful, they were certainly bothersome to the Germans.

---

* Between July 1942 and the end of 1943, 155 destroyers were added to the fleet.[27]

Then, too, the Big Inch (twenty-four inches in diameter), and the Little Big Inch—two oil pipelines that stretched from Texas to New York, via the Midwest—were completed. The Big Inch alone could carry three hundred thousand barrels of oil per day, thereby greatly lessening the need to move oil by tanker from the Gulf to the Northeast. The Germans were aware of this, for Adolf Piening in one of his reports explaining the scarcity of targets in the Gulf said, "Oil pipelines to the east coast are likely to have been finished . . . as well as utmost use of rail lines for supply to east coast."[28] The final section of the Big Inch was welded together on July 19, 1943—the day after *Pilar* returned from her last patrol.

Although figures vary, depending on the source, Germany suffered the bulk of her U-boat losses (578 boats) in the years 1942–44. This was worldwide, although the vast majority of U-boats were sunk in the Atlantic theater of war. Generally, when a U-boat was sunk, all hands were lost. Of the total U-boats lost, roughly half were sunk by aircraft and the other half by naval vessels. Some of these aircraft were land based, while others were flown from the decks of escort carriers. Quite often ships and aircraft coordinated their attacks, so that the resulting kill was a joint effort.

On the other side of the ledger, merchant-ship losses *in just the Gulf and Caribbean Sea frontiers alone* totaled 309 in 1942, by far the worst year of the war in terms of merchant-shipping casualties in those regions.[29] Of the two, the Caribbean suffered more losses that year (231 to 78). But when Adolf Piening in *U155* sank the *Lysefjord* and the *Gulfstate* in April 1943, and *U176* sank her two merchantmen in May, they were marking the virtual end of the U-boat war in the Gulf. The very last attack in the Gulf came in November 1943 when *U193* sank the tanker *Touchet*. From then on Dönitz sent no more U-boats to the Gulf—the cost-benefit ratio had become too unbalanced—and U.S. naval authorities decided that *Pilar* could retire with honor from her voluntary service.

* * *

Hemingway undertook a few unofficial cruises in the latter months of 1943—in-and-out ventures that were little more than fishing trips. Arguments with Martha about the usual subjects became a part of the routine, poisoning the atmosphere at the finca. Returning from the Floridita one night, Martha insisted on driving; an argument ensued, and Hemingway slapped her, whereupon she deliberately drove his treasured Lincoln into a tree and walked home, leaving Hemingway to deal with the remains.[30] Finally, in September, Martha went to New York as the first stop on her way to London, where she would be on assignment for *Collier's*. (Part of her reason for going was that they needed the money.) Hemingway asked for permission to shift his patrols to the Caribbean,[31] but nothing came of it.

As usual when he was alone, Hemingway was depressed and intensely lonely. He resented Martha's absence, although he perhaps understood he was at least partially responsible for it. He was doing no work. Martha returned to Cuba for a short stay in March of 1944, about the time that Hemingway finally realized his patrolling days were finished, and he contacted *Collier's* about becoming their frontline correspondent. It was a surrender of a kind, but it would at least fill the gaps created by loneliness and inactivity. The next several weeks with Martha were acrimonious, and she probably realized that their marriage was over: "We quarreled too much, I suppose. He does not understand about that; he pays no attention to quarrels or to any words spoken in anger. He expects every day to be new and the mind new with it. Unluckily mine is an old mind, which keeps all things about as they were; and the angry words have been ugly wicked little seeds which have taken root I guess and there is a fine harvest of mistrust to be reaped. It is all sickening and I am sad to death, and afraid, and as I said guilty and ashamed. But I cannot help it. I only want to be alone. I want to be myself and alone and free to breathe, live, and look upon the world and find it however it is; I want to escape from him and myself and from this personal life which feels like a strait jacket."[32] These quarrels were almost certainly fueled by alcohol; Hemingway may have expected to start anew each day because he did not quite remember what the evening's argument was about or what was said.

They went to New York together to organize passage to England, and in mid-May Hemingway flew to London on a military plane. He did not make arrangements for Martha, and she was forced to find her own way (she went by ammunition ship—the only passenger on a hazardous and uncomfortable journey of two and a half weeks). Since Hemingway had thought about U-boats for the last year and a half or more, his cavalier disregard of Martha's travel arrangements is a little surprising. Or perhaps it reflects the state of his feelings for her—an ammunition ship hit by torpedoes does not sink; it disappears.

Comfortably ensconced in the Dorchester Hotel on Park Lane, Hemingway fell in with the crowd of journalists and seemed to become happily reconciled to his new job. He met Mary Welsh even as Martha was still enduring her Spartan passage to England. He was susceptible, and Mary was receptive. Things advanced quickly.

That same May he wrote "First Poem to Mary in London." In the following excerpts he is reliving the not-so-long-ago days, retelling the incident with the U-boat and the *Marqués di Comillas,* and blending in the old themes of luck, anticipated death, and (imaginary) killings and nostalgia for his boat and for the sea and for his comrades and for the comradeship, which is a special kind of nostalgia familiar to anyone who has served, especially in wartime—and his love of the word and of writing, one of the few things that can last.

I loving only the word
Trying to make a phrase and a sentence
Something no bomber can reach
Something to stand when all of us are gone
And long after:
(Given a little luck at the moment of wording)
(Needing much luck then. Playing it out when I get it)
Come now to a new city.
(Owning no part of it. Shy from too long on the water. Killing
I know and believe in. Or do not believe in but practice. . . .)

His boat is in the far away sea. His people are dispersed
And his armament surrendered to the proper authorities. Duly
receipted and accounted for. . . .

No it is not a good ending. Not the end we had hoped for.
Not as when sighting her rising we closed dry mouthed but
Happy. Not as we thought it would be in the long nights on
the bridge with the head phones. Not as we thought it should
be each time we took her from the harbor. . . .

Where are you Wolfie now? * Where are you Paxtchi? . . .*

Then I am homesick for Paxtchi. . . . For
Wolfie standing on the flying bridge the muscles jumping in
his cheeks. Saying "Papa it's all right with me. Don't worry
for a moment Papa it's all right with me. . . ."

So now I sit in this town, homesick and lonely for the sea. . . .

---

* Winston Guest had joined the Marines.

For in the evening now, alone from choice, I watch the
Clock electrically tick and jump toward the hour
When she will come opening softly with the in-left key. Saying
"May I come in?" Coming small-voiced and lovely to the
Hand and eye to bring your heart back that was gone; to cure
all loneliness and bring the things we left behind upon the boat.[33]

It's hard to know what Mary must have thought of this. Lovers generally appreciate a poem now and then, but this one is so full of sadness and loss that she'd be forgiven for feeling a little depressed. But perhaps she focused on the ending, which says that only she can take away all this sadness and retrieve his heart from its melancholy place.

Regardless of what Mary thought about it, the poem suggests that Hemingway understood that something profound was over. (Perhaps he also sensed the onset of a deepening and worrisome tendency toward depression.) True, there would be more adventures ahead; a new love affair was beginning, the always exciting and intoxicating time when the woman in the flesh seems almost to merge with the image in your imagination; there was a war to cover and, with luck, to cover with as little supervision as possible. A book would come of it, surely. Martha would go her own way; she always had; there would be no trouble about that. The failure of their relationship was sad to think about, but he had much to look forward to.

Still . . . the navigator in him knew that the star fix he had made in Cuba, the fix that had placed him at the top of his arc, was no longer accurate. The "moth like stars" had moved on, and so had he. He was in another country now, "homesick and lonely for the sea."

Epilogue

~~~

THE MEANING OF NOTHING

The artist must imitate that which . . . discourses to us by symbols.

Coleridge

When I behold, upon the night's starr'd face,
Huge cloudy symbols of a high romance . . .

Keats

DESPITE what he said and possibly believed in later years, Hemingway did not find a U-boat. He may have seen one from a distance, but even that is open to question.

But it does not matter. The search is what matters—the quest, the adventure, the serious purpose, the voluntary service, the fun, the satisfaction of command and comradeship, the joy of being at sea, the craft of seamanship and navigation, the possibility of danger and the piquancy of not knowing whether it will come, the reality and the metaphor of an unseen enemy suddenly rising. All of that taken together is what mattered. Besides, if Hemingway had found a U-boat, it would have meant his death, most likely. And although at this time he may have had only occasional foreshadowings, writing that ending was something he was reserving for himself.

What was he thinking during those long hours on *Pilar*'s flying bridge? Imagining that may be presumptuous, but in some ways he was not all that different from other sailors standing watch on the bridges of other ships of war:

You volunteer your time and money and put yourself in harm's way not knowing when or if the enemy will appear, and you are prepared with your plans but you do not know whether you or your crew will be able to carry them out, or whether in combat you will master your emotions and do what needs to be done. There is no blustering in your own thoughts, just honest questioning. And the thing you seek may surprise you and be death, though you do not seek death; you seek to affirm your sense of self, and that is defined in part by your quest. And ironically on the bridge you think of happier times and happier places, of cafés in Paris, of the corridas of Spain, of pheasant hunting in Idaho and fishing in Michigan when you were a boy, and of the women you have known and others you would like to have known better. Yet even so, the bridge of your boat overlooking an expanse of sea that may conceal an enemy secretly observing you—that bridge is in many ways the best place of all to be. The sea gives you both the reality and the illusion of command, reality because you know your orders will be obeyed, which means they must be well-thought-out orders that do not ask the impossible; illusion because you command at sea only at the sufferance of the sea itself. You need luck to be able to do the things you plan to do. But you have been lucky before. And Pilar, *after all, is a wooden boat.*

* * *

The struggle itself toward the heights is enough to fill a man's heart. We must imagine Sisyphus happy.

Albert Camus

For someone who spent so much of his life in the public eye, Hemingway still seems elusive, perhaps because his public persona allows him to be so easily pigeonholed as the poster boy for macho writing, big-game hunting, deep-sea fishing, Homeric drinking and womanizing and assorted other frowned-upon behaviors. This cartoon of the man allows us to categorize and then dismiss him if we're so inclined, just as Martha dismissed his patrols. He was partly to blame for the way he was perceived, partly to blame for the way Martha perceived him. Everyone is always partly to blame.

But the patrols were representative of the man and his many facets. They were wartime forays against an enemy, literally an attempt by a wooden boat to take on an iron-and-steel machine of war. Ironically, for such a steadfastly apolitical man, this separate war had a political dimension. He went out to confront the weapon of a malignant totalitarian system whose ravages he had witnessed firsthand in Spain; his patrols were an affirmation of his own brand of individualism, his belief in liberty. If you believe in these things, you have no choice but to assert them in order to preserve them. Too many forces are ready to step up and take them away if you do not. And as a purely practical matter, his country was at war, and although he did not love war, he knew that once you were in one, you must win it.

That in itself is enough to legitimize the patrols. But to Hemingway the patrols must also have existed on an imaginative, metaphorical level, for the unseen, lurking menace of a U-boat represented the universe as he had come to know it, unpredictable, dangerous, often lethal, while his own resources to confront it, his own protective devices, were as fragile as *Pilar*'s wooden hull. Man in nature is almost always involved in a physical mismatch. Yet Hemingway went out anyway to confront the unknown. The U-boats were the sharks in *The Old Man and the Sea,* the wounded buffalo in "The Short Happy Life of Francis Macomber," the bulls in the ring at Pamplona, and all the memories that kept him awake at night. But the U-boats were also the object of a continuing quest, the cynosure of the imagination—like Santiago's great fish, or the glimmering girl of the Wandering Aengus. If this seems inconsistent, it does not matter. No one expects the imagination to operate logically; it operates in images, and "wisdom first speaks in images." Far from being meaningless, the patrols of *Pilar* reflect the complexity of a man who is often oversimplified and dismissed as someone who merely lived an interesting and exciting life and thereby drew attention to himself—attention, his critics say, that was out of proportion to his artistic merits. "I think of Hemingway as a man who developed a significant manner as an artist, a lifestyle that is important. . . . I don't think of Hemingway as a great novelist,"[1] said Saul Bellow. (Hemingway would have returned Bellow's comment with interest.*) But Bellow represents one critical faction, people who are put off by Hemingway's public persona and behavior, and who extend their disapproval to his work.

But just as his work was complex and often beautiful, so the patrols of *Pilar* were more than they seemed to be—a kind of synecdoche for his life and work. Like his famous iceberg theory, more was going on than what appears at first glance—most of it in Hemingway's imagination. Bernard Berenson's comment on *The Old Man and the Sea* might just as well apply to the patrols: "Every real work of art exhales symbols and allegories. So does this short but not small masterpiece."

Symbols and allegories—*Pilar* versus a U-boat; the individual versus a totalitarian state; man confronting the anonymous and murderous "they": man defiant and therefore undefeated. For the time being, at least.

Hemingway was obviously not alone in offering his service; he was one of millions. But that does not diminish his or anyone else's sacrifices. One has only one's self to offer up to the wooden god of luck. What Hemingway did for his country was nothing

---

* "You could put Lionel Trilling, Saul Bellow, Truman Capote, Jean Stafford and . . . Robert Lowry into one cage and jack them up good and you would find that you have nothing."[2]

more or less than what other volunteers did. But what he did he was also doing for himself. Imagining his life. Living his art. Being the Hemingway Hero, in all his various phases. Thinking of him there on the flying bridge of his well-loved *Pilar,* there by his own choice, willing and prepared to face the risk of combat, in command and accompanied by comrades who returned the affection he felt for them, it is easy to imagine Hemingway happy.

Notes

❧

Introduction

1   Hemingway, *Moveable Feast,* 210
2   Ibid.

Chapter One: A Serious Man

1   Hemingway, *Islands in the Stream,* 97
2   *Paris Review,* 45
3   Baker, *Hemingway Letters,* 474

Chapter Two: Martha and Spain: Love and War

1   Moorehead, *Gellhorn Letters,* 389
2   Moorehead, *Gelhorn,* 56
3   Ibid., 24
4   Ibid., 78
5   Ibid., 70
6   Ibid., 81
7   Moorehead, *Gellhorn Letters,* 450
8   Ibid., 461
9   Ibid., 313
10   Ibid., 236
11   Moorehead, *Gellhorn,* 111
12   Moorehead, *Gellhorn Letters,* 42
13   Gellhorn, *View from the Ground,* 72
14   Moorehead, *Gellhorn Letters,* 126
15   Moorehead, *Gellhorn,* 5
16   Ludington, *John Dos Passos,* 312

17   Shlaes, *Forgotten Man,* 262

18   Moorehead, *Gellhorn Letters,* 164

19   Ibid., 87

20   Moorehead, *Gellhorn,* 111

21   Moorehead, *Gellhorn Letters,* 125

22   Preston, *Spanish Civil War,* 27

23   Ibid., 293

24   Moorehead, *Gellhorn,* 135

25   Hemingway, *For Whom the Bell Tolls,* 253

26   Preston, *Spanish Civil War,* 134

27   Ibid., 274

28   Ibid., 121

29   Ibid., 103

30   Beevor, *Battle for Spain,* 94

31   Ibid., 94

32   Baker, *Hemingway Letters,* 460

33   Bakker, *Joris Ivens,* 249

34   Ludington, *John Dos Passos,* 378

35   *Paris Review,* 59

36   Hemingway, "The Gambler, the Nun and the Radio"

37   Hemingway, *Death in the Afternoon,* 4

38   Hemingway, *For Whom the Bell Tolls,* 175

39   Moorehead, *Gellhorn,* 135

40   Hemingway, *Fifth Column,* 66

41   Hemingway, "The Three Day Blow"

42   Preston, *Spanish Civil War,* 314, 315

43   Moorehead, *Gellhorn,* 147

Chapter Three: Two Kinds of Hunters

1   Hemingway, "Shakespeare and Company," *Moveable Feast*

2   Baker, *Hemingway Letters,* 404

3   Hemingway, "On the Blue Water"

4   Reynolds, *Hemingway: 1930's,* 230

5   Hemingway, "The Great Blue River"

6   Hemingway, "Marlin off the Morro"

7   Hemingway, *Death in the Afternoon,* 99

8   Ibid., 233

9   Gingrich, "Horsing Them in with Hemingway," *The Well Tempered Angler*

10 Baker, *Hemingway Letters,* 673

11 *Paris Review,* 369

12 Hemingway, "The Great Blue River"

13 *Paris Review,* 61

14 Dos Passos, *The Best Times,* 175

15 Hemingway, *Death in the Afternoon,* 192

16 Reynolds, *Hemingway: 1930's,* 92

17 Hemingway, "On the Blue Water"

18 Hemingway, *Death in the Afternoon,* 178

19 Hickam, *Torpedo Junction,* 240

20 Morison, *Battle of the Atlantic,* 282

21 Ibid., 308

Chapter Four: The Enemy in the Machine

1   Morison, *Battle of the Atlantic,* 413

2   Ibid., 10

3   Baker, *Hemingway: Life Story,* 374

4   Moorehead, *Gellhorn Letters,* 78

5   Gellhorn, *Travels with Myself and Another,* 81

6   Hemingway, *Farewell to Arms,* 115

7   Moorehead, *Gellhorn Letters,* 82

8   Moorehead, *Gellhorn,* 173

9   Moorehead, *Gellhorn Letters,* 117

10 Vause, *U Boat Ace,* 48

11 Savas, *Silent Hunters,* 28

12 Vause, *U Boat Ace,* 48

13 Morison, *Battle of the Atlantic,* 314

14   PAST Foundation, *U166* Web site

15   Morison, *Battle of the Atlantic,* 119

16   Wiggins, *Torpedoes in the Gulf,* 209

17   Morison, *Battle of the Atlantic,* note 130

18   Moorehead, *Gellhorn Letters,* 322

19   Gellhorn, *Travels with Myself and Another,* 59, 60

20   Wiggins, *Torpedoes in the Gulf,* 140

21   Hemingway, *Old Man and the Sea,* 107

22   Uboat.net

Chapter Five: Amateur Hour

1   Morison, *Battle of the Atlantic,* 124

2   Ibid., 208

3   Ibid., 127

4   Ibid., note 129

5   Moorehead, *Gellhorn Letters,* 113

6   Hemingway, *Fifth Column,* 38

7   Baker, *Ernest Hemingway,* 277

8   Baker, *Hemingway Letters,* 360

9   FBI memo, 6/13/43

10   FBI memo, 12/19/42

11   Hemingway, *For Whom the Bell Tolls,* 245

12   Baker, *Ernest Hemingway,* 369

13   FBI memo, 6/13/43

14   Mitgang, *Dangerous Dossiers,* 21

15   Baker, *Ernest Hemingway,* 356

16   *Paris Review,* 59

17   FBI memo, 6/1/43

Chapter Six: The Wandering Angler

1   Reynolds, *Hemingway: Final Years,* 59

2   Ibid., 58

3   Morison, *Battle of the Atlantic,* 200

4   Hemingway, *Islands in the Stream,* 455

5   Lawrence, *Seven Pillars,* 412

6   Hemingway, *Farewell to Arms,* 184

7   Hemingway, *For Whom the Bell Tolls,* 253

8   Hemingway, *Farewell to Arms,* 134

9   Hemingway, "On Writing," *Nick Adams Stories,* 237

10   Hemingway, "Big Two-Hearted River"

11   Hemingway, "A Way You'll Never Be"

12   Baker, *Hemingway Letters,* 187

13   *Paris Review,* 41

14   Moorehead, *Gellhorn Letters,* 380

15   Ibid., 456

16   Ibid., 210

17   Moorehead, *Gellhorn,* 187

18   Moorehead, *Gellhorn Letters,* 210

19   Ibid., 130

20   Ibid., 309

21   Ibid., 131

22   Ibid., 380

23   Ibid., 158

24   Gellhorn, *Travels with Myself and Another,* 60

Chapter Seven: Fathers and Sons

1   Baker, *Hemingway Letters,* 536

2   Moorehead, *Gellhorn Letters,* 124

3   Moorehead, *Gellhorn,* 225

4   Hemingway, "Short Happy Life of Francis Macomber"

5   Baker, *Hemingway Letters,* 537

6   Ibid., 514

7   Hemingway, *Farewell to Arms,* 327

8   Reynolds, *Hemingway: Final Years,* 64

9   Ibid., 68

10   Hemingway, "Fathers and Sons"

11   Hemingway, *Islands in the Stream,* 286

12   Baker, *Hemingway Letters,* 673

13   Ibid., 419

14   Hemingway, *Islands in the Stream,* 98

15   Ibid., 358

16   Baker, *Hemingway Letters,* 382

17   Ibid., 311

18   Reynolds, *Hemingway: The Homecoming,* 92

19   Hemingway, *Byline,* 358

20   Baker, *Hemingway Letters,* 374

21   FBI memo, 10/42

Chapter Eight: "And Faded Through the Brightening Air"

1   Morison, *Battle of the Atlantic,* 309

2   Reynolds, *Hemingway: Final Years,* 222

3   Ibid., 206

4   Reynolds, *Hemingway: 1930's,* 170

5   Hemingway, "Soldier's Home"

6   Hemingway, *Farewell to Arms,* 94

7   Baker, *Hemingway Letters,* 691

8   Moorehead, *Gellhorn,* 197

9   Hemingway, *For Whom the Bell Tolls,* 43

10   Reynolds, *Hemingway: Final Years,* 222

11   Phillips, *On Writing,* 5

12   Moorehead, *Gellhorn Letters,* 421

13   Ibid., 413

14   *Atlantic Monthly,* August 1965

15   *Paris Review,* 44

16   Morison, *Battle of the Atlantic,* 317

17   Hickam, *Torpedo Junction,* 229

18   Dönitz war-crimes-trial testimony

19   FBI memo, 6/13/43

20 Mitgang, *Dangerous Dossiers,* 62

21 FBI memo, 12/17/42

22 Hemingway, *Islands in the Stream,* 387, 388

Chapter Nine: In Another Country

1 Gellhorn, *Liana,* 130

2 Hemingway, *Islands in the Stream*

3 Hemingway, *Byline,* 184

4 Moorehead, *Gellhorn,* 196

5 Hemingway, *Fifth Column,* 84

6 Moorehead, *Gellhorn,* 209

7 Hemingway, *Islands in the Stream,* 336

8 FBI memo, June 1943

9 Ibid.

10 Ibid.

11 Baker, *Hemingway Letters,* 536

12 Bruccoli, *Only Thing That Counts,* 324

13 Moorehead, *Gellhorn Letters,* 309

14 Baker, *Hemingway Letters,* 536

15 *Paris Review,* 45

16 Hemingway, *Farewell to Arms,* 338

17 Baker, *Hemingway Letters,* 778

18 Hemingway, *Moveable Feast,* 91

19 Hemingway, *Farewell to Arms,* 45

20 Houk, "Sailor Looks," 41

21 Hemingway, *Islands in the Stream,* 350

22 Ibid., 346

23 Reynolds, *Hemingway: Final Years,* 78

24 Hemingway, *Islands in the Stream,* 393

25 Reynolds, *Hemingway: Final Years,* 89

26 Morison, *Battle of the Atlantic*

27 Ibid., 234

28 Wiggins, *Torpedoes in the Gulf,* 178

29   Morison, *Battle of the Atlantic,* 413
30   Moorehead, *Gellhorn,* 198
31   Reynolds, *Hemingway: Final Years,* 88
32   Moorehead, *Gellhorn Letters,* 163
33   Hemingway, *Collected Poems,* 103, 104

Epilogue: The Meaning of Nothing

1   *Paris Review,* 91
2   Baker, *Hemingway Letters,* 680

Bibliography

(The editions are those used for reference in the text.)

Baker, Carlos   *Ernest Hemingway: A Life Story* (Scribner's, 1969)
      Ernest Hemingway Selected Letters, 1917–1961
      (Scribner's, 1981)

Bakker, Kees   *Joris Ivens and the Documentary Context*
      (Amsterdam University Press, 1999)

Beevor, Antony   *The Battle for Spain* (Penguin, 2001)

Bruccoli, Mathew J.   *The Only Thing That Counts* (University of
      South Carolina, 1999)

Buchheim,
Luther-Gunther   *Das Boot* (Cassell, 1999)

Dos Passos, John   *The Best Times* (New American Library, 1966)

Fuentes, Norberto   *Hemingway in Cuba* (Lyle Stuart, 1984)

Gellhorn, Martha   *Liana* (Picador, 1993)
      Travels with Myself and Another (Putnam, 2001)
      The View from the Ground (Atlantic Monthly
      Press, 1988)

Gingrich, Arnold   *The Well Tempered Angler* (Plume, 1987)

Bibliography

Hemingway, Ernest   *Across the River and into the Trees* (Scribner, 1998)

Byline Ernest Hemingway (Bantam, 1968)

Complete Poems (University of Nebraska Press, 1992)

The Complete Short Stories (Scribner, 1987)

Death in the Afternoon (Scribner's, 1960)

A Farewell to Arms (Scribner, 1995)

The Fifth Column and Four Stories of the Spanish Civil War (Chas. Scribner's Sons, 1969)

For Whom the Bell Tolls (Arrow Books, 1994)

Islands in the Stream (Chas. Scribner's Sons, 1970)

Men at War (Bramhall House, 1942)

A Moveable Feast (Touchstone, 1992)

The Nick Adams Stories (Scribner's, 1972)

The Sun Also Rises (Chas. Scribner's Sons, 1954)

To Have and Have Not (Scribner, 1999)

Hickam, Homer   *Torpedo Junction* (Naval Institute Press, 1989)

Houk, Walter   "A Sailor Looks at Hemingway's *Islands*" (*North Dakota Quarterly,* Winter/Spring 2006)

Lawrence, T. E.   *Seven Pillars of Wisdom* (Anchor Books, 1991)

Lewis, Sinclair   *Babbitt* (Library of America, 1991)

Ludington, Townsend   *John Dos Passos, a Twentieth Century Odyssey* (Carrol and Graf, 1980)

Bibliography

Miller, Nathan   *War at Sea: A Naval History of World War Two*
                                  (Oxford, 1997)

Mitgang, Herbert   *Dangerous Dossiers* (Donald Fine, 1988)

Moorehead, Caroline   *Gellhorn: A Twentieth Century Life* (Henry Holt,
                                  2003)
                                  Selected Letters of Martha Gellhorn (Henry Holt,
                                  2003)

Morison, Samuel Eliot   *The Battle of the Atlantic, 1939–1943* (Castle
                                  Books, 2001)
                                  The Two Ocean War (Little, Brown, 1989)

The Paris Review   *The Paris Review Interviews*, vol. 1 (Picador,
                                  2006)

Phillips, Larry W.   *Ernest Hemingway on Writing* (Scribner, 1984)

Preston, Paul   *The Spanish Civil War* (Norton, 2007)

Reynolds, Michael   *Hemingway: The Final Years* (Norton, 2000)
                                  Hemingway: The Homecoming (Norton, 1999)
                                  Hemingway: The 1930's (Norton, 1998)
                                  Hemingway: The Paris Years (Norton, 1999)
                                  The Young Hemingway (Norton, 1998)

Savas, Theodore P.   *Silent Hunters* (Naval Institute Press, 1997)

Shlaes, Amity   *The Forgotten Man* (HarperCollins, 2007)

Vause, Jordan   *U Boat Ace* (Naval Institute Press, 1990)

Wiggins, Melanie   *Torpedoes in the Gulf* (Texas A&M University
                                  Press, 1995)

Acknowledgments

◊∾∾◊

ANY PEOPLE contributed to this project and deserve particular thanks: Susan Beegel, editor of *The Hemingway Review,* and Dr. Kirk Curnutt of Troy University and vice president of the Hemingway Foundation; Laurie Austin, who manages the audiovisual archives at the John F. Kennedy Presidential Library, where the Hemingway Collection is housed, was especially helpful in locating photographs. Susan Wrynn, also of the Hemingway Collection at the JFK Library, cheerfully provided access to the log of the *Pilar* as well as documents from Hemingway's life in Cuba. The staffs at the National World War II Museum in New Orleans and the PAST Foundation were generous with their time and their efforts to locate photos of *U166.* Colin Harrison, senior editor at Scribner, knows the difference between repetition and motif and will someday explain it to me. His enthusiasm for Hemingway was the driving force behind seeing this project to fruition, and his "never in a hurry" phone conversations were, and are, greatly appreciated. Colin's assistant, Jessica Manners, not only responded quickly to emails but also kept things moving along briskly. My son, Colin Mort, added his encouragement as did my wife, the estimable Sondra Hadley—no mean contribution. And finally, literary agent and friend, A. L. Hart, found the best possible home for this work, Scribner. Hemingway would have been pleased about that, at least.

Permissions and Photograph Credits

Index

Abraham Lincoln Brigade, 37
Across the River and into the Trees
    (Hemingway), 9–10
Adams, Nick (char.), 130–31
Aengus, 137, 138, 139, 229
Africa, EH's safaris in, 8, 10
aircraft, in antisubmarine warfare, 67,
    94–95, 96, 173–75, 177–78, 180,
    209, 212, 215, 216, 220, 221
air force, German, 39, 92
air force, Italian, 39
Amapala (freighter), 77
American Museum of Natural History,
    176
American Writers' Congress (1937), 45,
    116
anarchists, 35, 36, 42, 43, 44
Andrew Jackson (freighter), 142
Anegada Passage, 195, 203
Angelburg, 89
Anita (fishing boat), 50–51
Anselmo (char.), 167
anticlericalism, 36
antisubmarine warfare, 62, 75
    aircraft in, 67, 94–95, 96, 173–75,
        177–78, 180, 209, 212, 215, 216,
        220, 221
    depth charges in, 88, 89, 96, 105–6,
        174, 209, 212, 220
    HFDF in, 95–96, 172–73, 200,
        211–12
    radar in, 67, 94–95, 172, 173–75, 220
    sonar in, 79, 106, 172, 220
    visual surveillance in, 76, 96, 102,
        171–72, 176, 211
Ara (char.), 159, 192
Arditi, 165
Arias, Arnulfo, 180
army, German, 92
Army, U.S., 167
Army Air Corps, U.S., 102, 173–74

Aruba, 178
asdic, 88
Ashley, Brett (char.), 6, 133, 136
Atik, USS, 66
Atlantic, 169
Atlantis (German raider), 100n
Austria, 3, 4
Avenger, HMS, 202, 204

Babbitt, George, 27n, 139
Babbitt (Lewis), 27n
"Babbitts," 27, 30
Bahamas, 50, 70, 178n, 180
Bahía Honda, Cuba, 184, 203, 204
Baker, Carlos, 153, 165n
Baltic Sea, 89
Barcelona, 46, 48
Barkley, Catherine (char.), 2, 4, 7, 132,
    137, 208–9
Barnes, Jake (char.), 6, 7, 130, 133, 134,
    136, 159, 192
Basques, 35, 42, 122
Batista, Fulgencio, 117
Battle of the Atlantic, 87–88, 114
Battle of the Atlantic, The (Morison), 109
bauxite, 63, 194–95
bazookas, 164–65
BdU (U-boat command), 95, 98, 125,
    172
Beach, Sylvia, 3
Beevor, Antony, 41
"Belle Dame sans Merci, La" (Keats),
    135
Bellow, Saul, 229
Berenson, Bernard, 229
Beston, Henry, 13
big-game fishing, 50–51, 53, 57, 58–61
    appeal of, 54–56
    as metaphor, 60
big-game hunting, 150
Biscay, Bay of, 203

Bismarck (battleship), 87, 107
Bletchley Park, 95*n*
blimps, 96, 180, 215
Bogue, USS, 216
Boni & Liveright, 5
Bordeaux, France, 77*n*
Braden, Spruille, 114, 116–17, 118,
    119–20, 123, 163, 191, 200
Brandeis, Louis, 120
Brest, France, 77*n*
Brittany peninsula, 93
Bryn Mawr, 24, 25
Buena Vista, Bahía, 211
bullfighting, 56, 60, 207

Camus, Albert, 134, 227
Caporetto, battle of, 129, 132
Cardonia, SS, 101
Caribbean:
    German "blockade" of, 111
    Martha Gellhorn's reporting trip in,
        142, 143–44, 150, 152–53, 194–95
    U-boats in, 62, 64, 67, 70, 76–78,
        103, 142, 175, 180, 195, 203, 209,
        212, 221
Caribbean Sea Frontier, 178, 209, 221
Carmen (schooner), 97
Castro, Fidel, 117
Catalonia, 35, 48
Catholics, Catholicism, 6
    mysticism of, 206–7
    Spanish Nationalists supported by,
        35–36, 38, 42, 208
cayos, 210–13, 214
celestial navigation, 13–14, 93
censorship, 125, 195
Chambers, Whittaker, 27
Charles Scribner's Sons, 5, 6, 10, 52
checas, 41
Chiang Kai-shek, 143*n*
Chicago Tribune, 40–41
Chico, Cayo, 212
China, 8, 143
Chou En-lai, 143*n*
Churchill, Winston, 160
civilian antisubmarine patrols, 66, 75,
        102, 123–25, 164, 175, 195, 220,
        229–30
Club de Cazadores del Cerro, 151
Coast Guard, U.S., 125, 174–75
Cochrane, Thomas, Lord, 217

Coco, Cayo, 211
Cojimar, Cuba, 14, 203
Colebaugh, Charles, 112*n*
Coleridge, Samuel Taylor, 226
Collier's, 33, 37, 49, 84, 112*n*, 142,
    152–53, 222
communism, communists, 35, 41, 42,
    43, 116, 208
Communist Party, 27, 28, 116, 120, 121,
    122
    Spanish, 39, 42, 44–45
Compañía Transatlántica, 184
Condor Legion, 42
Confites, Cayo, 209, 210–11, 212, 216
Contemporary Historians, 43, 45
convoys, 63, 87–88, 90, 195, 202, 204,
    220
    wolf-pack strategy and, 76, 78, 95,
        172
Cooperative Commonwealth, 3
Correspondent in Spain (Knoblaugh),
    199–200
corvettes, 88
Crane, Stephen, 133–34
Crooked Island Passage, 70, 178, 209
Crook Factory, 8, 112, 113–14, 119–20,
    122, 153, 198–99, 200*n*
CS13, 209
Cuba, 9, 177
    as Allied nation, 111
    barrier islands (*cayos*) of, 210–13, 214
    corruption in, 117
    enemy agents in, 8, 126, 154–55, 210
    fascist sympathizers in, 9, 110–11,
        112, 122
    Fifth Column in, 110–11, 112, 114,
        154–55, 173
    naval air stations on, 178, 180
    Nazi activity in, 112
    proximity to Gulf Stream of, 50, 55
    Revolt of the Sergeants in, 117
    Spanish Republican refugees in, 111,
        113, 122
    supposed U-boat supply dumps on,
        68, 126, 153–55, 210
    U-boat patrols near, 67, 70, 77, 98,
        99, 142, 180
    U.S. embassy in, 112, 114, 116–17,
        118, 119–20, 123, 124, 163, 189,
        191, 200
Cuban Revolution, 117

Daily Worker, 121
Dangerous Summer, The (Hemingway), 11
Daniels, Josephus, 182*n*
Death in the Afternoon (Hemingway), 7, 62
Delgado, Luis (char.), 145–46
Delgado, Rameriz, 209
"Denunciation, The" (Hemingway), 145–46
depth charges, 88, 89, 96, 105–6, 174, 209, 212, 220
destroyers, 65, 88, 96, 220
Dominican Republic, 97
Dönitz, Karl, 87, 92, 125, 191*n*, 203, 221
    on aircraft attacks, 94, 175, 177–78
    on Allied losses, 64
    "Be harsh" order of, 50, 62–63, 79, 101
    regular reports required by, 95–96, 98, 99, 172–73
    wolf-pack strategy of, 76, 78, 95, 172
Dorman-O'Gowan, Eric Edward "Chink," 3, 165, 166, 168, 171, 218
Dos Passos, John, 33, 43, 44–45, 116, 121
    on EH, 60–61
Dunabeitia, Juan, 163

Emerson, Ralph Waldo, 209
Enigma code machines, 95*n*
Enrique (char.), 146
epiphany, 137
escort carriers, 220, 221
espionage:
    EH's interest in, 48, 112, 125, 198
    U-boats and, 125–26
Esquire, 52
Esso Bolivar (tanker), 101

Falangists, 36, 40–41, 110, 112, 122, 180
Farewell to Arms, A (Hemingway), 2, 4, 7, 84, 129, 131, 168, 208
fascism, fascists, 19, 20, 28, 34, 36, 37, 43
FBI, 143*n*
    anticommunist crusade of, 45, 115–16
    counterespionage as jurisdiction of, 120, 125

    EH and, 45, 114–15, 116–19, 122, 198–200, 220
    Marqués de Comillas incident and, 189–91, 203
    State Department and, 116–17
    writers given undue attention by, 120–21
Federal (tanker), 77, 80, 123, 153*n*
Fifth Column, in Cuba, 110–11, 154–55, 173
Fifth Column, The (Hemingway), 19, 47–48, 113, 119, 125–26, 196–97
Finca Vigía, 8, 9, 14, 49, 50, 194
Finland, 83
Finnish-Russian War (1939–40), 84
"First Poem to Mary in London" (Hemingway), 223–25
fishing:
    EH's love of, 138, 146
    as metaphor, 11
    see also big-game fishing
fishing boats, as source of fresh food for U-boats, 79
Fitzgerald, F. Scott, 3, 5, 19, 21, 58, 86, 135, 161, 201
Fitzgerald, Zelda, 5, 201
Flaubert, Gustave, 193–94
Florida Straits, 50, 61, 63, 97, 178
    U-boats in, 67, 68, 70, 100, 180, 184, 204, 215
Floridita (bar), 198
Forrester, C. S., 217
For Whom the Bell Tolls (Hemingway), 8, 14, 41, 46, 51, 83, 84, 121, 122, 124, 126, 132, 200
Fragoso, Cayo, 212
France, 38, 39, 48, 162
    German occupation of, 48–49, 65
Franco, Francisco, 33, 36, 38, 39–40, 43, 49, 110, 124
    political cleansing as policy of, 40–41, 48
Franklin, Sidney, 33
Fraser, George MacDonald, 189*n*
Freedom of Information Act, 118
French Resistance, 9
Fuentes, Gregorio, 163, 182, 200, 212

Garden of Eden, The (Hemingway), 11
gasoline and oil tankers, 63

Index

Gellhorn, Martha:
  "apocryphiars" disliked by, 29, 165,
    170
  bourgeois values disdained by,
    26–28, 31, 139
  Caribbean reporting by, 142, 143–44,
    150, 152–53, 194–95
  in China and Far East, 8, 143
  distortions in journalism of, 28–30,
    31
  divorce of EH and, 9
  on EH as lover, 139–40
  EH's relationship with, 8, 14, 20–21,
    31–33, 34, 47–48, 51, 83–86, 119,
    140–41, 142, 144, 152–53, 169,
    196–98, 201–2, 222–23, 225
  on EH's self-aggrandizement, 101,
    122, 142
  EH's U-boat patrols disparaged by,
    17, 83, 102–3, 140–41, 195–96,
    213, 217
  Eleanor Roosevelt and, 25–26, 29
  as European correspondent, 49, 83,
    84, 222
  hunting and, 85–86
  inconsistency of, 25–26
  individualism of, 30–31, 83, 197
  on legacy of Spanish Civil War, 35
  literalism of, 197, 218
  marriage of EH and, 8, 14, 21, 31
  on Nazi activity in Cuba, 112
  New Deal work by, 24–25
  pigeon shooting and, 148–49
  political ideas of, 26–28, 116
  sexuality of, 22–23
  as Spanish Civil War correspondent,
    8, 33–34, 37, 43, 46–47, 83
  Spanish Earth and, 44, 45
  as world traveler, 25, 31
  writing of, 21, 22–23, 193–94, 212
Germany, 37, 39, 111
  Allied bombing of, 62, 63
  intelligence agents of, 125
Gertrude (trawler), 99–100, 102, 103,
  141, 142, 153
Gingrich, Arnold, 52, 57, 58–59
Gold, Mike, 121
Golz (char.), 132
Grace, Princess of Monaco, 148
Graf Spee (pocket battleship), 87
Grahame, Kenneth, 53

Great Bahama Bank, 70
Great Bahama Channel, 210
Great Britain, 38, 39
Great Depression, 26, 30, 52
Great Gatsby, The (Fitzgerald), 5
Greene, Graham, 132
Green Hills of Africa (Hemingway), 8, 85
Greenland, 65
grenades, 81, 82, 126, 164, 186, 213
Grey, Zane, 54–55
Guantánamo Bay, Cuba, 178, 180, 209
Guernica, German bombing of, 20, 42
Guest, Frederick, 160
Guest, Lucy "CeeZee," 162–63
Guest, Winston, 160–61, 162–63, 182,
  189, 190–91, 200n, 212, 213, 224
Gulf Sea Frontier, 104, 124, 177, 178,
  189, 204, 221
Gulfstate (tanker), 204, 221
Gulf Stream, 14, 15, 50, 55, 61, 93
  U-boats and, 61–62, 90, 97, 204
Guttierez, Carlos, 59

Hammett, Dashiell, 120
Hatteras, Cape, 50, 62
Havana, 8, 14, 17, 49, 50, 55, 98, 99,
  100, 117, 119, 154, 155, 180, 189,
  216
Havana Post, 123
Hellman, Lillian, 33, 120, 121
Hemingway, Ernest:
  African safaris of, 8, 10
  antifascism of, 19, 20, 113, 228
  as autodidact, 60–61
  childhood of, 1–2, 206
  in China and Far East, 8, 143
  code of conduct of, 157–58
  competitiveness of, 57–58, 157
  conversion to Catholicism of, 6,
    207–8
  counterespionage efforts of, 8, 112,
    113–14, 117, 119–20, 122, 153,
    198–99, 200n
  depression of, 11, 14
  dream woman of, 138
  espionage as interest of, 48, 112,
    125–26, 198
  FBI and, 45, 114–15, 116–19, 122,
    198–200, 220
  fishing and, 138, 146; *see also* big-
    game fishing

heavy drinking of, 11, 59, 118, 170–71, 196, 223
on honor, 127–28
individualism of, 116, 208, 219, 228
injuries of, 2, 10–11
on killing, 56
leadership of, 158–60
in London, 9, 223
Martha Gellhorn's relationship with, 8, 14, 20–21, 31–33, 34, 47–48, 51, 83–86, 140–41, 142, 144, 152–53, 169, 197–98, 201–2, 222–23, 225
mastery admired by, 156–58
money worries of, 200–202
Nobel Prize won by, 11
"Papa" as nickname of, 161
paranoia of, 11, 118
in Paris, 3, 4–5, 7, 10, 51, 151–52
pigeon shooting of, 146–49
political ideas of, 45, 116, 208
public persona of, 15, 227–28
Pulitzer Prize won by, 10
romanticism of, 135, 139, 197, 218–19
scientific bent of, 60
self-aggrandizement by, 29, 59, 101, 119, 122, 142, 165–70, 171, 191, 218
as Spanish Civil War correspondent, 8, 17, 33–34, 43, 46–47, 83, 125–26
Spanish Earth and, 43–44, 45
suicide of, 1, 11, 57
as superstitious, 206, 208–9
truthfulness as ideal of, 166
world view of, 16
as World War I Red Cross volunteer, 2, 17, 165
as World War II correspondent, 9, 167, 216, 219, 222
on writers' politics, 121–22
on writing, 13, 15–16, 32, 59, 61, 158, 168–69, 219
Hemingway, Ernest, U-boat patrols of, 8–9, 19–20, 52, 75, 110, 158, 171–72, 202, 210–15, 216, 219
armament of, 80, 81, 82, 102, 126, 164–65, 213
assigned areas of, 180, 182, 184, 203, 204, 205, 209

attack plan of, 80–83, 100–102, 171, 176, 192, 218
crew of, 160, 162–63
EH's exaggerated accounts of, 168
EH's motives for, 16–18, 48, 124–28, 138
Gregory and Patrick on, 153–56
Marqués de Comillas incident in, 184–92, 198, 203, 223
Martha Gellhorn's disparagement of, 17, 83, 102–3, 140–41, 195–96, 213, 217
as officially sanctioned, 15, 124
as quest, 16, 128–29, 138, 140, 217, 218, 226, 228–29
riskiness of, 15, 16, 124, 125, 126, 175–76, 209
supply dumps and clandestine radios as target of, 68, 126, 153–55, 171, 183, 210–11, 212
unofficial patrols in, 183, 222
see also Pilar (fishing boat)
Hemingway, Gregory "Gigi," 7, 150–51, 213
mental problems of, 155–56
on U-boat patrol, 153–56
Hemingway, Hadley, *see* Mowrer, Hadley
Hemingway, John "Bumby," 3, 59, 150, 151, 153
Hemingway, Mary Welsh, 9, 10, 11, 171, 223, 225
Hemingway, Patrick, 7, 9, 150, 151, 213
on U-boat patrol, 153–56
Hemingway, Pauline Pfeiffer, 5–6, 7, 8, 21, 22, 32, 46, 49, 51, 151, 200–201
Hemingway Hero, 130–36, 137, 138, 159, 230
Henry, Frederic (char.), 4, 7, 129, 130, 131, 132–33, 134, 137, 159, 208–9
Herrera, Roberto, 163
HFDF (huff duff), 95–96, 172–73, 200, 211–12
Hickok, Lorena, 24
Hiss, Alger, 27
Hitler, Adolf, 38, 39, 48, 91–92, 111, 114
Homage to Catalonia (Orwell), 42n
Hood, HMS, 87, 107
Hooligan Navy, 66, 75, 102, 123–25, 164, 175, 195, 220, 229–30

Index

Hoover, J. Edgar, 115, 118, 119*n*, 120, 191
Hopkins, Harry, 24
Hoy, 122
Huckleberry Finn (Twain), 170
Hudson, Thomas (char.), 126, 130,
    155–56, 159, 192, 211
hunting, 54, 60, 150
Hürtgen Forest, 9
hydrophones, 96

Ibarlucia, Paxtchi, 163, 224
Iceland, 65
In Our Time (Hemingway), 4–5
International Brigades, 37, 46–47
Irene Forsyte, USS, 66
Islands in the Stream (Hemingway), 9, 11,
    126, 140, 155, 159, 191–92, 198,
    211, 216
Italy, 2, 3, 37, 111
Ivancich, Adriana, 9, 138
Ivens, Joris, 43–44, 45

Jacksonville, Fla., German spies landed
    near, 125
Japan, Pearl Harbor attack of, 64
Jay-Tee (cabin cruiser), 176*n*
Jordan, Robert (char.), 8, 84, 130,
    131–33, 134–35, 137, 167, 205–6
Jouvenel, Bertrand de, 24
Joyce, James, 3, 137
Joyce, Robert, 123

K74 (blimp), 215
Kansas City Star, 2
Kearny, USS, 65
Keats, John, 135, 226
Ketchum, Idaho, 1, 11
Key West, Fla., 7, 8, 21, 32, 49, 50, 51,
    104, 124, 177, 181, 189
Kiel, Germany, 89
King, Ernest, 66, 70–71, 102, 164
Knights Cross, 87, 90, 100
Knoblaugh, Ed, 199–200
Kriegsmarine, 39, 87, 92
Kuhlmann, Gertrude, 91, 93
Kuhlmann, Hans-Gunther, 86, 87, 88–89,
    90–93, 95–96, 97–99, 103–6, 108
Kurowsky, Agnes von, 2, 138

Lansky, Meyer, 117
La Pallice, France, 77*n*

Lawrence, T. E., 127
leadership, 158–60
Leddy, Raymond, 115, 117, 189–90
leftists, 29–30
Lend-Lease Act, 65
Leningrad, siege of, 114
Lerroux, Alejandro, 36
Lewis, Sinclair, 27*n*
Liana (Gellhorn), 193–94, 212
Liberty ships, 220
Life, 10
London, 9
Long Island, German spies landed on,
    125
Lorient, France, 77, 91, 92, 93, 202, 204,
    215
Loyalists, *see* Republicans, Spanish
Luftwaffe, 39, 92
Luth, Wolfgang, 89
Lysefjord (steamer), 204, 221

McAuslan in the Rough (Fraser), 189*n*
McCarthy, Mary, 121
Madame Bovary (Flaubert), 193–94
Madrid, 33–34, 39, 43, 48
Main Street America, Martha Gell-
    horn's disdain for, 26–28
Malraux, André, 23, 33
Maltese Falcon, The (Hammett), 121
Mambi (freighter), 209
mangrove swamps, 212–13
Manning, Robert, 169
March, Fredric, 44
Maria (char.), 8, 84, 132, 137
Marines, U.S., 65
marlin, 54, 55, 56, 58, 60, 61
Marqués de Comillas, SS (liner), 184–92,
    198, 203, 223
Marryat, Frederick, 153, 217–18
Marshall, George, 70–71, 102, 164
Marxism, 35, 36, 44
Matanzas, Cuba, 153, 154, 183
Matthews, Herbert, 34, 37
Mayo Clinic, 11
media, and public's right to know vs.
    military secrecy, 125
Megano Grande, Cayo, 212
Men at War (Hemingway, ed.), 16, 17,
    124
Men without Women (Hemingway), 7
merchant ships, 61, 63–64

armament of, 62
losses of, 64, 65, 66*n,* 70–71, 77, 100,
    109, 114, 221
neutral, 63–64, 111
Spanish, 111
see also convoys
Mesa, Fernando, 163
Mexico, Gulf of, 50, 63
    civilian antisubmarine patrols in, 62,
        123–25
    U-boats in, 8–9, 16–17, 18, 20, 62,
        64, 67, 68, 70, 76–78, 90, 95, 103,
        172, 175, 180, 184, 191*n,* 202,
        203, 215–16, 221
Miami, Fla., 178, 180
Midway, Battle of, 114
Mola, General, 41, 48
Mona Passage, 101
Montana, 7, 10
Monte Carlo, 148
Morison, Samuel Eliot, 66, 109, 111, 220
Morocco, 38
Morrison, Toni, 58
Moveable Feast, A (Hemingway), 4, 6, 11,
    140, 152, 162
Mowrer, Hadley, 3–4, 5–6, 20, 46, 51,
    146, 150–52, 157, 200, 201
Mowrer, Paul, 150, 152
Murphy, Audie, 167*n*
Murphy, Gerald and Sara, 161, 162
Mussolini, Benito, 48
Myth of Sisyphus, The (Camus), 134

Nationalists, Spanish, 34, 42, 48
    atrocities by, 41–42
    Catholic support for, 35–36, 38, 42,
        208
Navarez, General, 41
navy, Canadian, 65
navy, German, 39, 87, 92
Navy, U.S., 65, 66, 102, 173–75, 182*n,*
    220
    Caribbean Sea Frontier of, 178, 209
    Gulf Sea Frontier of, 104, 124, 177,
        178, 189, 204
    Panama Sea Frontier of, 180
Nazis, 20, 112, 124
Nelson, Horatio, Lord, 188*n*
Neutrality Act, 115
neutral shipping, as U-boat targets,
    63–64, 111

New Deal, 24–25, 39
Newman, John Henry, 208
New Yorker, 170
New York Times, 100, 123–25, 153*n*
Nickeliner (freighter), 209
"Night Before Battle" (Hemingway), 43
Nixon, Richard, 27
Nobel Prize for Literature, 11
North American News Alliance
    (NANA), 33
"Now I Lay Me" (Hemingway), 131
Nuevitas, Cuba, 209, 211, 212
Nuremberg trials, 64

O'Brian, Patrick, 217
oil and gasoline tankers, 63, 221
oil pipelines, 220–21
Olantha (freighter), 203
Old Bahama Channel, 209
Old Man, *see* Santiago (char.)
Old Man and the Sea, The, 10, 55, 106–7,
    127, 228, 229
Oneida (freighter), 97, 98
"On the Blue Water" (Hemingway), 50
Oregon, SS, 101
Orley Farm (Trollope), 156
Orwell, George, 37, 42*n,* 121
OSS, 9

Pacific, World War II in, 114
Pamplona, Spain, 5, 10, 152, 228
Panama, 180
Panama Canal, 7, 180, 184
Panama Sea Frontier, 180
Paris, 3, 4–5, 7, 10, 51
Paris Review, 13, 32, 101–102, 219
Pascal's Wager, 208
Pasionaria, La, 46
PBYs (flying boats), 96
PC566, 104–6, 107–8
Pearl Harbor, Japanese attack on, 64
Percival, Philip, 205
Perkins, Maxwell, 5, 152, 166, 201
Picasso, Pablo, 3, 42
Piening, Adolf, 202–3, 204–5, 221
Piening Route, 202–3
pigeon shooting, 146–49, 150–51
Pilar (char.), 51, 205–6
Pilar (fishing boat), 10, 14, 49, 217, 221,
    230
    blinkered searchlight on, 176

Pilar (fishing boat) *(cont.)*
  EH's purchase of, 8, 51–52
  HFDF on, 172, 173, 175, 200,
    211–12
  log of, 181–83, 185–88
  physical characteristics of, 52–53, 72,
    158, 188
  radar and sonar lacking on, 79, 172
  radio on, 175, 200, 212
  range of, 183
  repairs to, 200, 216
  research vessel disguise of, 176, 182
  as U-boat bait, 79–80
  see also Hemingway, Ernest, U-boat
    patrols of
Plimpton, George, 101–102, 170
Popular Front, 41
POUM, 42
Pound, Ezra, 3, 4, 5
Powell, Anthony, 123
Puerto Rico, 143
Pulitzer Prize, 10

Q-ships, 66, 165

radar, 67, 94, 172, 173–74, 220
Rawlings, Philip (char.), 119
Reader's Digest, 29
Red Cross, EH in, 2, 165
Republicans, Spanish, 35–36, 38, 42–43,
    44, 115, 124
  atrocities by, 41–42, 48
  internal conflicts of, 36–37, 42, 43,
    44–45, 112, 115–16
  as refugees, 48–49, 111, 113, 122
Reuben James, USS, 65
Revolt of the Sergeants (1933), 117
Reynolds, Michael, 165*n*
Richardson, Hadley, *see* Mowrer, Hadley
rifle, shooting with, 149–50
Rio Tercero (freighter), 125
Rivera, Diego, 162
Robert E. Lee (liner), 104–6, 108, 153,
    184–85
Rockwell, Norman, 30
Romano, Cayo, 211
Romanticism, 135
Roosevelt, Eleanor, 24, 25–26, 29, 66
Roosevelt, Franklin D., 39, 44, 120
Ross, Lillian, 170
Royal Air Force, 9, 93

Royal Navy, 65, 87, 88, 100*n*, 182*n*
Russell, Joe, 51, 181

saboteurs, 111, 112, 114, 125–26, 190,
    191*n*
Saint-Exupéry, Antoine de, 33
St. Louis, Mo., 26, 32
Saint-Nazaire, France, 77*n*
San Antonio, Cape, 203
San Juan, Puerto Rico, 178
San Julián, Cuba, 180
Santiago (char.), 10, 53, 106–7, 129, 130,
    133, 135–36, 159, 228–29
Saturday Evening Post, 30
Saturday Review, 21
Saxon, Don, 163, 176, 200, 211–12
Schacht, Harro, 77
Schnorchel, 68*n*
Schruns, Austria, 5
Scott, Winfield, 111*n*
Scribner, Charles, 153, 157
Scribner's, 5, 6, 10, 52
seamanship, 158, 217
secrecy, public's right to know vs., 125
Shafer, Henrich, 203–5
Shakespeare and Company, 3
shooting:
  rifle, 149–50
  shotgun, 149
"Short Happy Life of Francis Ma-
    comber, The" (Hemingway),
    158, 201, 228
shotgun, shooting with, 149
Sisyphus, 134, 135, 227
Sloppy Joe's (bar), 20, 31, 32, 51
"Snows of Kilimanjaro, The" (Heming-
    way), 161
socialism, socialists, 35, 44
sonar, 79, 106, 172, 220
"Song of the Wandering Aengus, The,"
    136–37
Spain, 3, 110, 111
  EH's love of, 20
  merchant ships of, 111
Spanish Civil War, 19–20, 32, 33–49,
    113, 115, 120, 124
  atrocities in, 40–42
  EH as correspondent in, 8, 17,
    33–34, 43, 46–47, 83, 125–26
  Martha Gellhorn as correspondent
    in, 8, 33–34, 43, 46–47, 83

Spanish Earth, The (film), 43–44, 45
Spectator, 29
Stalin, Joseph, 39, 43
Stalinists, 36–37, 42, 121
State Department, U.S., 116, 143
Stein, Gertrude, 3, 5, 6
submarines:
   living conditions in, 73–74
   submerged running of, 74
   see also U-boats
Sun Also Rises, The (Hemingway), 6, 162
Sun Valley, Idaho, 8, 86, 150
Suriname, 194–95
Switzerland, 3, 4

Tamm, Edward, 117–18, 122
tankers, 63
tanker submarines (milch cows), 68, 172
Tender Is the Night (Fitzgerald), 161
Thatcher, Margaret, 27*n*
Thetis, USCGC, 174
This Side of Paradise (Fitzgerald), 5, 135
Thomason, John, 82*n*, 163, 165*n*
Thompson submachine guns, 80, 81,
   82, 126, 164, 186, 213
Three Stories and Ten Poems (Heming-
   way), 4
To Have and Have Not (Hemingway), 21,
   51, 118*n*
To Hell and Back (Murphy), 167*n*
Toklas, Alice B., 3
Toronto Daily Star, 2, 3, 4
torpedo attacks, 97–98
Torrents of Spring, The (Hemingway), 6
Tortola, 143
Touchet (tanker), 221
Transatlantic Review, 4
Travels with Myself and Another (Gell-
   horn), 84
Trinidad, 63, 96, 104, 195
Trollope, Anthony, 156
Trotskyists, 36–37, 42, 43
Trouble I've Seen, The (Gellhorn), 21
True at First Light (Hemingway), 11
Twain, Mark, 164, 170, 171

U7, 88
U37, 86–87
U103, 62
U110, 95*n*
U123, 66

U134, 215
U155, 202–3, 204–5, 221
U157, 174
U166, 78, 89, 91, 92, 93, 99, 103–6, 108,
   142, 184–85
U176, 209, 221
U183, 203–5
U193, 221
U202, 125
U333, 176*n*
U506, 78
U507, 77–78, 80, 123, 153*n*
U527, 215–16
U580, 88–89, 90
U-boat command (BdU), 95, 98, 125, 172
U-boats, 72
   armament of, 63, 75, 78
   captains of, 62, 90, 92
   in Caribbean, 62, 64, 67, 70, 76–78,
      103, 142, 175, 180, 195, 203, 209,
      212, 221
   Cuba's north shore patrolled by, 67,
      70, 77, 98, 99, 142
   diesel engines of, 67–68, 76
   early successes of, 87–88, 114, 175
   electric batteries of, 67–68, 75
   espionage and, 125–26, 191*n*
   fishing boats as source of fresh food
      for, 79
   in Florida Straits, 67, 68, 70, 100, 180,
      184, 204, 215
   in Gulf of Mexico, 8–9, 16–17, 18, 20,
      62, 64, 67, 68, 70, 76–78, 90, 95,
      103, 172, 175, 180, 184, 191*n*, 202,
      203, 215–16, 221
   Gulf Stream and, 61–62, 90, 97, 204
   hydrophones on, 96
   living conditions in, 73–74, 89
   lookouts on, 93–94, 95
   losses of, 88, 108*n*, 221
   maximum diving depth of, 76
   as metaphor, 16, 127, 128, 228
   1942 as "Happy Time" for, 64, 205
   radio transmissions by, 95–96, 98, 99,
      172–73, 212
   range of, 65, 68, 75, 78
   submerged running, of, 68, 70, 74,
      78–79, 96
   surface running as necessity for,
      67–68, 75
   top speeds of, 75, 78

U-boats *(cont.)*
  torpedo attacks by, 97–98
  Type VII, 74–76, 91
  Type IX, 78, 91
  U.S. east coast patrolled by, 64,
    65–66, 70, 90, 103, 109
  wolf-pack strategy of, 76, 78, 95, 172
  in World War I, 66
  see also antisubmarine warfare
Ulysses (Joyce), 3
"Undefeated, The" (Hemingway), 133
United States:
  Catholic lobby in, 39
  Gulf coast of, 63, 102, 123–25, 164,
    188, 195
  isolationism in, 38–39
  Japanese attack on, 64
  neutrality of, 88
United States, east coast of:
  civilian patrols of, 66, 75, 102,
    123–25, 164, 195
  German "blockade" of, 111
  U-boat patrols along, 64, 65–66, 70,
    90, 103, 109

Valencia, 43
View from the Ground, The (Gellhorn), 29
visual surveillance, 72, 76, 93–94, 95, 96,
    102, 171–72, 177, 211

war, as metaphor, 132
Watch Officer's Guide, 181
"Way You'll Never Be, A" (Heming-
    way), 131
Welles, Orson, 44
Welsh, Mary, *see* Hemingway, Mary
    Welsh
Wilson, Edmund, 30, 119n
Windward Passage, 101, 180, 203, 204
Winner Take Nothing (Hemingway), 8
Winter, Werner, 62
World War I, 127
  EH in, 2, 17, 165
  U-boats in, 66
World War II, censorship in, 125
WPA, 30

Yeats, William Butler, 123, 136–38
Yucatán Channel, 70, 180, 203

About the Author

≈≈≈

Terry Mort has degrees in literature from Princeton University and the University of Michigan. At Princeton he studied with Hemingway biographer Carlos Baker and did his thesis on the Hemingway Hero. After graduate school he served as an officer in the Navy, specializing in navigation and gunnery. He spent two years in the Pacific, including a lengthy deployment to Southeast Asia during the war there, and a third year with an amphibious squadron patrolling the Gulf of Mexico and the Caribbean.

He is the author of three novels as well as a book on fly fishing. His short fiction has appeared in *Gray's Sporting Journal,* and he writes regularly for *Field & Stream,* reviewing classic sporting literature. He has edited works by Mark Twain, Jack London, and Zane Grey. He has traveled extensively, spending time in over thirty-five countries. He lives with his wife, Sondra Hadley, in Sonoita, Arizona, and Durango, Colorado.